AN INTRODUCTION TO TWENTIETH-CENTURY CZECH FICTION

To Lissy,
my favourite psychiatrist,
who thinks that Czech writers are slightly less mad
than Russian ones

An Introduction to Twentieth-Century Czech Fiction

Comedies of Defiance

ROBERT PORTER

sussex
ACADEMIC
PRESS

BRIGHTON • PORTLAND

2 4 6 8 10 9 7 5 3 1

First published 2001 in Great Britain by
SUSSEX ACADEMIC PRESS
PO Box 2950
Brighton BN2 5SP

and in the United States of America by
SUSSEX ACADEMIC PRESS
5804 N.E. Hassalo St.
Portland, Oregon 97213-3644

British Library Cataloguing in Publication Data
A CIP catalogue record for this book is available from the British Library.

Library of Congress Cataloging-in-Publication Data
Porter, Robert.
An introduction to twentieth-century Czech fiction : comedies of defiance / Robert Porter.
p. cm.
Includes bibliographical references and index.
ISBN 1–902210–80–8 (alk. paper)
1. Czech fiction—20th century—History and criticism. I. Title: Introduction to 20th-century Czech fiction. II. Title.
PG5011 .P67 2001
891.8'63509—dc21   2001043001

Typeset and designed by G&G Editorial, Brighton
Printed by TJ International, Padstow, Cornwall
This book is printed on acid-free paper

Contents

―――――

Preface vi
Acknowledgements viii

Introduction 1
Jaroslav Hašek: *Surviving the century* 4
Karel Čapek: *Whose point of view?* 27
Bohumil Hrabal: *Small people and tall tales* 52
Josef Škvorecký: *Fascism, Communism and all that jazz* 87
Ota Pavel: *Laughter in the dark* 123
Ivan Klíma: *Conscience and moral conundrums* 136
Daniela Hodrová, Michal Viewegh, Jáchym Topol: *New voices?* 162

Notes 184
Select Bibliography 192
Index 197

Preface

This book is not primarily intended for the small number of specialists in Czech literature in the English-speaking world. It is intended for the significant numbers of students and others who have a genuine interest in Czech twentieth-century fiction, but who have not yet read very widely in the field and who may be struggling with the language.

The purpose, in the first instance, is to offer a way into Czech literature through a number of "case studies", fixing on the essentials of each chosen author's creative work and concentrating on specific texts by way of illustration. Occasionally, especially and self-indulgently so in the chapter on Hašek, comparisons and contrasts are made with foreign writers, particularly English and Russian ones, on the assumption that many English-speaking students of Czech, for better or worse, come to their second Slavonic language from Russian. A secondary aim is to offer an overview of Czech twentieth-century fiction from the inter-war period (the "First Republic"), through the Second World War, the 1948 communist take-over, on to the "Prague Spring" of 1968, the years of "normalization" (as the reimposition of communism was officially dubbed), and ending with the "Velvet Revolution" of late 1989 and its aftermath.

This book by its very nature makes no claims to being definitive, treating as it does a mere handful of prose writers. Nor does it claim to be anything like definitive in its discussion of the chosen writers, some of whom have already had one or more whole monographs devoted to them by other critics. However, it is hoped that the mix of *tour d'horizon* and occasional close-up will urge students, off their own bat, towards more exploration of these authors and others, even if they have to learn Czech to do so.

The choice of writers will seem to specialists to be arbitrary. It reflects to a large extent my own limitations and tastes, but also the tastes of the wider reading public both among Czechs and others, and it has been made in informal consultation with a good many educated Czechs and teachers of Czech. Most, but not all, of the writers presented here have been translated into English. Where an English translation is readily available and reasonably competent I have quoted from that and supplied the Czech original, noting – if necessary – any slippage or discrepancy. Other translations are my own. Thus, the book will be an aid to students both of Czech language and literature, and will also be of use to those who have no stomach for the mental gymnastics and cerebral acts of contortion that are involved in acquiring Czech.

There are two glaring lacunae – two writers missing, whose absence requires more explanation than the foregoing and the conventional one about lack of space. They peep out of every nook and cranny in this book, demanding attention, threatening to upstage the chosen few. They are Franz Kafka and Milan Kundera. I allude fleetingly but repeatedly to both. Kafka, of course, disqualifies himself for having written in German, but his impact on Czech literature is undeniable and he has his self-confessed acolytes among the writers featured here and in his fellow absentee. Kundera is more problematic. I wrote a slight and very superficial book about him many years ago, and there have been several much more substantial studies published on him since. His emigration to France in 1975 was as much intellectual as geographical. One simple indication of this is to be glimpsed in the fact that allusions to his native land have grown less and less in his recent fiction. Moreover, his last two novels have been written in French and anyway, for many years he has – consciously and deliberately, it would seem – developed a style which many would argue facilitates translation.

Discoursing on the problems of translation and exiled writing, Stanislaw Baranczak writes: "One extreme solution, represented, I believe, by Milan Kundera, consists in minimizing the translator's potential interference. The author is to make his original work as translatable as possible – in fact he makes himself write in a deliberately translatable, clear, and unequivocal style, so that the translator will not be prodded into too many deviations from the intended meaning."[1] Kundera (and Kafka) might then best be understood within the broader context of European, especially Central European, culture. Kundera, with the possible exception of Škvorecký, has gone further than any of the writers featuring in this book to free himself from his specifically Czech cultural and linguistic baggage. At the same time, it can be argued that he has done more than any other modern Czech writer to put Czech literature on the map. I can only lodge a counter-plea that selection of material in a book of this nature is never easy.

Acknowledgments

———

I would like to express my gratitude for their help to all the people over the years who have responded to my queries and statements about Czech literature. Special thanks are due to Jan Čulík and Josef Fronek for their careful reading of the first fair draft of this book and for all their advice. Bohuslava Bradbrook has freely shared her expertise with me over many years. Her comments on my chapter on Čapek helped me refine my thoughts considerably, though her patience and wisdom are no match for my bone-headed obstinacy when it comes to value judgements and on occasion we will have to agree to differ. Gleb and Nicholas Zekulin have been of great help over a number of details. Ivan Klíma has been very kind in clearing up a number of points of detail for me, as has Jiří Holý in sending me much bibliographical material. Thanks come here too late for Zuzana Cockram, whose untimely death in June 2000 robbed me of a friend and helpmate. Karel Hynek Mácha will surely not mind if his overworked words – at various times inverted by the Poetists and by Kundera – are dragooned into service once again: I will recall my conversations with Zuzana "with faint laughter on my face and deep sadness in my heart".

In recent years I have subjected a number of young ladies, in particular Ilona Bílková and Marcela Reslová, to scandalous lexical harassment both in the work-place and elsewhere. My gratitude goes to them for the good humour, forbearance and intelligence with which they have tutored me in Czech. I promise them I am making every effort to improve. Isabel Clements-Jewery told me to include a "thank you" to a pal of hers for lending me a copy of *At The Mountains of Madness* and I am too frightened to argue with her, so thank you, Duncan MacGregor (and Isabel!).

Finally, if readers find, as they surely will, things wrong with this book, blame me.

Robert Porter
University of Glasgow
Autumn 2000

"What a fine comedy this world
would be if one did not play
a part in it."

Denis Diderot

Introduction

One purpose of this book is to draw some general conclusions about Czech literature and suggest affinities or otherwise with other European literary traditions.

In a celebrated essay, the eminent Czech critic, René Wellek, identified two traditions of Czech literature:

There are two main traditions in the history of Czech literature: one an artistic, poetic tradition which we see at its height in the fourteenth century, rediscover in the seventeenth and eighteenth centuries during the age of the baroque and in the fine oral literature, and we see emerge again in Mácha and in the modern symbolist poets. There is another stream, far more intellectual, rationalist, practical, pragmatical, which found literary expression in men such as Jan Hus, in the humanists and reformers, and again in the historian Palacký, and in Thomas Masaryk.

These twin streams continued into the twentieth century, but became overlain with the Modernist experiments that swept across Europe and America in the early decades of the twentieth century, and then by Socialist Realism, as imported from the Soviet Union after 1948. Most of the serious writers, and all those of that era addressed in this book, of course reacted with disdain to Socialist Realism, mocked it, or simply rose above it. We perceive the "artistic", "poetic" and "oral", with all sorts of qualifications, in Hašek, Hrabal, Topol and Hodrová. The other stream, the "intellectual", "rationalist" and "practical" – with all its connotations of civic-mindedness – is to be found in Čapek, Klíma, Škvorecký and Pavel. At times the two streams overlap.

Another way of looking at the fiction of the twentieth century might be in terms of comedy and the absurd. The Czechs' grim experiences have generated in many of them a finely honed sense of black humour, which is reflected to varying degrees in all the writers under discussion here. "Black comedy" is a term that has been bandied about in the second half of the twentieth century, not least in relation to Czech literature. It may, therefore, be as well to recall that the phrase was first coined by Jean Anouilh when he designated his plays either *pièces roses* or *pièces noires*. André Breton also produced in 1940 his *Anthologie de l'humeur noire*. In a recent edition of *A Dictionary of Literary Terms and Theory* we read: "Black comedy is a form of drama which displays a marked disillusionment and cynicism. It shows human beings without convictions and with little hope, regulated by fate or fortune or incomprehensible powers, in fact human beings in an 'absurd' predicament. At its darkest such comedy is pervaded by a kind of sour despair: we can't do anything so we may as well laugh."[2]

One might add that in the case of Czech literature, while situations and characters may seem blackly comic and even absurd, their essential reality is often not in question. The grotesque and fantastic are not *sine qua non*. Moreover, despair is not all-embracing – Švejk and his ilk will never cease marching.

In the chapter on Čapek I refer to the work of the philosopher Henri Bergson, whose descriptor of comedy surely applies just as well:

> The first point to which attention should be called is that the comic does not exist outside the pale of what is strictly *human*. A landscape may be beautiful, charming and sublime, or insignificant and ugly; it will never be laughable. You may laugh at an animal, but only because you have detected in it some human attitude or expression. You may laugh at a hat, but what you are making fun of, in this case, is not the piece of felt or straw, but the shape that men have given it – the human caprice whose mould it has assumed. It is strange that so important a fact, and such a simple one too, has not attracted to a greater degree the attention of philosophers. Several have defined man as "an animal which laughs." They might equally have defined him as an animal which is laughed at; for if any other animal, or some lifeless object, produces the same effect, it is always because of some resemblance to man, of the stamp he gives it, or the use he puts it to.
>
> Here I would point out, as a symptom equally worthy of notice, the *absence of feeling* which usually accompanies laughter. It seems as though the comic could not produce its disturbing effect unless it fell, so to say, on the surface of a soul that is thoroughly calm and unruffled. Indifference is its natural environment, for laughter has no greater foe than emotion. I do not mean that we could not laugh at a person who inspires us with pity, for instance, or even with affection, but in such a case we must, for the moment, put our affection out of court and impose silence upon our pity. In a society composed of pure intelligences there would probably be no more tears, though perhaps there would still be laughter.[3]

In Bergson's view, the ability to be laughed at is an essential component of the human condition and would also appear to be indispensable to intelligence, even "pure" intelligence. The volatile emotions that we encounter in so many of the works to be discussed can indeed lead to moral and intellectual ruin. In Kundera's first novel, *The Joke*, the hero poses a terrible challenge to the "seriousness" and "lyricism" of the totalitarian age with just a simple joke scrawled on a postcard. His own ensuing hatred of those who denounced him is finally checked by the laughter that his ill-fated attempt at revenge engenders.

It might be the case that despite the absurdity that many characters in Czech fiction find themselves afflicted with, they still retain some decency and reason. In this connection there is in Czech fiction of the twentieth century, not just a degree of urban bric-à-brac, which makes its world far more familiar to Western readers than say the world of Russian literature, but there is also a degree of *urbanity*. It is quite extraordinary that for all the mock epics and mock heroics, false-placed high-mindedness and self-deception that one encounters in so much Czech fiction, there is no word in Czech (or in Russian for that matter) for "bathos". Czech fiction may not have a strong epic tradition – despite the best efforts of Alois Jirásek (1851–1930), who produced a string of historical novels charting the defeats and ultimate revival of the Czech nation – but it does have some life-affirming traits, not least in its special brand of humour. It is in laughter – not, God forbid, to be equated or confused with happiness or optimism – that Czech fiction surmounts any provincialism that geography, history and language have pre-disposed it to.

Jaroslav Hašek
(1883–1923)
Surviving the century

———

The Good Soldier Švejk and his Fortunes in the World War (*Osudy dobrého vojáka Švejka za světové války*) has become so widely known and inextricably associated in the popular imagination with The Czech Republic, to the considerable profit of the tourist industry, that it is natural that it should have its detractors. Robert Pynsent writes:

> The titular hero is a cowardly, devious, unconsciously vulgar petty *bourgeois*, whom the reader may love as an I'm-all-right-Jack opportunist or loathe as an uncommitted amoralist. The work is an unfinished episodic novel, repetitive especially when Švejk himself is not speaking, and sometimes heavy-handed in its satire. It does succeed in reproducing the scorn of the thinking man for the nincompoopish Austrian military hierarchy and the officious incompetence of the civilian enforcers of Vienna's will. Whatever reserves one might have about this grotesque, one cannot but admit that it frequently gives one the opportunity of a healthy belly-laugh.[1]

Elsewhere, in a lengthy, erudite and informative article he concludes that Hašek is "a genius of crassness".[2] On the other hand, the former diplomat and latter-day scholar Sir Cecil Parrott devoted all of his academic career to Hašek, translating his *magnum opus* into, it must be said, a somewhat stilted English and producing critical and biographical works on him. In his collection of essays *The Art of the Novel* Milan Kundera called *The Good Soldier Švejk* "perhaps the last great popular novel".[3]

The Good Soldier Švejk is quite simply the story of a middle-aged, rheumatic Prague citizen volunteering for active service in the Austrian army when the First World War breaks out. Previously, he had been discharged from the military on the grounds of stupidity. We follow him on his travels and during his various encounters with fellow soldiers and those in authority. Through his apparent incompetence he drives his officers to distraction, but he always manages to extricate himself from

———

difficulties. He is gregarious by nature and forms casual friendships easily. He is an endless raconteur, but his real *forte* is survival.

Ordinary Czechs are often irritated at foreigners' charges against them of ("Švejkism" (involving subterfuge, cowardice, mealy-mouthedness, though could these last two qualities really apply to Švejk?). One notes that such charges could come from on high when powerful enemies became exasperated at the inability of military might alone to bring the smaller nation to heel. The Nazi quisling Emanuel Moravec, after Heydrich's assassination in May 1942, upbraided the Czechs for not collaborating whole-heartedly in the investigation. In his view the Czechs had the "diligence of an ant and the horizon of a slug. These are the facets of our unhappy national peculiarity which culminate in the disgusting figure of a calculating sloth and a titular idiot Švejk".[4] Gordon Skilling in his enormous book on the Prague Spring devotes several pages to a dismissal of "Švejkism" ("The supposed willingness of the Czech nation and its leaders to adapt passively to a given political system"), calling the Švejk myth a "facile, but unconvincing, interpretation of Czech history".[5] Perhaps it is a measure of Hašek's achievement that, if nothing else, his book, more than any other single work of literature anywhere, encapsulates not so much a set of national characteristics as the predicament and destiny of a nation.

However, much greater claims can be made for *The Good Soldier Švejk*. Whilst it is sometimes long-winded, diffuse and repetitive, it is also seminal in two ways. First, it initiates the darkly comic anti-militaristic theme, which dominates so much war literature of the twentieth century. Secondly, it reorders humanity's priorities.

Švejk's Legacy: First World War Literature and Anti-Militarism

Bertolt Brecht was to write his own updated stage version of Hašek's work, *Švejk in the Second World War* (performed 1956, published posthumously 1959). While there are considerable differences between the two novels, Voinovich's *Private Ivan Chonkin* (first two parts published in the West 1975) was widely acclaimed by reviewers as the Soviet *Švejk*. One can cite, since *Švejk*, a pleiad of novels that use black comedy to debunk war: Joseph Heller's *Catch-22* (1961) and Kurt Vonnegut's *Slaughterhouse-Five* (1969) to name but two. Nor should one forget the more popular and trivial forms such as Spike Milligan's volumes of war memoirs starting with *Adolf Hitler: My Part in His Downfall* (1972) and from the 1950s onwards the spate of film, television and radio offerings, perhaps the most salient of all these being the film *M.A.S.H.* (1970, director Robert Altman) and the subsequent TV series.

It is important to distinguish between this kind of writing and the merely anti-militaristic satire that can be traced back at least as far as Falstaff. Falstaff's comic deceit and cowardice are more than outweighed by the heroics and ultimate triumph of the king and the nation. Indeed, one notes in Shakespeare's history plays a confidence in the historical process. (The essential point about The Good Soldier Švejk and its legacy is that history itself is debunked; there is no progress and no victory, there is only momentary survival, and only on an individual basis. We are dealing with the very antithesis of epic here, and to that extent it will be useful to examine at some length other areas of First World War Literature.)

In brief, the main features of the "classical" Greek epic are as follows: it is the story of a nation's foundation, fundamental transformation and/or survival; mortals are pitted against gods and/or the natural elements; heroes are often created out of an illicit relationship between a mortal and a god or goddess, there may be the inadvertent slaughter of a relative or loved one; the hero is governed by his fate (*moira*) and if he or she challenges this through an act of *hybris* he/she will be punished; there is a strong oral basis to the epic, stemming of course from Homer; additionally, there are a number of set stylistic devices attaching to the epic: the story will frequently start *in medias res* rather than "at the beginning"; epithets will be repeated, in order no doubt, originally, to aid the memory of those listening to these traditionally long recitations; the epic simile will often take on a life of its own and lead the audience away from the object it initially seeks to describe; there may well be a number of set pieces involving sports, games, music, or some pastoral idyll, which give the audience and the main characters some respite from the inevitable military conflicts.

In the modern world one may distinguish between epics composed contemporaneously, or hard on the heels of the events they recount, and those which consciously use recorded history to investigate in fictional form an earlier period. Tolstoy's *War and Peace* was written in the 1860s, half a century after the Napoleonic wars it deals with; similarly Solzhenitsyn's *The Red Wheel*, dealing with the First World War and the Russian Revolution, was written largely in the 1970s. On the other hand, Mikhail Sholokhov's *The Quiet Don*, covering the same period as Solzhenitsyn's work, was begun in the late 1920s. The straight epic has proved remarkably resilient in Russian literature, even setting aside the ideologically contrived epics demanded by Socialist Realism. Vasilii Grossman's enormous novel of the Second World War *Life and Fate*, depicting Russia's very existence hanging by a thread during the Battle of Stalingrad, certainly deserves the epithet.

With one important exception, English and German literature addressing the First World War studiously eschews the epic and its comic antithesis. Elizabeth Marsland's wide-ranging study *The Nation's Cause: French, English and German Poetry of The First World War* identifies, broadly speaking, three categories of poems, nationalistic, propagandist and protest verse, and concludes:

> First World War poetry, whether it celebrates national identity, pleads for the humane standards endangered by total commitment to the nation, or reflects unprotesting compliance with the demand for sacrifice, is a comprehensive verbal response to the war in which nationalism came into its own.[6]

Yet would it not be true to say that in the most successful and lasting poems produced by the galaxy of English poets we are confronted more with individual horrors than with abstract concepts such as "nation" or "victory"? At times the warrior poets display as much sympathy for the enemy as for themselves (Wilfred Owen's "Strange Meeting" – "I am the enemy you killed, my friend"). Rupert Brooke's "The Soldier" ("corner of a foreign field/That is forever England") might be construed as much as homesickness as patriotism, and it was, of course, produced early on in the war, before doubts and exhaustion could set in. Siegfried Sassoon and Wilfred Owen outlived Brooke and became avowedly anti-war. The very rare moments of humour in the poetry of the First World War are grim indeed: Edgell Rickwood's "The Soldier Addresses His Body" ("I shall be mad if you get smashed about/we've had some good times together, you and I;") or more famously, Sassoon's "The General" ("He's a cheery old card, grunted Harry to Jack [. . .] /But he did for them both by his plan of attack").

When it comes to prose, in Robert Graves's memoir *Goodbye to All That* we are told bluntly: "Patriotism, in the trenches, was too remote a sentiment, and at once rejected as fit only for civilians, or prisoners. A new arrival who talked patriotism would soon be told to cut it out."[7] Shortly after this, Graves tells us that the last time he ever attended a church service (other than weddings and church parades) was Good Friday April 1916, while on leave (p. 165). Though continuing in active service, when after his serious wounding, to cease would have been easy, he came to oppose the war effort, though not as vehemently and publicly as his friend Siegfried Sassoon: "We no longer saw the war as one between trade-rivals: its continuance seemed merely a sacrifice of the idealistic younger generation to the stupidity and self-protective alarm of the elder" (p. 202). And Graves was horrified at the jingoism at home, which was based on total ignorance of conditions in the trenches. Ford Maddox Ford's tetralogy *Parade's End* is a deadly serious account of the British plutocracy's conduct and values before, during and after the war, as well as being a refined comedy of manners. Yet in the time that the hero, Christopher Tietjens, spends at the front there is almost none of the gore that we find in most other works addressing the same subject matter. Gifted man that he is, he simply comes to see the absurdity of the events; he is caused as much anguish by his wife's infidelities and his attempts to keep up appearances and maintain social convention.

It is interesting to note similar sentiments in classics written in other quarters. In the case of Erich Maria Remarque's classic *All Quiet on the Western Front*, a novel publicly reviled under the Nazis, but so universally famous as to have its title pass in to common parlance, food and daily survival outrank patriotism or heroism; at one point the hero and his companions behold with utter dispassion a dogfight between a British and a German airplane and place bets on who will win. Henri Barbusse's enduring novel *Under Fire* in similar vein told the harrowing story of trench warfare from the Frenchman's viewpoint. Like *All Quiet on the Western Front* its opening scenes are as much concerned with food, basic clothing and day-to-day survival as with "victory"; and one character argues that their German enemies are just as much people as they are. There is deep scepticism about the notes of jingoism and false optimism that the newspapers strike. A "Mother Courage" element creeps into the text, as it becomes clear that French civilians are profiteering from the war, and are happy for it to continue. A soldier returning from leave complains about the numerous able-bodied pen-pushers and malingerers he has encountered.

T. E. Lawrence's *Seven Pillars of Wisdom* ranks with the greatest of English First World War Literature. Even Richard Aldington, who charges the author with self-aggrandizement and outright falsification, allows that the work has considerable literary quality. Yet it is a glaring exception. Lawrence, translator of *The Odyssey* and lifelong admirer of *War and Peace*, has produced, as if from a template, a twentieth-century epic, every major feature of which is wickedly inverted or downgraded in *The Good Soldier Švejk*. One notes in passing that both works were written immediately after the events described and that initially both were published privately. Lawrence's tells us in his Preface:

> The *Seven Pillars of Wisdom* was so printed and assembled that nobody but myself knew how many copies were produced. I propose to keep this knowledge to myself. Newspaper statements of 107 copies can be easily disproved, for there were more than a 107 subscribers: and in addition I gave away, not perhaps as many copies as I owed, but as many as my bankers could afford, to those who shared with me in the Arab effort, or in the actual production of the volume.[8]

Lawrence ended the war as a national and international hero (the "Lawrence of Arabia" legend and his participation at the Paris Peace Conference in 1919 contrasting with his declining the Order of the Bath and the DSO and subsequently his self-imposed obscurity and anonymity). (Hašek returned to a newly independent Czechoslovakia, a model democracy headed by an urbane and cultivated philosopher-king, as a pariah – an ex-Bolshevik, a bigamist and an alcoholic. He wrote *Švejk* to earn a living, and at the outset could not find a publisher.)

The imperious and sombre tone of Lawrence's work, echoing notions in the opening lines of Milton's *Paradise Lost* – "Man's first disobedience"), is captured in the first sentence: "Some of the evil of my tale may have been inherent in our circumstances. For years we had lived anyhow with one another in the naked desert, under the indifferent heaven" (p. 27). And adopting the epic formula, the work begins when the events it addresses are already underway. By contrast *Švejk* opens with a conversation in the vernacular which tells of the assassination of the Archduke Ferdinand in Sarajevo and which in the space of a few exchanges equates him with a messenger at a chemist's shop and a collector of dog's droppings. Lawrence's work is subtitled "A Triumph", Hašek's "and His Fortunes in the World War" – a more literal translation of "osud" might be "destiny" or "lot". Lawrence's saga relates gripping military engagements and culminates in the rout of the Turks and the victorious entry of the Arab forces into Damascus (Švejk never encounters the enemy (though occasionally he sees the aftermath of battle), and this cannot be attributed simply to the work remaining unfinished at the time of the author's death. After all, Hašek has given us well over seven hundred pages of narrative.)

The teleological aspect of Lawrence's work: uniting the Arabs, waging guerrilla warfare, seizing Akaba by land, when British sea bombardment had proved so ineffectual, and finally entering Damascus, is Odyssean. The work is usually published with several maps showing Lawrence's travels. By contrast, the Czech editions of *The Good Soldier Švejk* provide no maps, and the English language version's maps serve to illustrate the hero's woeful sense of direction, intentional or otherwise. This ties in with the "reordering of human priorities" which we discuss below. The chivalric element of the epic is also on display: Lawrence claims that the Arabs would never attack civilians, and when the Turks perpetrate appalling atrocities on women and children, for the first time in his campaign he orders that no prisoners be taken when he and his Arab followers retaliate. On one occasion he comes across a sleeping Turkish soldier and spares him, riding away, more or less confident that he will not be shot in the back. Military prowess could, though, have its comic side:

> Auda came swinging up on foot, his eyes glazed over with the rapture of battle, and the words bubbling with incoherent speed from his mouth. "Work, work, where are words, work, bullets," . . . and he held up his shattered field-glasses, his pierced pistol-holster, and his leather sword-scabbard cut to ribbons. He had been the target of a volley which had killed his mare

under him, but the six bullets through his clothes had left him scatheless.

He told me later, in strictest confidence, that thirteen years before he had bought an amulet Koran for one hundred and twenty pounds and had not since been wounded. Indeed, Death had avoided his face, and had gone scurvily about killing brothers, sons and followers. The book was a Glasgow reproduction, costing eighteen pence; but Auda's deadliness did not let people laugh at his superstition. (p. 312)

(The only chivalry that might be found in *Švejk* is when the hero claims to supplement his boss's rations out of his own pocket. Death and violence are to be seen or recounted on practically every page of Hašek's novel, but they are domestic or are visited by officers on their own men (or *vice versa*), not on the enemy.)In Chapter One alone we have stories of the deaths of: Ferdinand, Elizabeth stabbed with a file by an anarchist in 1898,[9] an army captain is shot, the rebellious culprit hangs himself before he can be executed, the King of Portugal is shot, a general falls off his horse to his death, a cattle dealer is stabbed, no one will do business with his son as a consequence and so the son is driven to suicide (drowning), a gamekeeper is shot and so are his three successors, who all married the widow, the fourth kills her with an axe and is hanged; Švejk also reminds us that Rudolph, the son of Franz Joseph died in mysterious circumstances and that Ferdinand Maximilian, brother of the Emperor, was executed in Mexico. Some sixteen deaths in all, and that is without the various acts of non-fatal violence: Svejk trussed up (svázanej do kozelce) for two days while in solitary confinement for two weeks because of twenty buttons missing from his uniform, the condemned man biting the priest's nose while on the gallows, and so on. "Trussing" was a particularly nasty form of punishment in the Austrian army, whereby the victim's wrists were bound to his ankles. All this is without the predictions from various quarters of world war, widespread massacres and "all emperors and empresses" being assassinated. In stark contrast to the "epic" deaths in Lawrence (all in the cause of Arab liberation and unification), these deaths are all presented to the reader as utterly devoid of real reason, almost incidental to human endeavour; and if any detail is offered, it is largely irrelevant: "The bullet flew out of his back and damaged the office into the bargain. It smashed a bottle of ink which messed up the official documents" (Kulka vyletěla panu hejtmanovi ze zad a ještě udělala škodu v kanceláři. Rozbila flašku inkoustu a ten polil úřední akta).[10] This episode is deeply ironic, given that the Austrian Empire was bound together by officialdom and bureaucracy which paid scant attention to human individuals.

The angles of narration in the two books are diametrically opposed. Lawrence uses the first person, and in purely literary terms, his text is marked by an extraordinary candour and transparency. For our purposes, it is beside the point whether the historical facts have been manipulated, as some have claimed. The author recounts his setbacks as well as his successes; his own graphic account of his torture and rape at the hands of the Turks and his own tribute to the other participants in the struggle in his Introduction, at least to this commentator's mind, more than outweigh the conceit that any autobiography involves. More importantly, as the story progresses, Lawrence records his own growing doubts, both about British good faith *vis-à-vis* the Arab cause and his own psychological make-up and philosophy.

> Now I found myself dividing into parts. There was one that went on riding wisely, sparing or helping every pace of the wearied camel. Another hovering above and to the right bent down curiously, and asked what the flesh was doing. The flesh gave no answer, for, indeed, it was conscious only of a ruling impulse to keep on and on; but a third garrulous one talked and wondered, critical of the body's self-inflicted labour, and contemptuous of the reason for effort. (p. 461)

There are several references to his false position – a committed Christian purporting to lead a nation of Muslims, a man from the very cradle of civilization, education and culture at the centre of a primitive and nomadic society – before we come to

> The rankling fraudulence which had to be my mind's habit: that pretence to lead the national uprising of another race, the daily posturing in alien dress, preaching in alien speech: with behind it a sense that the "promises" on which the Arabs worked were worth what their armed strength would be when the moment of fulfilment came. [...] My will had gone and I feared to be alone, lest the winds of circumstance, or power, or lust, blow my empty soul away. (p. 514)

Later, feelings of ambiguity and uncertainty manifest themselves:

> It was evening, and on the straight bar of Sinai ahead the low sun was falling, its globe extravagantly brilliant in my eyes, because I was dead-tired of my life, longing as seldom before for the moody skies of England. This sunset was fierce, stimulant, barbaric; reviving the colours of the desert like a draught – as indeed it did each evening, in a new miracle of strength and heat – while my longings were for weakness, chills and grey mistiness, that the world might not be so crystalline clear, so definitely right and wrong. (p. 560)

Eventually, the author's self-questioning leads to considerations that teeter on the subversive, as far as our argument is concerned:

> I had had one craving all my life – for the power of self-expression in some imaginative form – but had been too diffuse to acquire a technique. At last

accident, with perverted humour, in casting me as a man of action had given me place in the Arab Revolt, a theme ready and epic to a direct eye and hand, thus offering me an outlet in literature, the technique-less art. Whereupon I became excited only over mechanism. The epic mode was alien to me, as to my generation. (p. 565)

(The third-person narration of *Švejk* facilitates the elusive nature of the character. Neither the hero's closest companions nor the reader are really able to ascertain if the prime feature of his personality is cunning. Certainly, he can manipulate others – after all, he earns his keep before the outbreak of war by forging dogs' pedigrees. But institutions write him off as an idiot and he persistently declares his own imbecility to such an extent that the book might well be retitled "The Seven Pillars of Stupidity". Švejk talks non-stop, but almost never about himself, and we are left to divine ? his character through his actions. Unlike in Lawrence as cited above, we find in the Good Soldier a remarkable degree of integration: his constants are, briefly, his garrulousness, his amiability and his talent for survival. Yet we know nothing about his family, save for a letter from his brother and passing mention of a common law wife, for both of whom he betrays very little emotional attachment. We see more of his landlady, Mrs Müller.)

Other features of the traditional epic that we find inverted in *Švejk* include the battle with the natural elements (including finding enough to eat) and manifestations – in songs and the cataloguing families and clans – of national consciousness. Of course, many pages of *Seven Pillars of Wisdom* are devoted to surviving outdoors in the extremes of climate that the desert offers: "The day seemed to be hotter and hotter: the sun drew close, and scorched us without intervening air [. . .] When it got near, the wind, which had been scorching our faces with its hot breathlessness, changed suddenly; and, after waiting a moment, blew bitter cold and damp upon our backs" (pp. 211–12). We may be treated to the odd description of some feast (e.g. pp. 272–5), the hero's diet often consists of little more than camel meat, and anyway:

> For years before the war I had made myself trim by constant carelessness. I had learned to eat much one time; then to go two, three, or four days without food; and after to overeat. I made it a rule to avoid rules in food; and by course of exceptions accustomed myself to no custom at all. (p. 476)

He goes on to tell us that he adopts the same attitude to drink and to sleep.

Compare all this to what we see in *Švejk*. As much of the action, if that is the right word, takes place indoors as out – in pubs, railway carriages, in bawdy houses and boarding houses, in prison cells. Before a grim account of beatings, lice and foul food, we read: "The night spent in the garrison gaol will always rank among Švejk's most affectionate memories" (p. 95).

(Noc strávená na garnizóně patří vždy k milým vzpomínkám – vol. 1, p. 105). Even during the hero's celebrated anabasis to try and join his regiment in Budějovice the emphasis is on banality and domesticity. The opening of the section is blatantly mock epic, with comparisons drawn between the hero and Xenophon, the Goths and Julius Caesar (English text, p. 241; Czech text, vol. 2, p. 31), before Švejk encounters an old lady who tells him he is going the wrong way. Švejk never complains about his physical conditions, unlike some of the other characters, notably the forever ravenous Baloun. The hero's rheumatism seems to disappear after the first few chapters. Yet alcohol and good company are top priority. Several passages in *Švejk* read like a full-blown parody of an epic feast. Baloun relates how gluttony runs in his family:

> My late papa once wagered in a pub at Protivín that at one go he would eat fifty smoked sausages and two loaves of bread, and he won. Once in a wager I ate four geese and two basins full of dumplings and cabbage. It happened to me at home that after lunch, I suddenly felt that I'd like to have a tiny bit more. So, I used to go into the larder, cut off a piece of pork, send for a jug of beer and in a minute I'd devoured two kilos of smoked pork. (p. 479).

> Nebožtík tatínek, ten se sázal v Protivíně v hospodě, že sní na posezení padesát buřtů a dva bochníky chleba, a vyhrál to. Já jsem jednou vo sázku sněd čtyry husy a dvě mísy knedlíků se zelím. Doma si vzpomenu po obědě, že bych chtěl ještě něco zakusit. Jdu do komory, uříznu si kus masa, pošlu si pro džbán piva a splivnu dvě kila uzený. (vols 3–4, p. 42)

Hašek tops off this inverted struggle for survival with the introduction of the occultist cook, Jurajda – cooks in armies (and prison camps) by tradition being more inclined to gastronomy than godly matters.

The preoccupations with nationalism offer us some of the most moving passages in *Seven Pillars of Wisdom*; and here there are some extraordinary parallels with Sholokhov's epic of the same period *The Quiet Don*.

> There came a warning patter from the drums and the poet of the right wing burst into strident song, a single inverted couplet, of Feisal and the pleasure he would afford us at Wejh. The right wing listened to the voice intently, took it up and sang it once, twice and three times, with pride, and self-satisfaction and derision. However, before they could brandish it a fourth time the poet of the left wing broke out in extempore reply, in the same metre, in answering rhyme, and capping the sentiment. The left wing cheered it in a roar of triumph, the drums tapped again, the standard-bearers threw out their great crimson banners, and the whole guard, right, left and centre, broke together into rousing regimental chorus. (p. 153)

Later Auda leads the singing himself:

To-night Auda was guide and, and to make us sure of him he lifted up his voice in an interminable "ho, ho, ho" song of the Howeitat; an epic chanted on three bass notes, up and down, back and forward, in so round a voice that the words were indistinguishable. After a little while we thanked him for the singing, since the path went away to the left, and our long line followed his turn by the echoes of his voice rolling about the torn black cliffs in the moonlight. (p. 240)

Moving in closer to Akaba, Lawrence tells us:

Our night-passage might have been through a planted garden, and these varieties part of the unseen beauty of successive banks of flowers. The noises too were very clear. Auda broke out singing, away in front, and the men joined in from time to time, with the greatness, the catch at heart, of an army moving into battle. (p. 307)

Later in the campaign we have the following:

Then began our flood of visitors. All day and every day they came, now in the running column of shots, raucous shoutings and rush of camel-feet which meant a Bedouin parade, it might be of Rualla, or Sherarat, or Serahin, Serdiyeh, or Beni Sakhr, chiefs of great name like ibn Zuhair, ibn Kaebir, Rafa el Khoreisha, or some little father of a family demonstrating his greedy goodwill before the fair eyes of Ali ibn el Hussein. (pp. 445–6)

Songs and cataloguing play a similar part in Sholokhov's epic. Near the beginning of the novel we have the song which inspired the American folk singer Pete Seeger to write his famous ballad "Where have all the flowers gone?":

> And where are the geese?
> They've gone into the reeds.
> And where are the reeds?
> The girls have mown them.
> And where are the girls?
> Married and gone away.
> And where are the Cossacks?
> They've gone to war . . . [11]

Many pages later, when all the Cossack clans – one is almost tempted to speak of a Cossack *nation*, such is the sense of tradition and community here – are in retreat from the Bolshevik forces, the hero Grigorii Melekhov, utterly fearless and no stranger to violence and death, breaks down in tears:

No less than two squadrons had passed, but the sound of hooves could still be heard; it must be a regiment that was passing. And suddenly the brave,

rather harsh voice of a song-leader soared up like a bird over the steppe:
Ah, how it was on the river, on the River Kamyshinka,
In the glorious steppes, the steppes of Saratov . . .
Hundreds of voices lifted the old Cossack song zestfully, and highest of
all rose a tenor descant of astonishing power and beauty. While the vibrant
heart-catching tenor still soared somewhere in the darkness, overriding the
basses, the song-leader began another line:
There the Cossacks lived, good men and free,
All of the Don, the Greben and the Yaik countries . . .
Something seemed to snap inside Grigory . . . A sudden fit of sobbing
shook his body and a spasm seized his throat. Swallowing his tears, he waited
eagerly for the leader to begin again, and soundlessly whispered after him the
words he had known since adolescence:
Their Ataman was Yermak, son of Timofei,
Their captain was Astashka, son of Lavrenty . . .
[. . .] An old Cossack song that had survived the centuries lived and ruled
over the dark steppe. (vol. 2, pp. 665–6)

Late in the autumn of 1917 the Cossacks return from the front and we have
a long list of individuals, many of them particularized concisely: "Anikei,
as hairless as ever", "Tall, ungainly Borshchev", "The Kalmyk-looking
Fedot Bodovskov" (vol. 1, p. 558). The purpose of the cataloguing device
in both Lawrence and Sholokhov is to give an impression of vastness and
might while at the same time engendering a notion of human identity,
heritage and tradition. Lawrence marshals his literary abilities, no less than
his military talents, to achieve victory for the Arabs. In Sholokhov's text it
is clear that we are dealing with the defeat of a near-nation, and the destruction of a way of life and of a culture. But in both works the faith in the
historical process is manifest.

In *Švejk* the patriotic songs and poems, such as they are, are deliberately
misplaced; indeed they are studiously counterbalanced by bawdy ditties of
the type that the blasphemous Chaplain Otto Katz renders (e.g. "Of all the
people in the world,/ I love my love the best./ I'm not her only visitor;/ I
queue up with the rest" –he is singing of the Virgin Mary, p. 86) (*Ze všech
znejmilejší/ svou milou já mám,/ nechodím tam za ní sám,/ chodí za ní
jiných více* – vol. 1, p. 95). In the second chapter, at Police Headquarters,
there is mention (English text, p. 16; Czech text, vol. 1 p. 24) of one detainee
having been arrested for wanting to play the Czech nationalistic "Hej,
Slované" at a charity concert when Austria was about to go into mourning
for Ferdinand. At the lunatic asylum the doctors ask Švejk to sing, and his
repertoire turns out to be a poorly remembered and indiscriminate mixture
of sentimental ballads, the future Czech national anthem *Kde domov můj*,
the Austrian national anthem and a hymn to the Virgin Mary (English text,
pp. 34–5; Czech text, vol. 1, p. 43), one of which he treats us to at some

length a few chapters later when he urges Mrs Müller to wheel him to the recruitment centre in a bath chair, his rheumatism having reasserted itself (English text, p. 56; Czech text, vol. 1, pp. 65–6). Given the general context that Hašek has established for it, the Austrian nationalist doggerel reads, intentionally or otherwise, like parody: "There once was a valiant volunteer/Who gave his life for his country dear" (English text, p. 301; Czech text, vol. 2, p. 92); but on occasion the author lends a helping hand to its absurdity: on the train journey through Hungary a corporal is leaning out of the carriage and bawling a highly nationalistic song, when he loses his balance and:

> flew out of the wagon and with the full force of his flight hit his stomach on the points-lever, on which he remained transfixed and hanging, while the train went on and while in the rear vans they were singing another song: "Count Radetsky, noble sword,/ Swore to sweep the savage horde . . . " (p. 484)

> a vylítl z vagónu a plnou silou narazil v letu břichem na páku u výhybky, na které zůstal nabodnut viset, zatímco vlak jel dál a v zadních vagónech zpívali zase jinou: "Graf Radetzky, edler Degen,/ schwur's des Kaisers Feind zu fegen . . . " (vols 3–4, pp. 47–8)

Of course, Czech nationalists would only sing such songs under coercion, while many non-committed Czechs would perform them only tongue-in-cheek or unthinkingly, in the way that the English might sing Scottish or Irish songs of a nationalist bent. Why does Švejk sing such songs when he is alone, executing his tortuous march to Budějovice? The answer could be that he is as genuinely unsure of his identity as has been the Czech nation itself. This in turn leads us to suggest that he is not so much a dissembler as a genuine "don't know", at least when it comes to political commitment. In many ways Švejk is far from stupid: he has a phenomenal memory, he attracts more people than he repels, he uses his initiative, often acting more commonsensically than the powers-that-be. Above all, he survives, when political institutions have presided over the mindless slaughter of millions. "Humbly report, sir, I belong and I don't belong to the 91st regiment and I haven't the faintest idea how I really stand" (p. 89) (Poslušně hlásím, pane feldkurát, že patřím i nepatřím k jednadevadesátýmu regimentu, že vůbec nevím, jak to vlastně se mnou je – vol. 1, pp. 98–9) is what the hero tells the chaplain in the garrison prison, thus prefiguring, albeit inadvertently, many outsiders in twentieth-century fiction.

In *Švejk* there are none of the epic catalogues that we noted in *Seven Pillars of Wisdom* and *The Quiet Don*. Instead, we have small groups of individuals creating momentary havens of tenuous well-being; there is no sense of national identity and common purpose, no faith in ultimate victory. In Hašek's work, the characters are motivated by other concerns. Before turning to these, we might add a coda of a sartorial nature on the anti-military theme.

Václav Bělohradský has written on *Švejk* in an article "The Retreat into Uniform and the Disintegration of Order" and attempted to define the universality of Central European culture through this element in the novel: "a uniform is the true God of metaphysics. Only in a uniform does human life achieve the dignity of an Idea. By means of a uniform it is possible to escape from the fragility and fuzziness of life to a world of permanent meanings and facts."[12] One might quibble here with such a broad generalization, but it cannot be denied that dress in military and anti-military literature plays a role that is more than fortuitous. Don Quixote spends a week manufacturing a plaster helmet, shatters it with a trial sword stroke, and then makes another helmet, but this time does not test it, not wanting to waste his labour a second time. Appearance ousts reality. Lawrence adopted Arab dress, and even sported it at the Paris Peace conference. He writes that after one bloody engagement some Arabs were left half naked and he went to strip clothing from the dead for them: "But the Bedouin had been beforehand with me, and had stripped them to the skin. Such was their point of honour. To an Arab an essential part of the triumph was to wear the clothes of an enemy: and next day we saw our force transformed (as to the upper half) into a Turkish force, each man in a soldier's tunic" (pp. 314–15).

Švejk is escorted to be batman to Chaplain Katz by a lanky guard and a short, fat one:

> Before they had discharged him they had given him an old military uniform which had belonged to some pot-bellied fellow who was taller than him by a head.
>
> As for the trousers three more Švejks could have got into them. An endless succession of baggy folds from his feet to where his trousers reached over his chest involuntarily evoked the admiration of the spectators. A vast tunic with patches on the elbows, covered with grease and dirt, dangled around Švejk like coat on a scarecrow. His trousers hung on him like a circus clown's costume. The military cap, which they had also changed in the garrison gaol, came down over his ears. (p. 99)

> Nežli ho propustili, dali mu starý vojenský mundúr, který patřil nějakému břicháči a o hlavu většímu, než byl Švejk.
>
> Do kalhot, které měl na sobě, byli by se vešli tři Švejkové. Nekonečné faldy od noh až přes prsa, kam až sahaly kalhoty, mimovolně způsobovaly obdiv diváků. Ohromná blůza se záplatami na loktech, zamaštěná a špinavá, klátila se na Švejkovi jako kabát na hastrošovi. Kalhoty visely na něm jako kostým na klaunovi z cirku. Vojenská čepice, kterou mu též na garnizóně vyměnili, šla mu přes uši. (vol. 1, pp. 109–10)

Incidentally the circus image is taken up and developed in Vonnegut's *Slaughterhouse-Five*, where the hero-narrator, captured by the Germans, is supplied by British POWs with a costume recycled from their pantomine production of *Cinderella*.

In a perfect-fit inversion of the episode in *Seven Pilllars of Wisdom*, the sartorial imagery in *Švejk* reaches its apotheosis when the hero dons the discarded uniform of the runaway Russian prisoner. It is one of those episodes in the book, like his singing military songs when there is no one to hear him, or pulling the communication cord on the train, when there is no convincing motivation. It is a simple, instinctive impulse, flying in the face of institutions, the rational world and all that "uniform" stands for. Švejk simply wants to know how the uniform would suit him (English text, p. 666; Czech text, vols 3–4, p. 236), but the consequences nearly lead to his execution for desertion.

The classical epics depicted mortals in combat with the gods. The twentieth-century's gods have been ideologies, and the social and political systems they engender. As Lawrence's doubts increase, he talks of "man-rational" and "man-instinctive", concluding that "to man-rational wars of nationality were as much a cheat as religious wars" (p. 565). Clearly, he is coming to recognize the conundrum (that goes back to the eighteenth century at least?) that instinct and scepticism, as embodied in *Švejk*, are part and parcel of rational man. The Good Soldier, man-instinctive, offers the most serious challenge to the gods. Lawrence, longing for the "moody skies of England" for "weakness, chills and grey mistiness", may really have been longing for the doubts and ambivalence which that other erstwhile serving soldier, prisoner and military leader, Jaroslav Hašek, never really abandoned.

Reordering Human Priorities

If war and history do not exist in the philosophical undertow of *The Good Soldier Švejk*, what are we left with? The answer can only be "the self", the individual, and this prefigures much existentialist thinking in the twentieth century. A Švejk-like digression is unavoidable here, but will, one hopes, unlike Švejk's anecdotes, illustrate a point.

Numerous commentators have pointed out that Hašek's near-exact contemporary and fellow citizen was Franz Kafka (born in Prague 1883, died in Vienna 1924). Max Brod, Kafka's closest friend, had praised Hašek's early work, and there was even a story that Hašek and his friends invited Kafka to a meeting of their infamous *Party of Moderate Change within the Boundaries of the Law* (Strana mírného pokroku v mezích zákona).[13] A highly efficient and conscientious white-collar worker in the "Workers' Accident Insurance Institute for the Kingdom of Bohemia",[14] Kafka adopted a lifestyle which could not have been more different from Hašek's. Yet both writers discovered the world of the self, Kafka in portraying a harrowing and ominous universe, slightly tinged with eroticism and dark comedy, Hašek by presenting us with a comedy whose bleak implications are undeniable.

As Ronald Gray remarks, in Kafka's diaries there are no references to speak of to the First World War or its aftermath, or to the revolutions in Berlin, Munich and Budapest.[15] There is a much-quoted entry in Kafka's diary for 2 August 1914: "Germany has declared war on Russia. – Swimming in the afternoon."[16] The shift from world events to utter banality echoes precisely the opening dialogue in *Švejk*. Gray tells us that "Kafka's self-torturing was seldom concerned with any particular evil, apart from self-love" (p. 46), and he refers to the author's "self-reproach", "self-criticism", "self-purification" and "self-damnation" (pp. 34–5). As we discuss later (see p. 139) in his novel *Love and Garbage* Ivan Klíma writes: "In his questioning Kafka stopped at the very first step, at himself, because even here he'd entered an inpenetrable depth."[17]

Karel Kosík creates an arresting image of Švejk being led under escort across Charles Bridge and meeting the hero of *The Trial*, also under guard coming the other way; the latter is being led to his death, the former, as it turns out, proves indestructible. Kosík concludes:

> In the first half of the twentieth century these two Prague authors offered two visions of the modern world. They described two human types, which at first glance seem far apart and contradictory, but which in reality complement each other. While Kafka depicted the materialism of our day-to-day human world and showed that modern man must live through and become familiar with the basic forms of alienation in order to be human, Hašek showed that man transcends materialism, because he is not reducible to an object, or to material products of relationships.[18]

Kosík points out how Švejk becomes a personality in the face of mindless authority (what the author calls the "Great Mechanism" – "Švejk without the mechanism is not Švejk, but only cheerful company, a joker, a fox"- p. 133), and this is a valid, uncontentious and perfectly understandable interpretation, especially given the "normalized" Czechoslovakia of the early 1980s; and Kosík touches briefly on the master–servant relationship in the novel. It is here, in our view, that the broader questions of self and the individual's priorities come into their own.

A curious feature of the picaresque novel, of which *Švejk* is a late, possibly the last, great example, is the love–hate, "see-saw" relationship between the ostensible underdog protagonist and his immediate superior.

Antecedents include, of course, Cervantes' Don Quixote and Sancho Panza, Diderot's Jacques and his Master, Fielding's Tom Jones and Squire Allsworthy; and its legacy in the twentieth century finds popular expression in Wodehouse's Woodster and Jeeves, or in a Czech context, we find something similar in Zdeněk Jirotka's humourous novel *Saturnin*, with the eponymous hero, his young employer and the avuncular Dr Vlach. Kosík, Pytlík and many other critics speak of Švejk in terms of Sancho Panza, and Hašek himself mentions him when setting the scene for Švejk and Lukáš to meet (English text, p. 162; Czech text, vol. 1, p. 175). This kind of situation comedy eventually transmogrifies into the popular "double-act", with a straight man and a fall guy, best exemplified in the Laurel and Hardy films.

There is an important aspect to such inescapable relationships. They constitute a *perpetuum mobile* in which the decisive individual, irrespective of social standing, physical prowess or apparent intelligence, loses sway, albeit momentarily, to the underling. The social fabric is stripped away and the individual is driven to rely on nothing but the "self". Indeed, decisiveness and the ability to act decisively play little part in the fate of either the superior or the subordinate.

Švejk becomes batman to Lieutenant Lukáš because he is gambled away by the drunken, licentious and blasphemous Chaplain Otto Katz; and in gambling, in games of chance, decisions are always upstaged by chance. The first encounter between Švejk and Lukáš leaves the latter disarmed. Lukáš is educated, an army instructor and is used to giving orders, but his immediate response to Švejk's first diatribe is to shrug his shoulders "like a man who did not know how to express a certain thought and could not immediately find words to do so" (p. 168) (jako člověk, který neví a nenalézá ihned slov k vyjádření určité myšlenky – vol. 1, p. 182). Later he thinks: "My God! I often talk drivel like this too and the only difference is the form I serve it up in" (p. 170) (Můj bože, vždyť i já často stejně mluvím takové blbosti a rozdíl je jen ve formě, kterou to podávám – p. 183). He is, in any event, uncertain about his personality:

> Lieutenant Lukáš was a typical regular officer of the ramshackle Austrian monarchy. The cadet school had turned him into a kind of amphibian. He spoke German in society, wrote German, read Czech books, and when he taught in the course for one-year volunteers, all of whom were Czechs, he told them in confidence: "Let's all be Czechs, but no one need know about it. I'm a Czech too." (p. 166)

> Nadporučík Lukáš byl typem aktivního důstojníka zchátralé rakouské monarchie. Kadetka vychovala z něho obojživelníka. Mluvil německy ve společnosti, psal německy, četl české knížky, a když vyučoval ve škole jednoročních dobrovolníků, samých Čechů, říkal jim důvěrně: "Buďme Češi, ale nemusí o tom nikdo vědět." (vol. 1, p. 179)

None of the misdemeanours that drive Lukáš to distraction is (ill-intentioned) though their perpetrator may freely admit to things going wrong: "Ever since I was little I have had bad luck like that. I always want to put something right, to do good, but nothing ever comes out of it except trouble for me and all around" (p. 172) (Vodmalička mám takovou smůlu. Vždycky chci něco vopravit, udělat dobře, a nikdy nic z toho nevyjde než nějaká nepříjemnost pro mne i pro vokolí – vol. 1, p. 186). This is the aftermath to his allowing the lieutenant's cat to eat the canary. When on the train he mistakes Major-General von Schwarzburg for a Mr Purkrábek of the Slavia Insurance Company and comments importunely on the senior officer's baldness, it is no more than the result of the hero's gregarious and garrulous nature (English text, p. 221ff; Czech text, vol. 2, p. 11ff.). And all his other mistakes *which are made while carrying out orders* are understandable: initially he will not allow Katy to enter the apartment; he has "fulfilled her every wish" (p. 183) (vyplnil všechna přání – vol. 1, p. 197), including about six carnal ones; when the letter of assignation he is delivering to Mrs Kákonyi for Lukáš falls into her husband's hands, he is prepared to claim it is his, and the ensuing fracas and public outcry are hardly his fault.

His delivering only the first part of the popular novel on which the army's secret codes are based is again understandable, as are the delays and frustrations created by his antics on the telephone. When caught by the tyrannical Lieutenant Dub while procuring a bottle of cognac for Lukáš, he saves himself and his superior by pretending it is ordinary drinking water and downing it in one (English text, p. 578; Czech text, vols 3–4, p. 144). The brawl that ensues when Švejk has to extricate Dub from the brothel is again hardly the hero's fault. Kundera has noted that Švejk merely mimics the inanities of the bureaucratic state.[19] Far more subversive that all these errors are those where Švejk simply acts out of intuition, where there is no rationale behind what he does, as we noted in the previous section (pulling a train's communication cord, putting on a Russian uniform).

(Švejk, as a product of the Modernist imagination, is not to be construed as a flesh-and-blood character, but more as a cardboard cut-out, a bundle of images or notions. Yet he frequently takes on more substance when he acts on impulse. After he halts the train he finds himself seated with a forlorn Hungarian soldier, and despite the language barrier, they form a bond, with Švejk shelling out for the drinks. More poignantly, after the mix-up over the code books, Lukáš cannot bring himself to tell Švejk exactly what is at stake, and the hero "feels respect for himself" (Měl sám před sebou úctu). Routinely, the hero confesses to his idiocy and incompetence, and we read: "It did not happen every day that he committed something so frightful that he must never be allowed to learn what it was"

(p. 476) (To se každý den nestane, aby provedl něco tak hrozného, že se nikdy nesmí dozvědít, co to bylo – vols 3–4, p. 39).

In the normal course of things Lukáš is just as capable of kind acts as of being a martinet. He would occasionally buy his men a barrel of beer; then he might have Baloun trussed up and afterwards feel remorse. Yet in his dealings with Švejk he develops from initial perplexity, as noted above, to exasperation, fury and then a kind of affectionate resignation. This is not purely attributable to the eternally ravenous Baloun, his replacement batman, forever stealing his food. It is worth pausing over their reunion after the Mrs Kákonyi débâcle:

> Švejk and the lieutenant were silent. Both observed each other closely for a long time. Lukáš stared at Švejk as though he were preparing to hypnotize him, like a cock standing in front of a chicken and waiting to spring on it.
>
> Švejk as usual looked at Lieutenant Lukáš with moist tender eyes as though wanting to say: "United again, heart of mine! Now nothing will separate us, my pet."
>
> And when the lieutenant remained silent for a long time, Švejk's eyes spoke with sorrowful tenderness: "Speak, my darling, say what you are thinking."
>
> Lieutenant Lukáš broke this embarrassing silence with the words in which he tried to inject a considerable dose of irony: "Hearty welcome to you, Švejk! Thank you for the visit. Well, now, what a precious guest we have!" (pp. 404–5)

> Švejk i nadporučík mlčeli. Oba se dlouho na sebe dívali a pozorovali se. Lukáš se díval na Švejka, jako by chtěl ho hypnotizovat, jako kohoutek stojící proti kuřeti a chystající se na ně vrhnout.
>
> Švejk, jako vždy, díval se svým vlahým, něžným pohledem na nadporučíka Lukáše, jako by chtěl mu říct: Opět pohromadě, má sladká duše, teď už nás nic nerozdvojí, můj holoubku.
>
> A když dlouho se nadporučík neozýval, výraz očí Švejkových promluvil s lítostivou něhou: Tak řekni něco, můj zlatý, vyjádři se!
>
> Nadporučík Lukáš přerušil toho trapné ticho slovy, do kterých snažil se vložit notnou porci ironie: "Pěkně vás vítám, Švejku. Děkuji vám za návštěvu. Vida, to jsou k nám hosti." (vol. 2, pp. 199–200)

Lukáš then carries out one of his usual explosions, retroactively controlled. The translation here makes a good job of rendering the inter-gender affection (Má sladká duše, můj holoubku, můj zlatý: my sweet soul, my little dove, my treasure). One notes, in passing, that there has been serious speculation about Hašek's sexual orienation, despite his two wives. By the time they reach Budapest Lukáš is missing Švejk as much as Švejk misses the lieutenant (English text, p. 509; Czech text, vols 3–4, p. 74). Later on, in a very rare glimpse we get into Švejk's private life (the only other salient one is the odd mention of his schoolmaster and reserve officer brother, English text, p. 526 and p. 528; Czech text, vols 3–4, pp. 91, 93), the hero reads to

Lukáš an old letter from his former girlfriend, breaking off their relationship. This is the kind of intimacy he would not share with his equals and chance drinking companions. Shortly before Švejk becomes separated from his own side and dons the Russian uniform, we actually have Lukáš *asking* Švejk to tell a story, instead of telling him to shut up (English text, p. 653; Czech text, vols 3–4, p. 222). Their final reunion is brief and comes after Švejk has been cleared of the treason charges against him (English text, pp. 734–6; Czech text, vols 3–4, pp. 304–6), and here, once again, Lukáš is forlornly pleading with Švejk to be brief and to the point. However, it would be safe to assume that had Hašek's text continued the mutual affection would not have diminished.

The lesson to be drawn from this account of the master–servant relationship in *Švejk* is that the "self" is more susceptible to emendation through interaction with other "selves" than through the agency of bureaucracies and military hierarchy. Such development in personality is likely to be more momentary and reversible, than linear, and to that extent may be compared with the novel's consideration of history. Radko Pytlík, in discussing Hašek's character, argues that the author was a child and remained one all his life, and "acted impulsively and decisively. In this way he opened his soul to surprising experiences, and concentrated all his spiritual energy into one instant, without regard to the circumstances. Thus to see the surrounding world in a bizarre, colourful light and in comic contrasts, unburdened by seriousness" (jednal vždy impulzívně a rozhodně. Tím otevřel duši překvapujícím zážitkům a soustředil veškerou duševní energii do jediného okamžiku, bez ohledu na okolnosti. Proto viděl okolní svět v bizarním, barvitém osvětlení a v komických kontrastech, bez zatěžující vážnosti) (pp. 100–1).

By the same token it can be argued that Švejk and Lukáš are the most complex characters in the book, the place where the author has concentrated most of his spiritual energy; thus other characters are more prone to stereotyping and, paradoxically, to grotesque distortion. Each is governed by one overriding trait. This is so, and yet it in fact aids a key trait in the novel that we have argued for, namely that the self takes precedence over abstract notions, even in those characters who profess such notions. It should be added too that the idea of "concentrating on one instant" is a *sine qua non* of the novel's scorn for the historical process, for large institutions, be they the army, the church or the judiciary, with all their concomitant plans, procedures and formulae.

Švejk is gregarious, has a prodigious anecdotal memory, attracts people as much as he repels others (usually his superiors – but could they survive without him?); he can defuse confrontations of any scale with his disarming smile and innocent blue eyes; he can act courageously and with violence on occasion – even if the results are not as intended, witness the manner in which he ejects the debt collector who calls for Chaplain Katz (English text, p. 145; Czech text, vol. 1, p. 158), or the way he knocks the impoverished Polish nobleman down the stairs in the brothel when he is trying to locate Lieutenant Dub (English text, p. 621; Czech text, vols 3–4, p. 190); he can be generous, buying the Hungarian drinks, or rapacious – after all, in civvy street he forges dogs' pedigrees to make a living. His powers of reasoning result in some delightful sophistries (e.g. that this war will last 15 years because now people are twice as clever as when they fought the Thirty Years War – English text, p. 739; Czech text, vols 3–4, p. 310), but no more erroneous than the thinking of the high command. Lukáš is a gambler, a womanizer and occasional drunkard, but never to the exclusion of all else. We note his other qualities above.

To judge these characters by their actions rather than their words, they are motivated by enlightened hedonism and survival instincts. This is true of all the other characters too, except that Hašek reduces their portraits, in most instances, to one cardinal trait. The predominant interest of those in the officer class, Colonel Zillergut, Lieutenant Dub, Captain Ságner and so on, is to exert their power over their subordinates. Do they spend any real time or energy on serious military matters in order to win the war? The chief representatives of the other ranks are each driven by individual concerns for their own survival, no matter how they may, or may not, dress them up: Baloun is ruled by his belly, Marek (clearly, as Parrott has pointed out,[20] another alter ego of Hašek – just as Švejk is – given his editing *The World of Animals* (English text, p. 323ff; Czech text, vol. 2, p. 114ff.) and the dossier on him) is powered by intellectual tail-chasing, as, in his capacity as official military historian, he writes up accounts of future glorious victories (English text, p. 580; Czech text, vols 3–4, p. 146). There is a deliciously prophetic element here: there was an old anti-Soviet joke that the prime duty of the Soviet historian was to predict history. Jurajda, the occultist cook, in civilian life had owned and edited an occultist journal and written on how no one should fear death and on the transmigration of souls. This does not prevent him from trying to avoid the front by writing a letter ostensibly to his wife, but largely for the benefit of the military censorship (English text, p. 457; Czech text, vols 3–4, pp. 18–19).

Cadet Biegler is the most intriguing of the minor characters, for he is the only man among the other ranks who genuinely embraces the military ethos, out-Heroding the officer class. He is introduced by the author as being monumentally stupid, and in his pursuit of military glory rather than victory *per se*, he achieves what no other character in the book does – temporarily he quits the real world. Cadet Biegler's dream represents one of the darkest passages in the novel. The depiction of Heaven turns out to be just another version of the hell that is earth. Angel-officers beat angel-recruits for not shouting "alleluia" adequately and "General" Biegler's audience with God reveals the latter to be none other than his former Captain Ságner. Meanwhile wretched lines of mutilated men, with bits of their bodies in their rucksacks, queue up to get through the pearly gates. If one wanted to seek moral lessons in all this, one would have to note that Baloun's filching to stave off his hunger displays an honesty that far outweighs Biegler's vanity. Baloun's belly, his "self", also denotes an ontological authenticity that is sadly lacking elsewhere.

Conclusion

Lieutenant Lukáš [. . .] cried out in a hoarse voice: "When is this going to end, Švejk?" (p. 406). (Nadporučík Lukáš [. . .] chraplavým hlasem zvolal: "Kdy bude tomu konec, Švejku?" – vol. 2, p. 201)

This is a plea as much as a question, and comes in the middle of one of the hero's excruciatingly diffuse accounts of himself and others. The digressions, the anecdotes and the sophistry which Švejk indulges in equate with the amorphous and incomprehensible nature of the modern world. They amount to a rejection of nineteenth-century rationalism and the conventional novel of that time, which demanded a beginning, middle and end. They also reflect the day-by-day suffering of the individual in war or peace. They are replicated by other characters in the book: when Katy's husband comes to confront Lukáš and to take his wife back home, the two men studiously avoid the pressing issue. The hop merchant bemoans the loss of his foreign markets, while Lukáš, perhaps uniquely in the entire text, discusses strictly military matters and the wider progress of the war (English text, p. 186ff; Czech text, vol. 1, p. 199ff). The two part most amicably and Katy leaves calmly with her husband.

The digressions in *Švejk* work outwards from the individual and the moment he is in. They are the antithesis of any overall plan for mankind, or for a society or state into which each individual must fit. They are anti-intellectual and highly anecdotal, relying on hearsay rather than sources (note the number of books and authors in the text that are cited in mocking tones; or, in one of the rare footnotes Hašek provides, a book is, thankfully, spurious: Udo Kraft's *Self-Education in Dying for the Emperor* (English text, p. 490; Czech text, vols 3–4, p. 54).

The anti-intellectualism of *Švejk* also accounts for its vernacular language, which annoyed some critics, especially at the time of the book's first publication. In fact, the demotic tones hark back at least as far as Shakespeare's bawdy or even Chaucer's and Boccaccio's toilet humour, and they foreshadow the vulgarity of much literature from the 1960s onwards. Hašek's linguistic registers seem positively chaste by comparison. It could also be added that Hašek's linguistic excesses, if that is what they were, played a part, albeit belatedly, in the democratisation of Czech literature, and in its internationalization.

The Other Prose

While it must be said that by comparison with *Švejk* the bulk of Hašek's other work is disappointing, it should be recorded that it was vast and that it represents an important cultural phenomenon, namely the intertwining of life and art. Hašek was a hack, a cabaret performer, a street artist, a raconteur. Hašek-šašek (Hašek the clown) became a common epithet. His public antics would have been called "happenings" in the late 1960s in Western Europe, while his greatest stunt, the founding of the Party of Moderate Change within the Boundaries of the Law, eloquently foreshadows the none-too-serious fringe parties which featured in British elections from 1960s, Screaming Lord Sutch's Monster Raving Loony Party being the best example. Hašek's political party consisted of no more than a few drinking companions who met at the Golden Litre pub in Balbín Street and then wandered further afield, to numerous other hostelries and wine cellars in Prague, before roaming the whole country and going abroad, sponging. Curiously, The Chalice, Švejk's local, was not a particular favourite of Hašek (Pytlík, p. 167). Hašek stood as candidate in the 1911 election in the Vinohrady constituency, though he was not officially registered and the 38 votes cast in his support were presumably spoiled papers. He campaigned under such slogans as "Down with the earthquake in Mexico!" and put forward policies on animal rehabilitation and nationalising concierges.[21] His *History* of the party was not published until 1963.

Hašek created a unique and seminal mock epic, he celebrated the victory of the individual over the system and in his lifestyle he blended street theatre with literature. It is unlikely that the debates about him, already voluminous, will go away. So instead of a conclusion, I cite just one example of his abiding appeal and relevance. In the immediate wake of the Velvet Revolution, *The Times* carried a prominent tribute to the Good Soldier and his creator, declaring:

> If you can laugh at the wicked, their fate is sealed. Jaroslav Hasek and his great creation laughed at every kind of obedience, order, structure, tradition, rank, respect, deference and law; they laughed because what they were laughing at deserved to be pulled down and burnt to ashes. In the annals of Czechoslovakia the good soldier Svejk should have a hallowed form and place. I ask President Havel: can you think of a more hallowed form and place for him than Wenceslas Square? Forward, the sculptors of Bohemia![22]

Primary Influences: presence of technology, Pragmatist thinking, Cubism (analytical)

Karel Čapek
(1890–1938)
Whose point of view?

———

Cubist artist

died *utopianism*

In the spring of 1911 Karel Čapek travelled from Berlin to Paris to join his brother, Josef. The former was on a break from his studies at Charles University in Prague, the latter from Art school. Karel attended lectures at the Sorbonne as well as enjoying, on his own admission, a good deal of the nightlife.[1] This trip proved to be the single greatest influence on him, for it buttressed his penchant for the avant-garde, for Cubism and for the thought of the charismatic Henri Bergson (1859–1941), the leading philosopher of the day. There was to be a curious kinship in the deaths of the French philosopher and the Czech author. Čapek died on Christmas Day 1938, heartbroken at the incipient occupation of his country by the Nazis and at the betrayal of Czechoslovakia by the Western powers. Bergson's last months in occupied France (he died in January 1941) remain in some obscurity, but there are stories that, being of Jewish–Polish extraction, he gave up his French honours, registered as a Jew and rejected a squalid offer from the Vichy régime that he become an honorary Aryan.[2] The dreams of both men were in tatters.

The idea of Bergson's most germane to an understanding of Čapek's fiction concerns mechanism and teleology: Bertrand Russell writes:

> Mechanism and teleology suffer from the same defect: both suppose that there is no essential novelty in the world. Mechanism regards the future as implicit in the past, and teleology, since it believes that the end to be achieved can be known in advance, denies that any essential novelty is contained in the result.
>
> As against both these views, though with more sympathy for teleology than for mechanism, Bergson maintains that evolution is truly *creative*, like the work of an artist.[3]

Here we see Čapek's preoccupation with the world of technology and

———

27

[handwritten top margin: fascinated by technology, but concerned & opposed to dehumanization.]

[handwritten left margin: father of contemporary education]

*[handwritten left margin: * Pragmatist Philosophy: ideas could not exist in isolation. ideas must be based in effects + action]*

[handwritten left margin: Dewey]

more specifically of mass production. On the one hand he readily recognizes the usefulness of the machine age and the ways in which life can be eased; yet on the other hand he is deeply disturbed at the dehumanizing aspect. Man's spiritual make-up, his ability to create and be free are under renewed threat at the start of the twentieth century from the latest upward twist in the industrialization spiral. The tank, the machine-gun, the aeroplane and poisonous gas all became innovatory features of the Great War.

The Czech writer was also much influenced by the American school of Pragmatist philosophy, represented primarily by William James (1842–1910) and John Dewey (1859–1952). Briefly, Pragmatist philosophy, in its heyday in the first two decades or so of the twentieth century, held that ideas could not exist in isolation and had to be based on action and experience. One of James' key assertions was that "If the hypothesis of God works satisfactorily in the widest sense of the word, it is true." Such a notion, not unsurprisingly, put pragmatism at odds with Catholicism. But it had its appeal for the practically-minded Čapek and it harmonized with the staunch anti-Catholicism of his friend Tomáš Masaryk, philosopher-king and founding president of Czechoslovakia. No doubt some philosophers would take issue with James' views, but in addressing the question of religion in Čapek's fiction, Pragmatism does seem to play a role. How often do Čapek's characters invoke the Almighty or quote directly from the Bible! Yet how scarce are the discussions on whether God really exists and what His nature is! Čapek seems to take God's existence for granted, using it, somewhat facilely it might be argued, as a moral yardstick. The simplicity with which religion is invoked in Čapek's attempts to establish an uncompromised moral code also echoes back to the Hussite tradition, and this too stands four square with Masaryk's own values.[4]

Yet in Pragmatist thinking, doctrine and fixed principles took second place, and such "liberalism", shading into scepticism and irony on occasion, is repeatedly to be glimpsed in the best of Čapek's writing. However, in his less satisfactory work one detects an element of "wanting one's cake and eating it". Čapek's ambivalent attitude towards technology is frequently in evidence; he will allow a scientist or a detective to be upstaged by a fortune-teller, but warns against mysticism. Further, caught in a moral maze of some kind, his decent-minded characters will make their exit simply by quoting from the Bible. This leads on to another weakness in the author. John Dewey's life-long commitment to education possibly rubbed off in an unfortunate way on the Czech writer, for Čapek is not infrequently open to charges of didacticism. Of course, educational preoccupations would be understandable within the context of the nation-building that the newly-born democratic state was engaged in.

Though Cubism is a term applied primarily to the visual arts, it also has its uses in discussing certain types of literature. Pablo Picasso was, of

[handwritten: tension between creativity + mechanical notions]

[handwritten: truth within truth: fragmentation of truth]

course, the prime mover, especially in the six or seven years leading up to the First World War. The Cubist painters rejected the traditional notions of perspective and texture, whereby art made an attempt to imitate nature; Cubism brazenly sought to expose the structure of their subjects. Sometimes planes overlapped and objects were fragmented and/or seen two-dimensionally but from different angles. So-called Analytical Cubism, which in particular emphasized *form*, was at its height in Paris from 1910–1912 – just the time when the Čapek brothers could witness it first-hand.

This kind of artistic relativism, by means of which multiple perception was made possible, could in the hands of the creative writer, allow more easily for the depiction of cognitive and moral complexities. One of the cardinal features of Čapek's best work is its ability to see truths behind truths, while maintaining perfectly accessible plots and characters.

Yet another influence on Čapek was to be G. K.Chesterton. The two men met only once and briefly, yet the Czech author was an avid reader of Chesterton and sought to draw him into correspondence on several occasions.[5] Readers of the "Father Brown" stories will certainly find echoes in *The Tales from Two Pockets* (*Povídky z jedné kapsy a z druhé kapsy*, sometimes collectively known informally as *Kapesní povídky*). Both authors delighted in the depiction of paradox.

One must note in Čapek the widely disparate, verging on the mutually exclusive, influences. There is the analytical, even clinical, cast of mind of the professional philosopher; the intuitive and subconscious processes of Modernism (in its Cubist manifestations); and then the Liberal values evinced by the English author. Chesterton's later Catholicism would of course run counter to Čapek's blander religious preoccupations. In all this one might detect a paradigm of the intellectual openness, much commented on by critics and historians, that Czechoslovakia has for centuries been prey to and indeed likes to trade on. Has it led to scepticism and even cynicism? Or has it resulted in the very best kind of broad and liberal intellectual orientation?

The Trilogy

Hordubal, *Meteor* and *An Ordinary Life* (*Hordubal*, *Povětroň* and *Obyčejný život*) are generally regarded as Čapek's masterpiece. He argued in his Afterword to them that they should be seen as a trilogy, concluding:

> Now we can respect a man because he is different from us and understand him because we are his equals. Fraternity and diversity! Even that most ordinary life is still infinite, immense is the value of every soul. Polana is beautiful,

Clear psychological understanding of psyche

had she been ever so boney; the life of a man is too big to have only one face, to be sized up at a glance. No longer will Hordubal's heart be lost, and the man who fell from the sky will live through more and more stories. Nothing ends, not even a trilogy; instead of ending, it opens wide, as wide as man is able.

Nyní můžeme ctít člověka, protože je jiný než my, a rozumět mu, protože jsme mu rovni. Bratrství a rozmanitost! I ten nejobyčejnější život je ještě nekonečný, nesmírná je hodnota každé duše. Krásná je Polana, byť byla sebekostnatější; život člověka je příliš veliký, aby měl jen jedinou tvář a mohl být přehlédnut najednou. Už se neztratí srdce Hordubalovo, a muž z nebe spadlý bude prožívat nové a nové příběhy. Nic se nekončí, ani trilogie ne; místo konce se otvírá doširoka, tak doširoka, pokud člověk stačí.[6]

This is no trilogy in the usual sense of the word, since the plots and characters are quite different and each novel can be appreciated in isolation. However, the three works together stand as the most eloquent enactment of the author's artistic and philosophical credo, and one detects in the Afterword a degree of optimism that Čapek could, with very good reason, never aspire to subsequently. There is also an intriguing parallel between the way that Čapek turns his attention in the trilogy from broader social and historical considerations (which are much in evidence in his famous early plays like *Rossum's Universal Robots* – or *R.U.R.* – and *From the Life of Insects* – *Ze života hmyzu*) to the individual's psychology, and the way that some natural scientists in the same period pointedly turned their investigations away from the "macro" questions of the nature of the universe which attracted Einstein and directed them to sub-molecular and then sub-atomic physics.

Hordubal is set, exceptionally for Čapek, well away from the urban and petty bourgeois world of shops, factories and offices. The hero returns, after eight years of working as a miner in America, to his native Ruthenia, the most Eastern region of Czechoslovakia, the most primitive and poorest. For centuries the area belonged to Hungary, but was ceded to Czechoslovakia in 1920, then to the Soviet Union in 1945 and is currently part of an independent Ukraine. (There was a joke in Čapek's day that this was the African part of Czechoslovakia.) Here then, in an area populated by Ukrainians, Hungarians, Jews and Gypsies, Hordubal tries to renew his relationship with his wife and daughter. However, his wife Polana has taken up with the hired hand and together they are making a good job of running the farm, though in ways of which the hero disapproves. Hafie (Hafia in the translation), the daughter, exhibits real affection for Štěpán (Stepan) and nothing but fear for her real father. Hordubal is unable to reintegrate into the family or even the village. He falls ill and dies, though there are grounds for thinking that he may have been murdered. That eventually is the verdict of the jury. Caught then between the New World and the Old, between East and West, between industry and agriculture, relative affluence and undeniable poverty, Juraj Hordubal is the most complex of individuals. Yet the social and economic considerations are peripheral, even though the story is grounded in fact – in 1932 the Czech press reported on one Juraj Hardubej, who, after eight years in America, was murdered by his wife's lover, Vasil Maňák, to whom the wife Polana had betrothed her 11-year-old daughter; the murderer confessed and was sentenced to life imprisonment, the wife to twelve years.[7]

Of much more interest than the bare facts and the socio-economic circumstances surrounding the crime are the various ways that the hero perceives himself and his situation, and how others perceive him and the events in his life. Of crucial concern here is the mode of narration. The first part of the novel is told almost exclusively from Hordubal's point of view, with his thought processes reported to us directly. Illiterate and largely inarticulate, he in fact *says* very little, though we are persistently informed of his imagined dialogues with whomever he meets. The manner runs close to *style indirecte libre* and even to stream of consciousness. Yet Čapek never relinquishes his hold on lucidity.

The text opens with several simultaneous snapshots of the hero: from the omniscient narrator, from the hero's own angle of vision and from that of his fellow passengers. However, the reader is only momentarily disorientated. Soon we are aware that the hero is returning to his native village from America. His crumpled foreign clothes symbolically foreshadow his inability to reintegrate, and he is continually referred to as "the American" by his fellow villagers. His recollections of life abroad never leave him, yet he is incapable of conveying them to old acquaintances. Hordubal invokes the Almighty so frequently as he tries to makes sense of his situation that it is tempting to conclude that there is more at work here than the mere taking of the Lord's name in vain in authentic rustic speech patterns. Čapek allows for the possibility of a Divinity (in contrast to his avowedly atheistic father) without seeking to define it. In the closing paragraphs of the work the village is likened to Bethlehem. At the same time Čapek recognizes the validity of human experience over faith. On his first excursion up into the mountains where he renews his acquaintance with the herdsman Míša (Misa), for once the hero is at peace:

> With his hands spread out Hordubal lay on his back. There is no Hordubal, or even a Polana – only the sky, the earth, and the sound of the cow-bells. The clouds melt away, and nothing is left behind, not even as much as when you breathe on the glass. The ox thinks what a struggle he has, and it is only cow-bells from afar. What's the use of knowing. Gaze. God gazes, too. What a big eye, peaceful like the eye of a beast. The wind, as if time itself were

flowing and roaring; where can it all come from? And what's the use of knowing. (p. 57)

Ruce rozpjaty, leží Hordubal naznak: není Hordubala, není ani Polany – jen obloha a země, vítr a zvonění stád. Rozplývají se oblaka a nic po nich nezbude, ani jako když na sklo dechneš. Myslí volek, cože má sháňky, a je to jen zdálky zvonění. Nač vědět? Zírej. I Bůh zírá. Jaké veliké oko, pokojné jako pohled hovada. Ten vítr, to jako by sám čas tekl a hučel; kde se ho tolik nabere? Nač to vědět? (p. 49)

Trapped between faith and reason, Hordubal can only question whether the knowledge gained by either of these routes is of any worth. In his misery Hordubal tries reasoning, explaining his wife's self-evident infidelity in ways to exonerate her. He acquires a love potion from a gypsy woman to try and win her back. He seeks work away from his own farm; he contemplates introducing new American-style innovations to the farm and he enquires about the possibility of returning to America. He resorts to violence in ejecting Štěpán from the farm, only to see him return. He contrives the betrothal of his daughter to save face. He means well, attempting to care for the horses and cope with domestic chores while Polana shuts herself away from him.

At every turn he is defeated. Yet Hordubal represents a kind of triumph. His epistemology is in fact far surer than that of the investigators in the subsequent, and far shorter, parts of the novel, who seek to establish facts and true motives. The experts cannot even agree on whether the hero was stabbed or shot, or whether the small hole in his heart was the cause of death or his pneumonia. Štěpán's apparently irrefutable responsibility for Polana's pregnancy is brought into question by her defense lawyer's scientific arguments. Was the motive for the murder amorous rivalry, hatred, money? Štěpán's confession in court is most likely inspired by his desire to protect Polana. The real truths reside elsewhere in this novel.

William Harkins has written incisively on the symbolism in the novel. Štěpán Manya is dark and Romantic, naturally associated with fleet-footed horses. Hordubal still clings to more traditional forms of farming, cows and crops. High up in the mountains one gains greater perspective, not just of terrain but also of human beings and the universe. The symbolism is not of the obtrusive, almost allegorical, kind that one sometimes encounters in Čapek. It blends with the realism of the work and with the highly evocative nature descriptions. The result is a demonstration of poetic, as opposed to empirical, truth.

The second and third parts of the work are quite deliberately devoid of poetry, as unimaginative policemen and lawyers go about their business. They do their duty to their own satisfaction, but the reader despairs at their ham-fistedness and egoism. The ignorance and moral paucity of the workaday world is driven home to the reader by the haunting final sentence of the book, set out as a separate section: "The heart of Juraj Hordubal was lost somewhere, and was never buried" (p. 149). (Srdce Juraje Hordubala se kdesi ztratilo a nebylo nikdy pohřbeno – p. 126).

And the moral conundrums in the novel are likewise never laid to rest. Whilst our sympathies are primarily with the hero, there is a culpability about his naivity. He never learnt to read or write in his own language, let alone in English. When his literate friend, whom he relied on for three years to communicate with his wife and send her money, is killed in an accident, Hordubal blithely continues for the next five years to work abroad. He then assumes that he can pick up the threads of his Ruthenian life as if nothing had happened. In America he was swindled out of three thousand dollars in savings, and perhaps it is true that given his lack of education there is nothing he could do about it. Back home he is deprived of his family, friends, dignity and eventually his life; but as we watch him in close-up here, as opposed to hearing his own long-range recollections concerning America, we feel his complicity in his fate. The outlandish, outrageous scheme to betroth his daughter Hafie to Štěpán (a conscious inversion of what happened in the Hardubej case) suggests that Hordubal's solicitude at times plays second fiddle to his self-esteem. The manner of the narration and the existence of the other two novels in the trilogy urge us to contemplate what the inner thoughts and feelings of Štěpán, Polana and Hafie might be, and how our sympathies for them, to Hordubal's moral detriment, could so easily be enlisted.

Meteor is the most programmatic of the three novels. As the victim of an air crash lies unconscious and dying in a hospital somewhere in Europe various other characters try to establish his identity and together with this, the facts of his life and even his moral standing. Why should he have essayed a flight in such a storm? (We should note, of course, that in the early 1930s, air was by no means the preferred method of travel that it is today.) There are essentially four different approaches in this exercise: the scientific approach of the surgeon and the specialist; the religious approach of the nun, which involves her recurrent dream and the notion of confession; that of the clairvoyant, in which telepathy and intuition predominate; and finally, and most extensively, that of the poet, where imagination and creativity form the chief method. Each approach is supported to an extent by its devotee's *apologia*, the weakest of which is the doctors':

> The specialist sniffed and raised his eyes. "Sugar?"
> "How do you know?" muttered the surgeon. "I had his water examined, of course . . . If there's no blood. Besides other things they did find sugar.

You recognize it by the smell?"

"I'm not often mistaken," said the specialist. "You can tell acetone. Dear me, our ars medica is 50 per cent intuition." (p. 192)

Internista začichal a zvedl oči. "Cukr?"

"Jak to víte?" bručel chirurg. "Já jsem mu ovšem dal vyšetřit vodu … není-li tam krev. Našli mimoto cukr. Vy to poznáte po čichu?

"Obyčejně se nezmýlím," děl internista. "Aceton se pozná. Holenku, naše ars medica, to je na padesát procent intuice." (p. 161)

Incidentally, "Dear me" in the translation is slightly inaccurate. The somewhat old-fashioned "Holenku" would be bettered rendered as "My dear chap". The medics can establish only so much, and then it is subject to conjecture: the patient ("Mr X") has been in the tropics, since he has yellow fever, probably somewhere where there are colonies, since he has coins of various European denominations on him; he has had a serious alcohol problem, and he has had a restless, wandering, possibly adventurous existence. The surgeon insists he will die of concussion and internal injuries, while the specialist is anxious that he should die of the far less mundane yellow fever ("Don't grudge him a famous exit" – p. 195; Přejte mu, kamarade, slavný exitus – p. 164). In this mildly comic exchange one detects the supremacy of the ego over the method employed and the underlying suggestion that objectivity is impossible.

The nun's philosophical position hardly needs stating: she has religious conviction, and in her recurrent dream she simply receives Mr X's confession. He has no recollection of his mother and relations with his wealthy father were hostile, while as a boy Mr X was, in his own words ("Lazy, obstinate and wicked" – p. 175; líný, vzdorovitý a neřestný – p. 147) and even as a boy he slept with the housemaids. He resolves to seduce a particular girl, and when he succeeds, he is shamed by her assertion that she will now be his. He flees abroad, and when too much wild living ("I could tell you of fifty lives, and they are all false" – p. 185; Mohl bych vám vypravovat padesát životů, a všechny jsou lež – p. 156) lands him in hospital, he comes to realise the importance of that early relationship, and hurries homewards to the girl, only to crash on route. From her account the reader can view Mr X as simply an old-fashioned repentant sinner (hackneyed in the extreme, given the moral ambiguities that much twentieth-century Czech fiction has thrown up).

The clairvoyant finds himself suffering from the same symptoms as Mr X and cannot help but concentrate on him. He attempts an explanation of his powers:

"Let's say, imagine a circle – a circle of brass wire." Here he drew a circle in the air. "A circle is a visible thing. We can think of it abstractly, we can define it mathematically, but psychologically a circle is something we *see*. If I blind-folded you you could touch that wire, and you would say that it is a circle. You would have the *sensation* of a circle. And there are people who with closed eyes can discern with the ear what form the body has that is vibrating. In our case they would *hear* a circle if we hit that wire with a mallet [. . .] Telepathy is nonsense, we can't perceive things at a distance; we must approach them, approach the stars with number, matter with analysis, and the microscope; and when we have eliminated sensation and bodily presence we can approach anything by concentration. I admit that there may be premonitions, dreams, apparitions and visions; I admit that, but on principle I do not want to have anything to do with it. I decline it and reject it. I am no visionary; I am analytic; full reality does not disclose itself to us; it must be won with arduous labour, by means of analysis and concentration. You admit that the brain is the instrument of analysis, but you guard yourself from the conception that perhaps it is a lens which brings objects nearer to us, although we do not move from the spot or open our eyes." (pp. 201–2)

"Dejme tomu, představte si kruh – kruh z mosazného drátu." Přitom nakreslil ve vzduchu kruh. "Kruh je věc viditelná. Můžeme si jej myslet abstraktně, můžeme jej definovat matematicky, ale psychologicky je kruh něco, co *vidíme*. Kdybych vám zavázal oči, mohli byste ten drát ohmatat a řekli byste, že je to kruh. Měli byste *pocit* kruhu. A jsou lidé, kteři dovedou se zavřenýma očima rozeznat sluchem, jaký tvar má těleso, které zvučí. V našem případě by *slyšeli* kruh, kdybychom do toho drátu uhodili paličkou [. . .] Telepatie je nesmysl, nemůžeme poznávat na dálku; musíme se věcem přiblížit, přiblížit si hvězdy číslicemi, hmotu rozborem a drobnohledem; a když vyloučíme smysly a tělesnou blízkost, můžeme se čemukoliv přiblížit soustředěním. Připouštím, že jsou snad předtuchy, sny, zjevení a vize; připouštím to, ale metodicky to odmítám, popírám a zavrhuju. Nejsem vizionář, jsem analytik; pravá skutečnost se nám nezjevuje; musí být vytěžena přísnou prací, analýzou a soustředěním. Připouštíte, že mozek je nástroj analýzy, ale bráníte se představě, že by mohl být čočkou, která nám přibližuje věci, aniž bychom se hnuli ze svého místa nebo otevřeli oči." (pp. 170–1)

The clairvoyant's explanations of his method, abbreviated here, are still none the less long-winded, somewhat pedantic and arguably a little contra-dictory; perhaps this signals misgivings on the author's part similar to those he has concerning the doctors' "scientific" approach. That said, there is some substance here, as the clairvoyant echoes concepts first propounded by Gottfried Leibnitz back in the seventeenth century concerning the human mind as a telescope,[8] and also picks up on the notion of synaesthesia. Čapek would have been more than familiar with the ideas of the French and Russian Symbolist poets around the turn of the century regarding the interaction of the five human senses and the possibility of arriving at trans-sense cognition (see p. 75 on Hrabal).

The clairvoyant goes on to offer another telling analogy, this time one
that might chime in with ideas of relativity:

> It is as if you made a film of a man's life from the moment he was born until
> now, and then placed all the pictures on top of each other and projected them
> all at once. You say, what a medley! Yes, for the present coalesces with the
> past, covers everything over, and only the form of the life remains as some-
> thing indescribable, and immensely individual; something like a personal
> aura, in which everything is contained [. . .] Everything, *the future as well*
> [. . .] That man won't live. (p. 203)

> Je to, jako byste filmovali život člověka od narození až do tohoto okamžiku,
> a pak všechny ty obrázky položili na sebe a promítli je všechny současně.
> Rekněte; jaká změť! Ano, neboť splývá přítomnost i minulost, všechno se
> překrývá, a zbývá jen tvar života, něco nepopsatelného a nesmírně osobního:
> něco jako osobní aura, ve které je uloženo vše [. . .] Všecko, *i budoucnost*
> [. . .] Ten člověk nebude živ. (p. 172)

Later, during his account of Mr X's life, the clairvoyant tells the doctors that "events" do not interest him, and that he looks at life in its
totality. In his account, the patient was deprived of his mother as a child
and had a difficult relationship with his father. He became a chemist, fix-
ated with molecular and atomic structures, but on proposing a new
chemical formula, was rejected by the leading chemist of the day. He seeks
his fortune abroad. Much later he sees his ideas published in a scientific
journal and rushes back home to unearth his own notebooks, but the
plane crashes.

Empirical science, religious faith and a straightforward sense of right and
wrong, extrasensory powers coupled with an awareness of some very
modern scientific thinking – all these yield only so much. The lion's share
of the novel is handed to the creative writer.

The poet's journal states that he is inventing a story about X, "one of the
thousand stories that I have not written and shall not write" (p. 228) (Jednu
z tisíců povídek, které jsem nenapsal a nenapíšu – p. 193; note the slight
mistranslation: "thousands"). He is constructing just one possible reality
and using his fantasy to do it. He admits:

> Phantasy for its own sake seems immoral and cruel, like a child; it indulges
> in horror and ridicule. How often have I led my fictitious beings along the
> paths of sorrow and humiliation so that I could pity them the more! Such are
> we, we creators of phantasy; to add glory or value to a man's life we inter-
> fere and bring in a portentous destiny, and we overburden him with trouble
> and adversity. But after all, doesn't it bring with it a special glory of its own?
> To show that he hasn't led a barren and empty life, a man nods his head and
> says: "I've lived through a lot." (p. 232)

Karel Čapek   *Whose point of view?*

Fantazie sama o sobě se zdá imorální a krutá jako dítě; libuje si v hrůzách a *aware of* směšnosti. Jak často jsem vedl své fiktivní osoby cestami hoře a ponížení, abych je mohl tím hlouběji litovat! Takoví my jsme, my výrobci fantazií, abychom oslavili nebo zhodnotili život člověka, nadrobíme mu těžký osud, uvalíme na něho zápasy a útrapy v míře vrchovaté. Ale což v tom opravdu není zvláštní sláva života? Člověk, který chce ukázat, že nežil nadarmo a jalově, kývá hlavou a praví: Mnoho jsem prodělal. (p. 196)

And later he states that what he invents becomes *his own life*: "I am the sea and that man, that kiss blown from the dark shadow [. . .] I am the man who has not finished his flight" (p. 241). (Já jsem to moře i ten muž, ten polibek vydechnutý z temného stínu [. . .] já jsem ten člověk, který nedoletěl – p. 204).

In the poet's version of events we have a melodramatic story, in which Mr X is physically assaulted on Cuba and loses his memory. He is taken in by a successful, if shady businessman, becomes his personal assistant under the name George Kettelring, and is despatched to Haiti to oversee the building of a sugar factory. Business takes him further afield, to other islands. He grows in power and wealth. On his return to Cuba, a romantic liaison develops between him and the American-educated daughter of his boss. She tries to help him recover his true identity. Vowing to return to Maria Dolores ("Mary"), but as someone else, he leaves, defeating her father commercially, and later falling on hard times himself. While writing to Mary his memory returns. He recalls falling out with his rich father, falling low in the world and ending up pimping his mulatto common-law wife. This leads to a fight, he is stabbed and another man is killed, presumably by a revolver shot. So the poet's story comes full circle. Mr X was hurrying home, like the prodigal son (as in several of his works, here Čapek quotes directly from the Bible), when the plane crashes.

This narrative, as well as being far lengthier than the other two, is heavily laced with local, exotic colour and dramatic events. There is more psychological development in the hero. Yet in itself the plot line is well-worn, and despite all the poet's explanations of how and why he writes, we have a feeling that he is dangerously mediocre. Čapek deftly upstages him with a minor *coup de théâtre* at the end: it appears Mr X was registered as a Cuban, not an American, as all parties had assumed.

Meteor is more ponderous than the other two novels, arguably more tract than fiction, yet it forms a key link in the overall pattern of the trilogy. *Hordubal* is set on the very edge of Czechoslovakia, even of Europe. *Meteor* is set only ostensibly in Europe (we are never told exactly where the hospital is) and all the narratives take place largely in the West Indies. Given this, *An Ordinary Life* can almost be seen as a counterbalance to the Czechs' questioning as to their national identity and as a reassuring answer to the question posed in the opening words of the Czech national anthem: "Where is my home?" (Kde domov můj?)

An Ordinary Life is set undeniably in the Czech Lands before and during the First Republic. It moves from the provinces to Prague and back again. Its unnamed hero stands in complete contrast to the protagonists of the previous two novels, in that he is materially successful, articulate and well-educated. Ostensibly we come to know a great deal about him. His life, viewed externally, seems utterly conventional and happy. He lives long and dies a natural death, having had enough warning about his end to write an autobiographical sketch (which forms the bulk of the text). Thus the work appears to fit the derogatory description of Czech literature which Čapek felt compelled to challenge in an article of 1936:

> Sometimes in Czechoslovakia various people frown and complain that we are not seeing the birth in our country of a world literature, but rather only a sort of Czech, domestic, provincial (some also say petty-bourgeois) literature which lacks so much by which it might acquire that special quality which is called world renown. It was said recently that the Czech novel when it is compared with the French, English, Russian (and perhaps even the Italian or Portuguese, but I don't remember exactly) is characterized by a sort of mediocrity and petty bourgeois quality.

> Občas se u nás leckdo zasmuší a požaluje si, že se nám nerodí literatura zvaná světová, nýbrž jenom taková česká, domácí, provinciální (někteří říkají také maloměstská), které toho mnoho chybí, aby nabyla zvláštní kvality, jež sluje právě světovost. Nedávno bylo řečeno, že český román, pokud je srovnáván s francouzským, anglickým, ruským (snad i italským nebo portugalským, ale to už si přesně nepamatuji), se vyznačuje jakousi průměrností a maloměšťáctvím.[9]

Čapek demonstrates in his trilogy the crudity of such a charge, perhaps in part by default: *An Ordinary Life*, despite its narrow geographical and social parameters, strikes more universal resonances than *Meteor* does with all its far-flung locations and exoticism.

The hero's preliminary account of his childhood, youth, brief period as a student in Prague and his various appointments in the railway company is naturally coupled with his reminiscences of his parents and acquaintances, his loves and his childless, though ostensibly happy, marriage. However, on perhaps half a dozen occasions his candid and unassuming monologue is suspended and he speaks of himself in the third person, and this technique paves the way for the thoroughgoing and disturbing reappraisal of his life which is to follow. Initially the autobiography maintains a neutral tone and the element of self-justification inherent in the genre is not obtrusive – indeed the occasional shift to third person narration rather guards against it. The overall picture is of a decent, modest man, whose periodic lapses are nothing untoward, notably his dropping out of university and the parental recriminations. Moderately successful in his career, moderately happy in his private life, the hero writes with sensitivity and perception about himself. Of his eight years at secondary school he says:

> In those years how ardently and keenly does a boy appreciate the things that do not belong to school; anything that is not a "preparation for life" but *is* life itself: whether it be friendship or the so-called first love, troubles, reading, religious crises, or romping about. This is something to which he may give himself heart and soul, and what is his now and not till after the certificate, or until, as one says at school, "when he has finished". (p. 347)

> Jak dychtivě a silně prožívá chlapec v těch létech cokoli, co není škola; cokoli, co není "příprava pro život", nýbrž *jest* život sám: ať je to přátelství, nebo takzvaná první láska, konflikty, četba, náboženská krize, nebo skotačení. Tady je něco, do čeho se může vrhnout cele a co je jeho už teď, a ne až po matuře nebo až, jak se na škole říká, "bude hotov". (p. 295)

These notions – almost word for word – anticipate by more than twenty years the principle which guides the hero of one of this century's most famous novels: the eponymous hero of Boris Pasternak's *Doctor Zhivago* declares to his heroine, Lara, that "man is born to live, not to prepare for life".[10]

There is a certain symbolism in the hero's career. As in Hašek and Hrabal, the railway seems to present a particular appeal, hardly surprising when one considers Czechoslovakia's geographical position and the fact that all major railways there lead to foreign parts. The hero applies for a job on the railways as an act of defiance when his father berates him for wasting his time writing poetry at university instead of studying. He is surprised at landing a post in the Franz Josef Station (known subsequently as Praha-Hlavní – Prague Main Station) in Prague in the dispatch department. A bout of consumption causes him to be transferred to a small station in the mountains, where the climate is more congenial to his health. This is literally the end of the line ("The last station in the world [. . .] then comes the universe. Right behind these buffers" – p. 362; A toto je opravdu poslední stanice na světě [. . .] pak už je vesmír. Hned za tím nárazištěm – p. 307). In one of his fits of third-person narration, the hero informs us that he did not simply become reconciled to this out-of-the-way place, but rather was anxious to demonstrate his superiority in coming from the capital (English text, p. 363; Czech text, pp. 308–9). The orderliness appeals to him (now he is on the right track and all seems predetermined).

Soon he is transferred to a model station, where the stationmaster is an orderly German. The hero is liked by his fellow workers and a romance develops between him and the stationmaster's daughter. Again, in a spate of third-person narration, the hero tells us about the importance of playing, of his childhood games in his father's yard.

A game is a serious matter, it has its rules and its binding order. A game is an absorbed, tender, or passionate concentration on something, on something *alone*. [...] And therefore I think a game likes to be on a reduced scale; if something is made small and tiny it is removed from that other reality, to a greater and deeper extent it is a world of its own, in which we can forget that there still is another. Well, and now we have succeeded in tearing ourselves away from that other world, now we are in the middle of a magic circle which separates us; there is the child's world, school, the Bohemian poet's party, there is the last station in the world, the prim station [...] the little garden of the retired man. (pp. 372–3)

Hra, to je věc vážná, má svá pravidla a svůj závazný řád. Hra je pohřížené, něžné nebo náruživé soustředění na něco, na *jenom* něco [...] A proto, myslím, má hra zálibu ve zmenšeném měřítku; je-li něco uděláno malinkým a zdrobnělým, je to vyňato z té okolní skutečnosti, je to víc a hlouběji světem pro sebe, naším světem, ve kterém můžeme zapomenout, že je ještě nějaký jiný. Tak, a teď se nám podařilo odtrhnout se od toho druhého světa, nyní jsme uprostřed čarovného kruhu, jenž nás odděluje; je svět dítěte, je škola, je bohémská parta básníkova, je poslední stanice na světě je čisťounké nádraží [...] nakonec je zahrádka penzistova. (p. 316)

Here then we have an apologia for the entire novel. In choosing to concentrate on a single life Čapek is in fact achieving the universality that some critics in the 1930s felt was lacking in Czech literature. In suggesting that each segment of the hero's life is a "game" the author is foreshadowing far more recent perceptions of the novel.

The hero marries, moves to a larger station and then eventually acquires his own station. The success in his career means that his personal life diminishes in importance: they decide not to have children, their sexual life is somewhat restrained. "You lie in bed and don't sleep, neither do I, but we do not speak in case we might suggest that something is lacking" (p. 384) (Pak ležíš a nespíš, ani já nespím, ale mlčíme, aby snad nepadlo slovo, že tu něco chybí – p. 326). Immediately following this we have another shift to third-person narration: "And the gentleman in the official cap walking up and down the platform ("pán v úřední čepici, přecházející po peróně) and addressing himself: "What can I do? In the end, a man is most at home in his work." ("Co dělat, nakonec muž je nejvíc doma ve svém díle.")

After the war the hero is transferred to a job in the Ministry in Prague and eventually retires. One notes then that in terms of his career he ends up where he started – in Prague, so arguably his real achievements, if there are any, reside elsewhere. During the reappraisal of his life he readily admits that it was the romanticism of the railways that appealed to him, but in an intellectual sleight of hand or act of *mauvais foi* he seems to under-mine himself:

> Well, yes, romanticism; but just because of that I liked the railways, because the romantic was in me; it was because of that peculiar, slightly exotic mist that railways possess, for that sense of distance, for the everyday adventure of arrivals and departures. Yes, that was something for me, that was just the fabric for my eternal dreaming. That other, that real life, was more or less a routine, a well-running mechanism; the more perfectly it clicked, the less it disturbed me in my day-dreams. (p. 422)

> Nu ano, romantika; ale vždyť právě proto jsem měl železnice rád, že ve mně byl ten romantik; to bylo pro ten zvláštní, trochu exotický opar, který železnice mají pro tu náladu dálky, pro to každodenní dobrodružství příjezdů a odjezdů. Ano, to bylo něco pro mne, to byl pravý rám pro mé nekonečné snění. Ten druhý, ten skutečný život, to byla víceméně jenom rutina a dobře běžící mechanismus; čím dokonaleji klapal, tím míň mě rušil v mých vysněných příbězích. (p. 360)

The hero never enacts fully his daydreams. The drama in the novel is in his mind, as indeed are the moral issues raised: at school he is a model pupil but has a secret admiration for the painter's son who is forever in trouble and is the constant bane of the teacher's life. On one occasion this boy injures his hand, yet refuses to weep, and spurns ("with proud, ... mocking eyes ... 'It's not your business'" – pp. 334–5; pyšnýma [...] výsměšnýma očima ... "Co je ti po tom?" – p. 284) the hero's question as to whether it hurts. The hero's response to this snub is deliberately to squeeze his hand in a vice, until pain gives way to rapture. He asks himself if the resulting self-inflicted, permanent injury is "a recollection of "childish hatred" or of "passionate friendship" (pp. 334–5) (památka dětské nenavisti, nebo vášnivého přátelství – p. 284) One recalls Hamlet's words that "there is nothing either good or bad but thinking makes it so", which anticipate by more than three centuries the primacy of existentialist subjective investi-gation which has come so much to the fore in Čapek's century.

War with the Newts

War with the Newts (*Válka s Mloky*) was published in 1936 and marked effectively Čapek's shift from out-and-out relativism to a more polemical stance, best exemplified by the late plays *The White Plague* (*Bílá nemoc*) and *Mother* (*Matka*). In the last chapter of *War with the Newts*, despite the double bluff of its title ("The Author Talks to Himself" – Autor mluví sám se sebou) the game is wholly given away: " ... Listen, is he *really* a Newt?" " ... No, Chief Salamander is a human being. He is actually called Andreas

Schultze and during the World War he was a sergeant-major somewhere"
("Poslyš, je on *opravdu* Mlok?" "Ne. Chief Salamander je člověk. Jmenuje
se vlastně Andreas Schultze a byl za světové války někde šikovatelem").[11]
The Czech word the author uses here for "sergeant-major" is a deliberately
obscure one (*šikovatel*). Adolf Hitler's father was illegitimate and at first
he used his mother's surname, Schicklgruber, a surname revived by Hitler's
political opponents in the 1930s. The parallel is unmistakable. It was
natural that during the Communist era the novel should be billed unre-
servedly as an anti-fascist work and it could be more easily accommodated
by Marxist ideology than a good deal of Čapek's other writing. For
communist critics, it also had its relevance in the post-Second World War
period, when capitalism and imperialism (cf. the escalating American
involvement in Vietnam from the early 1960s until defeat in 1975) still
needed to be challenged. Clearly, the novel is anti-fascist, but there are
aspects to the work which lend it more universal appeal, and some of its
preoccupations are eerily topical. A tract it may be, but its targets are not
narrowly focused.

It is also significant that while sharpening his political sword, Čapek
simultaneously returned to the fantastic/science fiction genres which had
attracted him so powerfully in the 1920s in such plays as *Rossum's
Universal Robots*, *The Insect Play* and *The Makropulos Secret* (*Věc
Makropulos*), or in the neologistically titled novel *Krakatit*. In pitching his
narrative a fair way beyond the borders of the everyday, he was, like so
many other practitioners of the genre, liberating it from the immediate
social or political conditions which provided the initial impetus. J. R. R.
Tolkien in the Foreword to his *The Lord of the Rings*, the epic fairy tale
that enjoyed cult status in the 1960s, rejects the notion that the work has
any "message":

> I cordially dislike allegory in all its manifestations [. . .] I much prefer
> history, true or feigned, with its varied applicability to the thought and expe-
> rience of readers. I think that many confuse "applicability" with "allegory";
> but the one resides in the freedom of the reader, and the other in the purposed
> domination of the author.[12]

The same could be claimed for *War with the Newts*: the author's conversation with himself ends with speculation that the newts will destroy
themselves and that humans will once more gain the ascendancy, but that
he does not know what will happen after that.

Indeed, for a work that might be construed as a tract, there is a lot of
irony and ambiguity in it. There is no hero as such, but a number of protagonists, the first being Captain J. van Toch. He is purported to be Dutch,
speaks of the bosses back home in Amsterdam who want whatever pearls
he can lay his hands on, has a Dutch ship under the singularly un-Dutch

name of the *Kandong Bandoeng*, yet he turns out to be Czech (a nation not known for its seafaring . . .). Moreover, his salty language (he speaks several) is the vehicle for his unreconstructed racism and xenophobia, as he curses at Jews, heathens and natives. However, he emerges as kinder than the other human protagonists when it comes to dealing with the salamanders. Only when he dies, probably of a stroke, does the Jewish tycoon, G. H. Bondy (his old school pal whom he used to persecute) decide to go in for wholesale exploitation of the newts. The original deal had been that the newts would supply the humans with pearls in exchange for weapons to defend themselves from sharks. Now Bondy, who has never even seen one of these newts, decides that they can be used for all manner of hydro-engineering projects. This, in his view, has become necessary because of the fall in the price of pearls.

If van Toch and Chief Salamander are not what they seem, the same is true in other areas. Much of the public debate about the newts is conducted on the basis of prejudice, not knowledge. The natives, who refuse to visit the bay where they live, regard them as devils. Once contact with the human world has unlocked their extraordinary intellectual potential, the newts are championed or denigrated by all manner of religious and political groups, and questions are raised as to whether they have souls and should they have full trade union rights. The scientific establishment decides that the newts are simply normal and boring, while it becomes clear that in fact the newts' intelligence represents a serious challenge to the humans' intellectual prowess.

Human vanity is Čapek's prime target, and in this regard he cannot resist a number of topical references, which lend the work a *roman à clef* element: in a transparent allusion to the 1933 film *King Kong*, Lily Valley, the putative film star tells Abe, when they are relaxing on their yacht, how she would like to star in a film, in which she is abducted by a gorilla. Her and her companions' encounter with the newts engenders all manner of heroic, and highly dubious headlines. When one of the early specimens of the talking salamanders is interviewed by British specialists (Sir John Bertram, Professor Ebbigham, Sir Oliver Dodge, Julian Foxley (English text, p. 70; Czech text, p. 77) one is tempted to attempt some decoding: Bertrand Russell, Sir William Hodge, Julian Huxley? Professor Vladimír Uher's article about the newts attracts a private correspondent who encloses a cutting suggesting that the discovery of the newts was made some hundred years before (English text, pp. 80–1; Czech text, pp. 86–7. Incidentally, the antiquated Czech spelling in the original can only be conveyed in the English version by using an old-fashioned looking typeface) – would it be too outlandish to suggest that this could be a tangential allusion to Tomáš Masaryk's exposure of the Zelenohorský and Královédvorský manuscripts as forgeries?

Elsewhere there are explicit references to prominent people of the day (the French writer Paul Adam, the English authors Aldous Huxley and H. G. Wells, this latter, of course a long-standing friend of Čapek (English text, p. 92; Czech text, p. 100). The reference to H. G. Wells is particularly apt, given his seminal *War of the Worlds* (1897), in which a Martian invasion leads to the destruction of London and the near subjugation of human society, until earthly bacteria, irrespective of the humans' effort to resist, defeats the enemy.

Elsewhere there are some deliberate or, with the passage of time, clearly inadvertent, misnomers: a "Mr Bellamy" (English text, p. 116; Czech text, p. 120) trades shamelessly in newts, just as people did with negroes two hundred years before – the resonances of the name, if any, for Čapek's contemporaries would be of Edward Bellamy's *Looking Backward* (1888), an immensely popular utopian fiction, which advocated non-revolutionary socialist reform. Čapek would have relished, but could claim no credit for, the current resonance (David Bellamy, the botanist and staunch conservationist); but as I discuss below, there are other prophetic aspects to the book which can justly be credited to the author. Towards the end of the book, with German nationalist feelings running high, we have a Dr Hans Thüring and a Dr Johannes Jakob Scheuchzer arguing for the superiority of the German newt, while one Sir Francis Drake, First Lord of the Admiralty in Great Britain, vows to meet any German challenge, and a prominent French journalist called Marquis de Sade weighs in (English text, pp.171–2; Czech text, pp. 172–3). Earlier, "Comrade Molokov" of the Communist International has issued a manifesto exhorting all newts to revolt (English text, p. 139; Czech text, pp. 141–2). (cf. Vyacheslav Molotov (1890–1986), top-ranking Soviet leader until his political demise in 1957).

The playfulness which Čapek exhibits in (mis)naming his characters reinforces the overriding concept that nothing is as it seems, that the essence of a being or even a situation is to be sought well beneath its label. At one stage the newts split between the Young and the Old factions, in a light-hearted jibe at the history of the movement closest to Čapek's own heart, the National Revival. The author focuses his attack on German fascism only in the Third Book of the novel, the implication being that its seeds are to be found in the usual human defects – greed, materialism, ignorance, prejudice and the blinkered self-interest of nations and businessmen. Captain van Toch, on his meeting with Bondy, rather puts his finger on another human foible that might lead to fascism: he explains the Czechs' natural inquisitiveness by the fact that "we Czechs don't want to believe in anything" (p. 26) (my *Češi nechceme v nic věřit* – p. 32). Given all the spurious beliefs that the development of the newts generates in the subsequent pages, such scepticism and open-minded curiosity might be seen as a virtue. However, Čapek was only too aware by the time that he was

[handwritten: he captures the way society works]

[handwritten: discusses relationship between Germany & CS (Czechoslovakia)]

writing the novel that virtuous scepticism could easily become perilous passivity.

Indeed, the novel's muted warning about the dangers of complacency might be glimpsed in the way in which some of its events have taken on a chilling topicality. The grim vision of a world being steadily engulfed by the seas chimes readily with present-day concerns about global warming, damage to the ozone layer and so on. The flooding in Central Europe affecting Poland and Moravia in the summer of 1997, when the Oder and Morava rivers burst their banks, lends a darker note to the concerns (English text, p. 206; Czech text, p. 206) voiced about the Newts making it up the Elbe and along the Vltava. When the newts blockade Britain's shores, the only recourse is to an airlift, pretty much reminiscent of the Berlin airlift of 1948.

In two particulars, Čapek picks up on themes that he raised in his early works: first, the dangers not so much of technological advance per se, as of mass production (cf. *Rossum's Universal Robots* or the last act featuring the ants in *The Insect Play*) and the concomitant abolition of individual creativity:

[The newts] have their overcrowded factory districts, their harbours, transport and agglomerations of millions. [. . .] Although their turbines were supplied to them by humans, the Newts know how to use them; but what else is civilization than the ability to make use of things invented by someone else? Even if, for the sake of argument, the Newts have no original ideas of their own they can perfectly well have their own science. True, they have no music or literature of their own but they manage perfectly well without [. . .] never before has so much been manufactured, constructed or earned as in this great age. Say what you will, the Newts have brought enormous progress to the world, as well as an ideal called Quantity. (pp. 146–7)

[Mloci] mají své přeplněné tovární čtvrti, přístavy, dopravní linky a miliónové aglomerace; turbíny jim sice dodali lidé, ale oni jich dovedou užívat; což je civilizace něco jiného než schopnost používat věcí, jež vymyslel někdo jiný? I když Mloci, řekněme, nemají svých vlastních myšlenek, mohou mít docela dobře svou vědu. Nemají sice své hudby nebo literatury, ale obejdou se bez nich dokonale [. . .] Ještě nikdy v dějinách lidstva se tolik nevyrábělo, nebudovalo a nevydělávalo jako v této veliké době. Nic platno, s Mloky přišel do světa obrovský pokrok a ideál, který se jmenuje Kvantita. (pp. 149–50)

The second concern is about human reproduction, and here too one might reflect on the current debates about birth control, genetic engineering and especially cloning.[13] The Appendix concerning the sex life of the newts has a passing reference to Wells and Aldous Huxley. And in this section the researcher Miss Blanche Kistemaeckers reaches the conclusion that the sex life of the newt is a "Grand Illusion, his erotic passion, his marriage and sexual tyranny, his temporary fidelity, his ponderous and slow ecstasy – all these are really unnecessary, outdated" (p. 94) (Veliká iluze; jeho erotická vášeň, jeho manželství a pohlavní tyranie, jeho dočasná věrnost, jeho těžkopádná a pomalá rozkoš, to vše jsou vlastně zbytečné, přežilé [...] úkony – p. 102). As the narrative progresses the newts vastly outbreed the humans, though in France, where the French newts are bought off by wine and apples, while their copulating increases, their fertility wanes (English text, p. 165; Czech text, p. 167). In *Rossum's Universal Robots* human beings cease to reproduce, while the robots go forth and multiply, and eventually acquire souls.

Čapek's preoccupation here is with the ostensible supplanting of mankind by another species, which itself may take on all the characteristics of humankind. One detects in this the author's worries about the general "dumbing-down" of humankind and the eradication of the intellectual. However, in Čapek the Promethean threat, explored in modern literature from Mary Shelley onwards, in fact contains a certain optimism: life will undergo harrowing changes, but will never disappear.

This optimism/wishful thinking brings us to one of those small men, so frequent in Čapek, who are inadvertent heroes. Mr Povondra, doorman to the magnate E. H. Bondy, within his own small compass, is responsible, thinking, conscientious, slightly self-important and rather pedantic. He stands in stark contrast to all the scientists, politicians and artists whose dogmatism and iconoclasm prove so dangerous.

The artistic avant-garde is depicted as no less extreme than some of the fascist thinking on display:

> The future belongs to the Newts. The Newts are the cultural revolution. No matter that they have no art of their own: at least they are not weighed down by idiotic ideals, dry-as-dust traditions and all that bombastic, boring, pedantic old rubbish that went by the name of poetry, music, architecture, philosophy, and culture generally – senile words that turn our stomachs. (p. 180)

> Budoucnost náleží Mlokům. Mloci, toť kulturní revoluce. Ať nemají svého umění; aspoň nejsou zatíženi idiotskými ideály, zaschlými tradicemi a celou tou ztyřelou, nudnou, školometskou veteší, které se říkalo poezie, hudba, architektura, filosofie a vůbec kultura – senilní slova, při nichž se nám obrací žaludek. (p. 181)

The words here can, in a Czech context, be taken as sheer parody, yet they are just as uncompromising as those of the Russian Futurists' manifesto of 1912 "A Slap in Face of Public Taste". This document had called for Pushkin, Dostoevsky and Tolstoy to be thrown overboard from the steamship of modernity. The prime mover, Vladimir Maiakovskii, became *the* poet of the Bolshevik Revolution and darling of the Left throughout the world.

Povondra, on his own initiative, allows van Toch access to Bondy, and later he comes to blame himself for all the woes that ensue. As a compulsive collector of newspaper cuttings on the subject of the newts, he provides much of the material for Čapek's prolix footnoting, which itself is clearly a parody of academic work. Here Čapek is adept at indulging in some avant-garde writing himself, as the footnotes on occasion engulf the main narrative (the reader can choose which text to read first), while simultaneously mocking the excesses of the avant-garde. In the closing stages of the book we meet three generations of the Povondra family, this in itself being an optimistic sign, with the patriarch sanguinely pontificating about the international situation and bemoaning his wife's inability to understand politics.

Throughout the book the satirical voice is always there, at its most bitter when confronting fascism, at its most indulgent and gentle here, when depicting and challenging the "little Czech" (malý, český člověk), with all his well-reasoned parochialism. (We hear the indulgent voice on other occasions too, as when Čapek chides his beloved France or Britain.) The scene of the Povondras calmly fishing on the Vltava with newts appearing around them, with Brazil engulfed, with Egypt, India and China totally inundated, with Russia and Germany all but destroyed (the Black Sea now extends all the way to the Arctic Ocean) strikes several chords today. After the 1968 Soviet-led invasion of Czechoslovakia there was a spate of jokes concerning the ephemeral status of superpowers. Most poignant perhaps though are old Povondra's words about the Germans:

> Those Germans, they were an odd sort of nation. Educated, but odd. I knew a German once, he was a driver at a factory, terribly rude man he was, that German. But kept his vehicle in order, I'll say that for him. So Germany too has disappeared from the map of the world. And the hullabaloo it used to make! Really dreadful: it was the army first and last, nothing but soldiering. (p. 204)

> Tihle Němci, to byl moc divný národ. Vzdělaný, ale divný. Já jsem znal jednoho Němce, on byl šoférem v jedné továrně; a to byl takový hrubý člověk, ten Němec. Ale vůz měl v pořádku, jen co je pravda. – Tak vida, Německo už taky zmizelo z mapy světa [. . .] A jaký fofr dřív dělalo! To ti byla hrůza: samá armáda a samá vojna. (p. 204)

While this comment stands as a pale reflection of the racism and intolerance that we witnessed in Captain van Toch at the outset, it also summarizes in the language of the man in the street the complex relationship throughout the centuries between the Germans and the Czechs. Czech culture may have been all but obliterated after the Battle of the

White Mountain (1620), and Nazi occupation visited unspeakable horrors on the Czech population, but in the wake of the Velvet Revolution of 1989 and the collapse of communism, President Havel's first official trip abroad was to Germany. Here there arises the very broad question of the role and future of any small nation in the modern world. *War with the Newts* has a light-hearted episode where a Czech language primer for newts is produced, just to satisfy national pride, but a nation's place in the world, Čapek would no doubt argue, comes at a higher price than that. His own down payment is to be found in the best of his writing.

Conclusion

"You have no idea, sir, what a lot of mysteries there are in this world. Every house, every family is a mystery." (p. 132)

"Nemáte ponětí, pane, co je na světě záhad. Každý barák, každá rodina je záhada." (p.109)

"Why don't You Yourself do the judging?" [. . .]
"Because I know everything. If judges knew everything, they couldn't judge either: they would understand everything and their hearts would ache." (p. 159)

"Proč vlastně vy . . . proč ty, Bože, nesoudíš sám?" [. . .]
"Protože všechno vím. Kdyby soudcové všechno, ale naprosto všechno věděli, nemohli by také soudit; jen by všemu rozuměli, až by je z toho srdce bolelo." (pp. 131–2)[14]

The *Tales from Two Pockets*, which were completed in 1929 and have been published in a variety of volumes and collections, represent the best rehearsal of Čapek's most successful fiction. The two extracts provided above establish succinctly their chief themes. The vast bulk of them are detective stories, reminiscent of Chesterton's "Father Brown" narratives. It must be said that the "whodunnit" element in most instances is deliberately facile; yet this is in keeping with the real purpose of the tales, which is not so much to do with the ascertaining of some *a priori* truth as with the moral and philosophical ramifications of a given situation or action. More than in the other fiction of Čapek's we have addressed, in the *Tales from Two Pockets* we can perceive the nuts and bolts of his art.

Čapek is intrigued by irrational human foibles, and very often in the *Tales* truth is arrived at through intuition or luck rather than through – or sometimes in open defiance of – logical deductions and established, bureaucratic procedures. These are gently mocked throughout: "Someone's been shooting at you, sir" (To vám sem někdo střelil, pane) says a police inspector to Mr Tomsa in "An Attempt at Murder" (Vražedný útok), on examining the bullet holes in the would-be victim's window (English text, p. 181; Czech text, p. 149). In "The Fortuneteller" (Věštkyně), a story set in England, a story that, we are informed, could never take place in France, Germany or Czechoslovakia, since in these countries "judges are obliged to try sinners and punish them in accordance with the letter of the law, rather than in accordance with their own discretion and conscience" (p. 27), (soudcové jsou povinni soudit a trestat hříšníky podle litery zákona, a nikoliv podle svého rozšafného rozumu a svědomí – p. 18) a judge berates the accused: "Rubbish. The ten of spades means expectations. Journeys are the jack of clubs; when the seven of diamonds turns up with it, it means a great deal of travel resulting in profit. Don't try to hoodwink me" (p. 31). (Nesmysl. Zelena desítka znamená naději. Cesty jsou zelený spodek; když s ním jde kulová sedma, znamená to veliké cesty, ze kterých kouká zisk [. . .] mne nenapálíte – p. 22).

The good-natured comedy belies some serious moral conundrums, such as in "The Crime on the Farm" (Zločin v chalupě) where a peasant freely admits to axing his father-in-law to death because of the victim's cantankerous inefficiency, but stubbornly refuses to plead guilty, insisting that he is an honest man, and that it "was all in our family" (p. 164) (dyť to bylo v rodině – p. 136). The most eloquent expression of the relativism and ambiguity in the stories is to be seen in the fact that most of them open with, or feature prominently, straightforward dialogue, underscoring the notion that there is always another point of view. Of the twenty-four stories "from the first pocket" twelve open with direct speech, three have direct speech in the second sentence, and four in the second paragraph. Of the remaining five, two ("The Last Judgement" and "The Disappearance of an Actor" (Poslední soud; Zmizení herce Bendy") have direct speech in the fourth paragraph, "Mr Janik's Cases" (Případy pana Janíka) has direct speech in the third paragraph, while "Footprints" and "Oplatka's End" (Šlépěje; Oplatkův konec) feature direct speech only in the sixth paragraph. Anyway, in both these last two stories dialogue is very restricted. The twenty-four "tales from the other pocket" all start with direct speech, and, with the obvious exception of the first, each purports to be a response to the one preceding.

All the narratives feature officers of the law, and Police Captain Dr Mejzlík figures in several stories. However, a few of them play down drastically the motif of detection. "Oplatka's End" concentrates on the various policemen vying with each other to kill the hunted man, and they emerge with little more to recommend them morally than the criminal himself. "The Last Judgement" takes us on a unique excursion in the collection into the realms of the fantastic. A killer with nine murders on his hands is shot dead by police and finds himself on trial in Heaven. God presents all the facts and can point to his good deeds as well as to his crimes: he committed murder "From anger, from greed, deliberately and by chance, sometimes with pleasure and sometimes from necessity. He was generous and sometimes he helped people. He was kind to women, he loved animals, and he kept his word" (p. 158) (Ze zloby, z chtivosti peněz, s rozvahou i nahodile, někdy s rozkoší a jindy z nutnosti. Byl štědrý a někdy pomáhal lidem. Byl hodný k ženám, měl rád zvířata a držel své slovo – p. 131). Yet omniscient God, as we noted above, is unable to pass judgement, and it is left to those who were judges on Earth to consign the man to Hell at the end of the trial. In the context of all Čapek's oeuvre we see laid bare in this story the problem of taking relativism to its logical consequences; in his more mature writing, especially in the *Trilogy*, one can argue, the author overcomes an "excuse-all" position by authentic character portrayal, and by clinging to the notion that our other opening quotation emphasized, namely, ubiquitous mystery. Indeed, one of the weaknesses of the *Tales* is that the characters are by and large no more than vehicles for ideas, they lack depth and psychology, and it must be said, the outcome of many of the "mysteries" is predictable, once one slips into the author's mindset.

This could not be said of one of the most haunting, and most "detection-free", "The Ballad of Juraj Čup" (Balada o Juraji Čupovi). The very title alerts us, for it eschews the more favoured title keywords (case, crime, murder – případ or příběh, zločin, vražda) which designate events, for something arrestingly lyrical. Set in Ruthenia among gypsies and featuring a murder and mention of dollars sent from the victim's husband working in America, it foreshadows *Hordubal*. Police Captain Havelka abandons almost entirely the noetic, empirical approach of the law to recount his story. The stress is rather on intoxication by alcohol and music. Drinking in the village pub and driven by the gypsy's violin-playing, the narrator is ready to kill or make love: "It's like they're dragging your soul right out of your body. I'm telling you, that music of theirs, it's unearthly, it's depraved" (p. 286) (tu vám zrovna vytahuje duši z těla; já vám říkám, ta jejich hudba, to je nějaká strašná a tajemná neřest – p. 235). Juraj Čup readily confesses to cutting his sister's throat because God has told him that she is possessed by an evil spirit (English text, p. 287; Czech text, p. 236). He then makes a near-impossible journey through the snow to give himself up to the authorities, which he waits patiently some six hours out in the freezing weather to do, while the narrator is carousing. The narrator and a police colleague then make the journey through the mountains to investigate, and hear how the victim lived long enough to identify her assailant.

The smallholders in the settlement wear sheepskin coats, which, to the narrator's mind smell stifling and have something of the Old Testament about them (English text, p. 289; Czech text, p. 238). This story then represents the very antithesis of "The Last Judgement". Little is known or understood; the narrator talks about the miracle of the arduous journey from and to the settlement and of the power of gypsy music, yet the events are perfectly credible and realistic, albeit without proper explanation; and clearly it is accepted that God, as per the Old Testament, will judge and punish, unlike the all-knowing, and therefore all-forgiving, God of the New Testament (as taken to his logical, and ludicrous, extreme in "The Last Judgement").

The satire, the search for moral absolutes, the concurrent acknowledging of the value of relativism, the reservations about the modern world with all its bureaucracy and rank, all these traits in the *Tales* are developed in the later fiction. At the same time, there is the author's fixation with the common man: *Tales from the Other Pocket* show a marked increase in the use of the vernacular. There is also the humbling concept that anyone can be proved wrong and that things are never as they seem; this humbling aspect goes further in *War with the Newts*, crystallizing into the notion that mankind is only on the earth on sufferance, and that he can easily be supplanted. The motif of disguise that we find in the pocket story "Disappearance of an Actor" echoes Chesterton's novel of 1908 *The Man Who Was Thursday* without, on this occasion at least, reiterating his colleague's concerns with political extremisms.

It may be that Čapek, being the first modern Czech writer to become widely translated and known abroad, has been to an extent overvalued. Yet his influence at home and abroad has been strong, and to many Czechs, especially those of a certain age, the First Republic without him, would be unthinkable, so closely was he involved with the National Theatre, with responsible journalism, with the President, with humanism and middle-of-the-road politics. It is true that, as Robert Pynsent has said, he could never think of satisfactory endings for his works (and one accounts for this by reference to his occasional didacticism, the need to spell out a moral dilemma or a message, when it would be best left unstated). But is it fair to say, as Pynsent has, that his most lasting works are the literary essays *Marsyas* or his translations of French poetry?[15]

All of his major works have regularly been in print in Czechoslovakia; and three major volumes of his works were issued in English translation in the 1990s. There are two major critical works in English on him. His fellow countryman Ivan Klíma has written extensively on him. So, despite William Harkins' claims for the *Trilogy*, might it be fairer to describe Čapek, as G. K. Chesterton was, as "the genius who never wrote a masterpiece"?

Given the history of Czechoslovakia this century, and some of the achievements of other modern Czech writers, a graver criticism might be levelled at Čapek – that all his moral-searching and civic concerns notwithstanding, he never *really* understood the nature of evil. His thoroughgoing decency was his ultimate enemy.

Bohumil Hrabal
(1914–1997)
Small people and tall tales

Introduction – Pábení

Along with Milan Kundera, Bohumil Hrabal is generally regarded as the greatest Czech prose writer of the post-war period. One might think that his proletarian pedigree and the varied manual jobs he had before taking up writing full time would have endeared him to the communist regime. Yet his writing is such that it is extremely difficult to categorize, and the communist establishment's attitude to him was largely one of suspicion. No doubt, to some degree the feeling was mutual, but it would be more accurate to say that Hrabal's artistic preoccupations simply soared above political demarcation lines. As the critic Igor Hájek put it: "While Páral skilfully steered clear of politics and ideology, Bohumil Hrabal was one of those who simply ignored them. Whenever he got into difficulties with censors or editors, it was because of the eccentric nature of his writing."[1]

At the heart of this "eccentricity" is "pábení", and before attempting a definition of the term, let alone an English translation, it is appropriate to consider briefly Hrabal's biography and lifestyle. Born in Brno in 1914 on March 28, he traced his origins back to a French soldier who was wounded in the locality during the Napoleonic Wars, stayed and became involved with a Moravian girl . . . Bohumil himself was born out of wedlock. His mother met František Hrabal, an accountant in the brewery in Polná in 1917, and this small town, about forty miles north-west of Brno, saw the beginnings of a conventional family life for them. Stepfather progressed in the brewery business, coming to run the brewery in Nymburk nad Labem, some twenty miles east of Prague by 1920, when the young Bohumil started school. The boy was a wayward son and pupil, forever running off, wandering about and listening in on the conversations of the maltsers. He did badly at the *reálné gymnásium* (secondary school) in Brno and his stepfather transferred him back to school in Nymburk. He sometimes accompanied his stepfather on business excursions to pubs in the vicinity. He eventually graduated from the "reálka" in Nymburk in 1933 and moved to Prague, where he was enrolled in the Law Faculty from 1935 to 1939. However, he seems to have been more interested in poetry, especially the French poets Mallarmé, Rimbaud and Verlaine. He had displayed an unusual facility with languages when he had had to undertake a course of Latin to get into Law School. Now, at university, he also showed a lively interest in philosophy and the visual arts.

The Nazi occupation saw the closure of all the institutes of Higher Education in Czechoslovakia, and, unable to complete his formal studies, Hrabal was obliged to return once again to Nymburk. There then followed an even more chequered career. From December 1939 until August 1940 he was a white-collar worker in the notary's office in Nymburk; from then until the end of January 1941 he attended Eckert's private business school in Prague and was simultaneously employed in the offices of the Railway Cooperative in Nymburk; from February 1941 he was a warehouseman in Nymburk; from March 1942 he was a railway worker and later dispatcher in the small station of Kostomlaty between Lysá and Nymburk. After the war, from September 1946, he was an insurance agent in Prague; in the following September he started a career as a travelling salesman; in June 1949 he was a foreman in the steel works in Kladno. In July 1952 he suffered a severe head injury when a wheel slipped out of a pulley on a crane and he was incapacitated for months. Yet by October 1954 he was once again working full time, now in a paper recycling works in Prague. In February 1959 he started work in the S. K. Neumann Theatre in Prague as a scene-shifter and extra. By 1946 he had finally completed his Law Degree from Charles University. On a cultural visit to Britain in 1990, he listed as one of his interests "meeting people with unusual jobs". It was only from 1962–3, at the age of 49, that Hrabal became a full-time writer. Throughout his adult years – and even a bit before – his social life was largely taken up with beer drinking in common-or-garden pubs, while listening and talking to fellow imbibers.

All of these biographical details can be readily glimpsed in Hrabal's major fictional works. All of them fit in beautifully with the crass ideology of socialist realism, imported from the Soviet Union in the post-1948 period, which insisted that a writer should "know life"; thus far, Hrabal's proletarian credentials were immaculate. However, socialist realism also required that a writer should depict "the truth in its revolutionary development", and "educate the toiling masses in the spirit of socialism" – we are quoting from the original statutes of the Union of Soviet Writers. Here, Hrabal's prose presented the hack communist critic with, to put it mildly, acute problems.

To return to *pábení*, Radko Pytlík, who has written extensively on

Hrabal, suggests that the term possibly originates from the folk dialect term *bábení*,[2] which we might translate as "women's gossip". The faintly pejorative tone is typical of Hrabal's penchant for irony. The title of his early work *Pábitelé* has been rendered as "The Palaverers", and even, rather eccentrically, as "The Enthusiasts"; but given Hrabal's flights of fantasy and his colourful turn of phrase (or more particularly, those of his characters/narrators), perhaps "yarn-spinners" or "natterers" might be more viable alternatives. After all, "palaver" has connotations of tedium as well as of pointlessness, and Hrabal's writing is anything but tedious, while its pointlessness is only ostensibly so, just like Švejk's anecdotes. Milan Jankovič's study (1996) cites Hrabal's own explanation of the term. Apparently the author once asked the poet Jiří Kolář what he was doing and he replied "Já pábím." And immediately Hrabal sensed "that pábení is a certain type of poetic activity, which deviates from hitherto current activities, that it will rather attempt the prohibited, the uncertain and the incomprehensible and what cannot be got at by rules and whose meaning becomes clear only afterwards. From then on I started to use that little word and depending on the situation I started to call certain types of people *pábitelé* and their activity *pábení*. Jankovič cites this from the 1969 edition of the book.[3] Here is Hrabal's own definition of the term, as it appears elsewhere:

> A *pábitel* is a person against whom there is always welling up an ocean of intrusive thoughts. His monologue flows constantly, sometimes like an underground stream in a hollow of thought, sometimes gushing out of his mouth. *Pábení* is like a flaming torch that is passed on by the relay team of human speech from mouth to mouth. A *pábitel* is an instrument of language, which enriches itself on all the endearments and tricks that the linguist is interested in. As a rule, a *pábitel* has read almost nothing, but on the other hand has seen and heard a great deal. And has forgotten almost nothing. He is captivated by his own inner monologue, with which he wanders the world, like a peacock with its beautiful plumage. A *pábitel*, when he isn't indulging in talking to people, entertains himself with his own talk, giving himself information about incidents whose significance is exaggerated, displaced, in the wrong order, because the *pábitel* filters reality through the diamond eyelet of inspiration. The *pábitel* is filled with wonder at the visible world, so that that ocean of beautiful sights allows him no sleep. He is so obsessed with narrating that it seems as if the tongue has chosen the *pábitel*, so that through the *pábitel*'s mouth it can see itself and show what it is capable of. The *pábitel* knows how to make his news extraordinary by taking a pair of scissors to it, he knows how to cut off a discourse at a certain moment and to paste it on to an event surprisingly unrelated. He knows how to maintain the temperature and the temperament of his text in a state of tension of which he feels he is the hero.

So while the wise and the cautious carefully disinfect themselves, *pábitels* smell of human flesh. While the wise and the cautious hang leaden weights on their wings, the *pábitels'* pinions are on their return journey from an expedition, their plumage plucked and singed. So *pábení* means getting even with the rituals of education. When all's said and done, real education finds its ultimate triumph in both *pábitels* and *pábení*. Lao-tzu: knowing how to not know. Socrates: I know that I know nothing. Nicholas of Cusa: Docta ignorantia [Learned ignorance – R.P.]. Erasmus of Rotterdam: In praise of folly. Etc.

Pábitels prove that life is worth living.

Tak pábitel je člověk, proti kterému se neustále vzdouvá oceán dotěrných myšlenek. Jeho monolog teče pořád, tu jak ponorná říčka v dutině mysli, tu zase se řine ústy ven. Je to pábení, které jak hořící pochodeň je podáváno štafetou lidského jazyka od úst k ústům. Pábitel je nástrojem jazyka, který obohacuje sebe sama o všecky něžnosti a finty, o něž má zájem jazykověda. Pábitel zpravidla skoro nic nečetl, ale zato se hodně díval a hodně slyšel. A skoro na nic nezapomněl. Je zaujat svým vnitřním monologem, se kterým chodí po světě, jako páv se svým krásným peřím. Pábitel, když se nedává do řeči s lidmi, baví hovorem sám sebe, podává informace o případech, jejichž význam je zveličen, přesunut, zpřeházen, protože pábitel cedí skutečnost přes diamantové očko inspirace. Pábitel je naplněn obdivem k viditelnému světu, takže ten oceán krásných vidin mu nedává spát. Je tak posedlý vyprávěním, že to vypadá, jako by jazyk si vybral pábitele, aby jeho ústy spatřil sebe sama, a dokázal si, co dovede. Pábitel dovede ozvláštnit svoje zprávy nůžkami, dovede přestřihnout hovor v jistou chvíli a navázat na událost překvapivě nesouvisející. Dovede udržet temperaturu a temperament textu v napětí, ve kterém se cítí hrdinou.

Tak zatímco moudří a opatrní se pečlivě desinfikují, pábitelé voní člověčinou. Zatímco moudří a opatrní si věší na svá křídla olověná závaží, perutě pábitelů už se vracejí z výpravy s oškubaným a popáleným peřím. Tak pábení je vyrovnávka proti obřadnosti vzdělání. Ostatně pravé vzdělání nakonec odolává až v pábitelích a v pábení. Lao-c': umění neumět. Sokrates: vím, že nic nevím. Mikuláš Kues: Docta ignorantia. Erasmus Rotterdamský: Chvála bláznovství. Atd.

Pábitelé dokazují, že život stojí za to, aby byl žit.[4]

The author's dust-jacket note to one edition of *Pábitelé*, reproduced here nearly in its entirety, provides a key to Hrabal's method. Here there are resonances of "stream of consciousness" and Joyce, of erudition mixed with earthiness, of irreverence and personal freedom, of poetry in prose, of legitimizing the individual's perception of the world.

In his own efforts to define the term, Pytlík notes that while Hrabal has suggested that he simply records and regurgitates what he has heard in pubs, in fact Hrabal's approach allows him "to capture by accessible and comprehensible means the complex sensibility of modern man" (dovoluje zachytit přístupnými a srozumitelnými prostředky složitou senzibilitu moderního člověka – p. 117). The technique involves montage and collage, and especially the ability to capture "people's talk ("hovory lidí") "in a blinding moment" (v bleskovém okamžiku – p. 118). The photographic metaphor is used by another critic Emanuel Frynta when he speaks of the "leica-style" of Hrabal. Hrabal has acknowledged a debt to his old Uncle Pepin, whose story-telling and speech mannerisms always enthralled him. Of course, Uncle Pepin figures prominently in several of Hrabal's fictions, notably *Cuttings* (published in English as *Cutting it Short – Postřižiny*) and *The Little Town Where Time Stood Still* (*Městečko, kde se zastavil čas*). The English translator solves the problem of Pepin's bawdy dialect and neologisms by using Scottish brogue.[5] Pepin's colourful stories also have a more obvious literary antecedent, Jaroslav Hašek. Pytlík takes the discussion further:

> Hrabal in fact uses Uncle Pepin's original story-telling only as a thematic point of departure; he accentuates the dynamics of testimony and integrates it with modern poetry. By means of all this, his *pábení*, which on the surface seems like a "common man", folk tradition, becomes a powerful instrument for the poetic expression of the complex feelings of modern man.
>
> Of course, it is not a question of citing or actualising a myth, as in a James Joyce novel, nor of monumentalising the common man or comic figure as in Hašek's *Švejk*. *Pábení* is founded on the oscillation between a plebeian cynical nihilism and the stifling beauty of a world, which is illuminated for us by a crazy imagination. It is Hrabal's autoprojection, but at the same time it is also a poetic automystification. (p. 129)

> Hrabal tedy užívá původní vyprávění strýce Pepina jen jako tematické východisko; akcentuje dynamiku výpovědi a uvádí ji v souvislost s moderním básnictvím. Tím vším činí ze svého pábení, jež se tváří napovrch jako "lidově" folklórní podání, pružný nástroj pro básnické vyjádření složitých pocitů moderního člověka.
>
> Nejde ovšem o citaci či aktualizaci mýtu jako v románu Joyceově ani o monumentalizaci lidového typu či komické postavy jako u Haškova Švejka. Pábení je založeno na oscilaci mezi plebejským cynickým nihilismem a mezi zalykavou krásou světa, který nám osvětluje bláznivá fantazie. Je Hrabalovou autoprojekcí, ale současně i básnickou automystifikací.

The wordiness here should not obscure the central point, namely that Hrabal invents and fantazises, but does so on the basis of the most palpable of verbal material. Those with a knowledge of Russian literature will recognize a similar technique in Mikhail Zoshchenko's stories of the 1920s, where the linguistic register owes so much to the vernacular, but still has an invented quality about it. Another point of comparison might be the fictions of Flann O'Brien or the regular column he wrote for the *Irish Times* under the pseudonym Miles na Gopaleen. The linguistic register is all-important, an essential springboard for the outlandish plots and images.

At times the reader becomes the tongue-tied "interlocutor". Puns, neologisms and malapropisms there may be, but above all – in particular for a non-Irish reader – the sheer dynamism and energy of the language are the most salient features. In Hrabal let us note just one example here of the linguistic virtuosity: in *The Tender Barbarian* (*Něžný barbar*) he attributes to his friend, the philosopher and writer, Egon Bondy, the coinage "Kurva fix", a neat hybrid of two obscene registers ("Kurva" – fuck it and "Krucifix" – damn it).[6]

Thus, the difficulties of reading Hrabal in the original, let alone translating him, should be readily apparent. *Hrabalovština* springs from a variety of identifiable social milieux, but it is also the product of an individual's inventive imagination. Like some of the analogues we note above, it addresses the horror of the modern world, as well as the comedy, absurdity and insanity that occur when lofty aspirations collide with mundane reality. However, arguably, more than these other writers, Hrabal captures the beauty of the modern world and stands in awe of it. *Hrabalovština* is a metaphor for the modern world, as is language as a whole for Joyce. The best example of a Joyce connection and the clearest instance of linguistic experimentation is in *Dancing Lessons for the Elderly and Advanced* (*Taneční hodiny pro starší a pokročilé*). This can be seen as a tongue-in-cheek genuflexion to "stream of conscience" in general and more directly to Molly Bloom's monologue. Nearly a hundred pages long, it consists of only one sentence, and roams freely between eroticism and comedy. As paradoxically as Joyce, by fixing on the ostensibly parochial, Hrabal achieves an extraordinary universality.

The thirteen stories which make up the 1964 edition of *Pábitelé* (in the Collected Works "Christmas Eve" is omitted) are each free-standing in terms of plot, with just an occasional narrative link: in the last story "Christmas Eve" (Štědrovečerní), there is a reference to Demeter, the gipsy girl's father from the previous text, "Romance" (Romance). What binds the stories is their imaginative power as expressed through Hrabal's special language. How do these operate?

Several of the stories work on three levels. "Jarmilka" (Jarmilka) is told in the first-person, with the narrator recounting his current activities and perceptions as a worker in the steel foundry in Kladno, while through conversations we learn of Jarmilka's illegitimate pregnancy and other personal problems, she being a girl working in the canteen, while a workmate, Vašek, persistently relates his experiences in a concentration camp during the war. Three human dramas intertwine in a matter-of-fact way to form a perfectly accessible, credible, yet slightly grotesque, collage. Jarmilka's man turns his attention to another woman at a dance and is challenged by Jarmilka's sister:

"Ain't you even a bit ashamed, you scum-bucket? You bang up my sister and then you're carrying on with someone else!" Jarmila got up. "And he gave her a clout while they were dancing! Tell me, uncle, is it right to give a dancing lady a clout?"

"To se ani trochu, ty drbane, nestydíš? Sestru mi zbouchnout a pak se takhle dívčit s jinou!" Jarmila se zdvihla. "A on jí dal v kole facku! Řekněte, strejdo, sluší se to, dát dámě v kole facku?"[7]

The Czech here is particularly colourful: "you scum-bucket" is "ty drbane", "drbat" usually meaning "to sling mud at someone", but in Moravia the word can mean "to fuck". "Zbouchnout" goes happily into English as "bang up". "V kole" here means "in a dance" or "on the dance floor". "Carry on with" is similarly quaint: "dívčit se" is presumably derived from the word for girl. After details of her fluctuating marriage prospects and the approaching pregnancy, the narrator and his friend eventually go to visit her in her home village. Her baby boy is in care, she is alone and apparently in deep depression. Nearly all of this information is delivered courtesy of Jarmilka's vernacular or something very similar, as from the old woman the hero questions in the heroine's home village.

The hero's speech register is different, mainly neutral, as he records his conversations with others and his work or trip to see the heroine. Not infrequently he parades the technical and localized technical/slang terms involved in his work, making few concessions to any readers who are not Kladno-based foundry workers: "Between the smelting room and the tempering shop I turned over a pile of rusty shavings. Then I loaded the shavings into the skips for the blast furnace [. . .] I climbed over a heap of crowbars (Mezi týglovnou a diadurem jsem překopával haldu zrezivělých špon. Potom jsem nakládal ty špony do sázecích koryt [. . .] Přelezl jsem hromadu cáglí). One notes that "smelting room" and "crowbar" are more commonly "šmelcovna" and "sochor".[8] Vašek, covered in filth from their labours, calls their work "angelic" (andělská práce – p. 152), and calmly recounts how the SS would organize a "Children's Day" (Dětský den – p. 153), when they forced prisoners to dance or jump until they were too exhausted to go on, and they would then be killed. The narrator sees no mark of his sufferings on him. When they see a rat, Vašek goes on to tell how the SS fed rats bread, and one prisoner stole some of it, was bitten by a rat and died (p. 153).

The purpose of each of these speech registers is to establish the autonomy of each character, and to illustrate the rich complexity of each moment: memory, current work and Jarmilka's human comedy/tragedy all come together. Hrabal acknowledged that André Breton's novel *Nadja* of 1928 was an inspiration for this story (Pytlík, p. 59). Breton's work is based on his brief but intense liaison in the autumn and winter of 1926–7 with a

Purpose

mysterious girl who went by the name of Nadja. Shortly after the break-up of the relationship she was committed to a mental asylum and died, apparently of cancer, in 1941.[9] Breton and other French surrealists were taken up very promptly by the Czechs, notably, the poet Vítězslav Nezval (1900–58) and *Nadja* was translated into Czech in 1935 (an English version appeared only in 1960). Undoubtedly Hrabal was inspired by the "confession" and "artistic credo" aspects of the work – in effect a manifesto of Surrealism – as well as by the image of a downtrodden heroine who inspires arresting images and juxtapositions. Of course, Jarmilka herself is a far cry from the artistic, intellectual and other-worldly Nadia as she appears in Breton's work.

The same technique of varying levels or layers of narration is to be seen in "The Notary" (Pan Notář) as the eponymous hero dictates to his secretary his last will and testament with elaborate funeral arrangements, while recalling how an old man he sees outside the window was responsible in his younger days for the macabre deaths of his two wives. These thoughts are interlaced with accounts given by the peasant and his wife about the goings-on in the village. Again, the macabre is dealt with in matter-of-fact tones – this time to unequivocal comic effect. The notary is assured that life in the village is tedious, apart from such incidents as: the foal that comes into the kitchen and smashes up the furniture and kicks a little boy, who has to go to hospital and have his leg amputated, but then he dies and the parents are shocked when they find the leg lying alongside the corpse in the coffin; or the cattle trader who tried to rape the religious studies teacher, but she kicked him in the testicles and then carried on kicking him, as he wheeled his bike, all the way to the police station, and then slapped him into making a confession; or the neighbour poisoned on slivovice who is hung upside down to drain it out of him, all to no avail.

Such blood-curdling incidents abound in other stories: the title story "Pábitelé" features a hero-narrator visiting a friend in a village and witnessing the friend's father accidentally driving a sickle into his head. The family take the incident in their stride and recount a number of other mishaps which the accident-prone father has sustained; it then emerges that the son inflicts a degree of physical suffering on himself to aid his artistic endeavours (he paints). The discourse is interspersed with explosions as the army nearby holds training sessions in grenade throwing, and with assurances that the air in these parts is extraordinarily healthy, despite the fact that everything is coated in dust from the nearby cement works. In "Cafe 'World'" (Automat "Svět") the proprietor of a snack bar cum pub finds a hanged girl in the toilet, and calmly deals with this would-be crisis while dispensing beer. Music and jollity keep coming through from the wedding reception upstairs; a young man comes in to talk about his missing fiancée, who has always been suicidal; a policeman comes to take care of the corpse, the newly wedded girl wants her groom back, but he's been arrested for blacking the policeman's eye; she offers to sleep with him, and with the young man (on this, her wedding night). The young man tells how he made a death mask for his fiancée; the closing scene has the bride wanting him to do the same for her, as he tears the remains of her wedding dress off her.

In all these outlandish happenings, where magic moments are found in the lives of ordinary people, it is important to note that there is nothing of the fantastic. Everything is rationally motivated, but the stark juxtaposition of events, parallel lines of discourse and matter-of-fact reactions among the stories' participants make for a grotesque. The notion is akin to the manner in which Arnošt Lustig's holocaust victims resign themselves to unspeakable horrors. But in *Pábitelé* hrabalovština staves off any immediate moral dimension and invests the narrative with comedy. The reader's surprise is in inverse proportion to the protagonists' complacency. Where death and violence do not loom large, casual sex does. In a delightful inversion of all the clichés, in "Romance" a sordid act of prostitution between a gypsy girl and a young man, whose stated ambition is to be Fanfan La Tulipe (a reference to the French comedy film of 1952 starring Gérard Philipe) (vol. 4, p. 335) leads to what appears to be a stable relationship, as he is accepted by her father and the gypsy clan – shades of Pushkin's "Gypsies" or Bizet's *Carmen* but ending with a happy beginning. Just occasionally, there is a *coup de théâtre*, as at the end of "Diamond Eye" (Diamantové očko) where the sixteen-year-old heroine on the train to Prague is suddenly revealed to be on her way to an operation to cure her blindness; or at the end of "Bambini di Praga 1947" (see below).

"Bambini di Praga 1947" is the longest story in the collection. The title refers in the first instance to Jezulátko, the baby Jesus and hideously baroque statue of the same in the Church of the Victorious Virgin Mary (Chrám panny Marie Vítězné) in Prague. The Italian nickname "Bambino di Praga" presumably derives from the style best exemplified by Italian artists and associated with the Catholic counter-reformation. The motif reappears (as do several other motifs in *Pábitelé* in later works) in *I Served the King of England*. In the same way that some writers develop favourite names or favourite characters, Hrabal holds particularly dear certain motifs. However, though there is one reference to Jezulátko (vol. 4, p. 205) the title here has more to do with the protagonists, all "infants" of Prague. One might also reflect that 1947 was the last year that Hrabal's country was to enjoy any childlike joy and innocence after the Nazi occupation before the communist takeover.

The episodic narrative owes something to the picaresque tradition, in which a loveable rogue or group of rogues undertake journeys and make a variety of acquaintances in an attempt at material self-benefit. In "Bambini di Praga 1947" we have four representatives of the insurance company

"Support in Old Age" (Opora v stáří) in a bid for more custom selling largely unsuitable policies and encountering some serious eccentrics along the way. There is the same combination of the grotesque and the everyday as we see in the other stories, and a developing erotic element. Part of the huge joke – and much of Hrabal's writing can be construed as such – is that the insurance men are anything but the staid individuals that are usually associated in the popular imagination with the profession. Mr Bucifal has been on trial with the firm for a week, having, according to his own account in the opening sequences at Mr Hyrman's butcher's shop, been sacked from the "Church Services" Co. after a row with a priest, when several statuettes of St Teresa got damaged during delivery (vol. 4, p. 200). Then, there is Viktor Tůma, a handsome man who looks like a Berber (krasavec berberského typu) (vol. 4, p. 198) and who is already paying two lots of child maintenance and gets jealous over pregnant women who are not in that condition because of him (vol. 4, p. 200). Antonín (Tonda) Uhde is "a natty dresser, with a rose between his fingers and his dainty top coat thrown casually over his slender shoulders ("elegán s růží v prstech a svrchníčkem jen tak přehozeným přes ramínka" – vol. 4, p. 199). The use of diminutives in the Czech here can hardly be captured in English, and is one means by which Hrabal achieves, as he often does, a notion of people as cartoon characters, a notion which becomes increasingly prevalent in the scenes involving violence or physical mishap. For example, Mr Krahulík, the boss of the firm, in trying to see what a lady passing by has written on the wreath she is transporting, knocks (literally, "sweeps" ("smetl")) the slight Tonda Uhde off his stool and kicks him in the head (vol. 4, p. 199).

This scene in the butcher's shop is characterized by the gory details of slicing up pigs' heads and scooping out their brains, while Mr Bucifal tries to sell Mr Hyrman a grave. He endeavours to overcome the latter's fear of being buried alive by telling him of a gadget that the supposed corpse can activate to alert the cemetery authorities. Pábení at this level runs seriously close to the medical condition of confabulation, whereby the sufferer does not consciously tell lies, but genuinely believes the lies he tells. In Hrabal, all that matters is the joy and slapstick comedy that the far-fetched word-spinning evokes. The "layers" that we have noted in other stories are also present here, as the sexually-charged Mrs Hyrman, skirt riding up, parades the spices she uses in her sausages, boasts about her husband's enormous fat fingers that can yet play the ukulele, and invites the assembled to a "Venetian Night" (Benátská noc). This turns out, in the third chapter, to be a trip to the fairground, involving side shows and boating.

Chapter two presents us with a pure example of pábení, unencumbered by multiple characters and incidents. Viktor sells insurance to two customers and has some brief encounters – with a girl wearing a Tyrolean hat and selling artificial water lilies (she reappears later in the story), an opera-singing road sweeper and some peripheral children bathing. Both his customers are grotesque: Mr Krause who runs an artificial flower business and has two artificial arms, and Mr Kot'átko, the aged cooper in the local brewery. But the real stuff of the chapter is in the verbal play and free association. Viktor tells his first customer that he is a student of philosophy, on release by the government for the important task of selling pensions:

"Young man, what philosophy do you study then?"
"Metaphysics."
"A beautiful science! But what kind of metaphysics? Ante rem? In rebus? Post rem?"
"Ante rem, platonic ideas."
"A splendid science!" said Mr Krause becoming beautiful at this news, and the reflections from his spectacle lenses ran down his cheeks like little silver fishes. "So, young man, the indolence of the Chaldeans and the pure spirit of Hellas have transformed Judaic wisdom for us beautifully ... ah! That's why I love King Solomon and his position apparently divided between two poles, between Ecclesiastes and the Song of Songs."

"Mladý muži, tak jakoupak filozofii studujete?"
"Metafyziku."
"Krásnou vědu! Ale jakou metafyziku? Ante rem? In rebus? Post rem?"
"Ante rem, platónské ideje."
"Parádní věda!" zkrásněl pan Klause tou zprávou a reflexy čoček mu běhaly tváří jak stříbrné rybičky. "Tak mladý muži, zahálčivost Chaldeů a jasný duch Hellady nám krásně transformovaly židovskou moudrost ... ach! A proto mám rád krále Šalamouna a ten jeho stav zdánlivé roztříštěnosti mezi dvěma póly, mezi Knihou Kazatel a Písní písní." (vol. 4, pp. 210–11)

Mr Krause's elevated style ("Chaldeans" would be roughly synonymous with the much more recognisable "Babylonians", and he prefers "Hellas" to simply "Ancient Greece") goes hand in hand with his willingness to soar above mundane discussions of life insurance. Yet the substance of his remarks offers another gloss on the spirit of *Pábitelé* as a whole: the oscillation between purity and licentiousness, between the sacred and the profane, which is where the wisdom of Hrabal, if not of Solomon, resides. Mr Krause goes on to express his affection for Philo of Alexandria ("a philosopher as irrational and fragile as my flowers" – "filozofa iracionálního a křehkého jako ty moje květiny" – vol. 4, p. 211) and Hermes Trismegistos, and the verbal jousting continues with puns on the Ten Commandments ("Desatero") and the tenth class of insurance on offer, and the seven-armed candelabra. We recall that the seven-branched *menora* is mentioned in the *Talmud* and is the most widely recognized symbol of Judaism. King Solomon's Seal is the Emerald Table, according to the conversation they have; and Viktor outlines two interconnected triangles, i.e. the Star of David, which is also known as Solomon's Seal. These emblems of the Jewish faith form a subtle contrast to the Catholic imagery inherent in the story's title. In these exchanges a small businessman becomes a philosopher, and an alleged student–philosopher becomes an insurance agent. The idea of changeable identities and social masks is echoed in the figure of the road sweeper: "That's the adagio lamentoso from the *Pathétique*! (To je Adagio lamentoso z Patetické!)" exclaims Viktor, while the sweeper replies: "And I am Václav Juřička from Písková Lhota (A já jsem Václav Juřička z Pískový Lhoty – vol. 4, p. 215)", roughly the equivalent of "I'm Joe Bloggs from round the corner". One should also note that the Old Testament references recall the idea at the back of the ancient Hebrew texts the Kabbala and the Zohar that Hebrew was a language endowed with mystical powers, that the Zohar described a language that set supernatural forces in motion.[10] Hebrew was a language that "did", not simply "said". In this connection one recalls that in the story "Do You Want to See Golden Prague?" ("Chcete vidět zlatou Prahu?") the poet admires the undertaker for his effortlessly summoning up of images, but it is the poet's words which in fact produce an effect and have the firemen turn on him for his banter. Given Hrabal's difficulties with the censorship despite his utterly apolitical writing, it is easy to subscribe to the (supernatural?) power of his style.

The further adventures that the infants of Prague experience are similarly subject to flights of lyrical fantasy, transitions from the macabre to the sublime, from vaudeville comedy to something darker. At the fairground, the boss tries to hide from a dissatisfied customer, a barber, who explains in gruesome detail what he will do to the insurance agent when he catches him. Meanwhile, all around there are scenes of merriment and music – carousels, candyfloss and mandolins playing on a river trip (an oblique reference back to the first chapter, where we are told the butcher will be playing at the Venetian Night). Nadja, the vendor of stain remover, teams up romantically with Viktor; the boat sinks when the irate barber kicks one of its planks in.

The subsequent scene in the hotel, where the protagonists dry out and engage in some semi-eroticism elaborates the notions established in the previous scene, namely the element of playing. Nadja, half-naked, performs bits of sales patter, eventually falls asleep drunk in a pram in the corridor which knocks over a potted plant. Playing and play-acting, cardinal traits in Hrabal, tie in with the mercurial nature of the characters and their shifting identities. Recordings by Benjamino Gigli, the greatest tenor of the day, play on the gramophone while the clowning continues (again, an oblique affinity is made with the previous chapter). Hrabal maintains the element of surprise throughout here: Viktor is in fact with the other girl, Uršula, the one selling the water lilies, in the next room, while Nadja cavorts with the boss and Antonín Uhde. And moreover, there is ultimately no sexual activity, though everything about the episode suggests that there should be. "A big baby (Tak velký dítě)", is the comment made by the awakened elderly resident regarding Nadja asleep in the pram; and the closing words of the chapter are: "Over the little town hung the moon and in the fountain the jet of water played with a pingpong ball . . . " (Nad městem visel měsíc a v kašně si pohrával vodotrysk s bílým pingpongovým míčkem . . . – vol. 4, p. 242). In this one lingering image, emphasized by the use of *points de suspension*, we have beauty, lyricism, innocence and, above all, a defiant eternity, which we see time and again in Hrabal.

The following episodes take us to the countryside, where we encounter a painter of grotesque pictures, a very accident-prone chemist, and then another village scene where most of the inhabitants are bastards of the local nobleman, and where there is some slapstick violence in the local pub: when he tries to calm things down, the priest is punched and emerges with a diamond shape drawn on his back, this being the common graffito in the Czech Republic designating the female genitalia. From here we move to the "dancing lessons for the elderly and advanced" and on to the grounds of the local lunatic asylum. Here Mr Bucifal reveals himself to be an undercover policeman who has been set to ensnare the fraudulent insurance men. This second *coup de théâtre* in the book closes "Bambini di Praga 1947". Taken as a whole the various episodes in this story form a pattern of alternation from the world of work to that of play, and back again: 1. work (the first two chapters); 2. play (chapters 3 and 4 – fairground and hotel); 3. work (chapters 5 and 6 – selling insurance to the painter and later to the chemist); 4. play (chapters 7 and 8 – the pub and the dancing lessons); 5. a fusion of work and play (chapter 9 – in the madhouse grounds).

The rich comedy in the story is backed by a wealth of symbolism, only a small part of which is noted here. It should be pointed out that several more motifs are taken up in other works by Hrabal: the "dancing lessons" become a whole one-sentence novel; the "bambino" features prominently in *I Served the King of England*; and likewise this novel also picks up on the motif of a less than deified First President (Masaryk of course, though he is never mentioned by name) – in "Bambini di Praga 1947" he urinates in the bushes, accidentally soaking an undercover policeman (vol. 4, p. 274). In the story "The Lady of the Camellias" ("Dáma s kaméliemi") two old women discuss the abdication of Edward VIII in 1936, and this finds a vague echo in the curious title "I Served the King of England".

How can one explain the epigraph to *Pábitelé*: "Some stains cannot be removed without damaging the fabric of the material"; Některé skvrny nelze vyčistit bez porušení podstaty látky)? The sentence occurs twice in "Bambini di Praga 1947" as Nadja has to warn any would-be customers of the limitations of her wares; but the real significance could well be a double-edged warning – to the overly assiduous literary critic trying too hard to analyse Hrabal's art, and to the censors and editors under whose vigilance Hrabal had to labour – after all, two of his earlier books, "The Lost Little Street" (Ztracená ulička) and "Lark on a Thread" (Skřivánek na niti), of 1949 and 1959 respectively, were pulped, the latter eventually coming out as "A Pearl on the Bottom" (Perlička na dně) in 1963. Finally, Hrabal's infants of Prague engage the world with childlike wonder, and the author's achievement in recreating that wonder for the adult is forever under threat from stain-removing utilitarians and philistines anywhere.

Closely Observed Trains

If not his most accomplished work, the short – and for Hrabal, remarkably conventional – novel of 1965 *Closely Observed Trains* (*Ostře sledované vlaky*) is none the less the author's most famous, not least because of the film based on it, directed by Jiří Menzel, which won an Oscar in 1966. Its popularity is readily understood, since it contains many of the hallmarks of *pábení*, and yet has a staightforward enough plot line, and characters who are by and large credible, albeit with some endearing quirks. Though richly laced with black comedy and sex, the book could still just about be interpreted in terms that the regime, in any case by now surprisingly liberal, would find convenient. However, to see the work primarily as the story of a young patriot's stand against the Nazis would be to render the author a disservice.

It is worth recounting the essentials of the plot, since the surface events suggest conventionality. Miloš Hrma, aged twenty-two, is a trainee signalman at a small railway station in Bohemia – Hrabal was a dispatcher in the little station of Kostomlaty, between Lysá and Nymburk towards the end of the war, and this is in effect where the action of the novel takes place. It is 1945, the Germans are losing the war and the climax of the novel coincides with the Allied bombing of Dresden (about 20 miles from the Czech border) in the February – when the city was devastated and as many as 50,000 people thought killed. We learn that Miloš slashed his wrists three months before the novel opens because he was unable to perform sexually with his sweetheart Máša (Masha in the English translation). On returning to work he is confronted with two crises: the dispatcher Hubička is in trouble for frolicking with the telegraphist Zdena Svatá and using the office rubber stamps to adorn her buttocks; and one of the trains "under close surveillance" (i.e. carrying military supplies, primarily Tiger tanks) has been delayed by half an hour, and the Germans are likely to take reprisals. Miloš is taken away by two SS men, and it seems probable that he is to be shot, but when they notice the cuts on his wrists they let him go. Hubička displays a devil-may-care attitude to life, until the climax of the novel. He confides in Miloš that he is part of plan to blow up a train carrying ammunition. A girl arrives at the station with the bomb, and Miloš agrees to drop it into the passing train from the top of the signal tower, Hubička having more or less lost his nerve. Miloš has all the confidence he needs now, having been deflowered by the resistance worker, Viktorka – clearly in some areas she does not do much resisting at all. Miloš manages to drop his bomb, but he and a soldier on the last wagon of the train shoot each other and both end up dying in a ditch. The train is successfully sabotaged.

The only somewhat unsatisfactory element about the narrative is that, being delivered in the first person, it rather detracts from what is ostensibly a realistic plot – how can the hero tell us his story when he is dead? The crack is papered over to some extent by what appears to be the hero-narrator's delirium when he is in his death throes. In addition, the hero seems to be remarkably skilled with his firearm, when there is no evidence in the text that he has ever handled a weapon before. But these are really only quibbles, given that the substance of the work is to be found outside the realms of conventional narrational realism.

Closely Observed Trains is not so much a war story as a comic exploration of an individual's existential anguish. As such it centres on a number of defining moments in his life, and sets aside any consideration of logical patterning in history or social life. To this end, one of the key features of the book is the recurrent technique of "fanning out" from a relatively small detail to a broader picture. Consider the opening of the novel:

> By this year, the year 'forty-five, the Germans had already lost command of the air-space over our little town. Over the whole region, in fact, and for that matter, the whole country. The dive-bombers were disrupting communications to such an extent that the morning trains ran at noon, the noon trains in the evening, and the evening trains during the night, so that now and then it might happen that an afternoon train came in punctual to the minute, according to the timetable, but only because it was the morning passenger train running four hours late.[11]

> Tenhleten rok, rok pětačtyřicet, Němci už neovládli prostor nad naším městečkem. Natožpak nad celou krajinou, zemí. Hloubkaři narušili dopravu tak, že ranní vlaky jezdily v poledne, polední večer a večerní za noci, takže se někdy stalo, že odpolední vlak přijel podle jízdního řádu na minutu včas, ale to bylo tím, že to byl čtyři hodiny opožděný dopolední osobák. (vol. 5, p. 59.)

The movement here from the particular to the wider picture, plus the Joseph Heller-like absurdity of the trains' "punctuality" suggests that the individual takes pride of place over social considerations and that there is more than an element of Hašek-like anti-war comedy. The novel's opening sentence is repeated several pages later when the narrator pedals off on his bike to see the crashed German aircraft, and this time there is an arresting image of a ticking clock, all the more poignant, given the idea that lineal time itself has been turned into an absurdity in the novel's first paragraph.

> When I rode along the footpath to the fuselage of the aircraft the snow was glittering on the level fields, and in every crystal of snow there seemed to be an infinitely tiny second hand ticking, the snow crackled so in the brilliant sunlight, shimmering in many colours. Then it seemed to me that I could hear these tiny hands ticking away not only in every crystal of snow, but somewhere else as well. There was the ticking of my watch, of course, I heard that quite distinctly, but I could hear another ticking, too, and this one came from the aeroplane, from this heap of wreckage in front of me.
>
> And there it was, the clock on the instrument panel, actually still going, and it even showed the exact time, I compared it with the hands of my watch. (pp. 13–14)

> Když jsem pěšinkou přijel až k trupu letadla, sníh se třpytil na pláních a v každém krystalku sněhu jako by tikala malininká vteřinová ručička, tak ten sníh na prudkém slunci praskal ve všech barvách, a já slyšel, jak nejen v každém krystalku tikají ručičky, ale ještě i někde jinde. Moje hodinky tikaly zřetelně, ale já slyšel ještě jeden tikot, a ten tikot vycházel z letadla, z té hromady.
>
> A tam opravdu tikaly palubní hodiny, dokonce ukazovaly přesný čas, který jsem srovnal s ručičkami mých hodinek. (vol. 5, pp. 62–3)

Immediately the narrator's attention here fixes on a glove, and he "feels" (Já jsem dobře cítil) that there is a hand inside it, which is "not alone" (není sama), but is attached to an arm, which is attached to a human body. With the "all the weight of my body" (váhou těla), the narrator pedals on, the repetition of the word "tělo" here creating a link between the living hero and the dead enemy.

In at least two other areas the motif of time is taken up. First, there is the marble clock in the Station Master's office, which has three balls instead of a conventional pendulum and whose beautiful chimes everyone comments on (Czech text, vol. 5, p. 65; English text, p. 19); more significant though, is the sign that stands over the entrance to Mr Noneman's photographic studio "Finished in Five Minutes" (English text, p. 40) (Za pět minut hotové – vol. 5, p. 79). The phrase occurs twice more in this chapter, and again, when the hero seeks advice about sex from Mrs Lánská, the Station Master's wife (Czech text, vol. 5, p. 99; English text, p. 70). The photographic studio is all but destroyed in an air raid, and the sign is blown down, thus the promise of efficient service is rendered absurd by the scenes of people and things being blasted away. Miloš's problems with premature ejaculation ("I was finished, even before I had begun" (English text, p. 70) (jsem byl hotov ještě dřív, než jsem začal – vol. 5, p. 99) similarly display an ordering of his priorities which sit ill on the shoulders of a conventional war hero.

Rather than in the sabotaging of the train, Miloš's real triumph is in the loss of his virginity, a scene which can be compared with his earlier sexual disgrace and the air raid, and which in its way is just as explosive. One notes in particular how the individual moves outside himself, encompassing all around:

> I was overwhelmed by a flood of light growing ever more brilliant, I was marching, marching uphill, the whole earth shook, and there was the rolling of thunder and storm, I had the impression that it didn't come from me or from Viktoria's body, but from somewhere outside, that the whole building was shaking to its foundations, and the windows rattling. I could hear even the telephones ringing in honour of this my glorious and successful entry into life, and the telegraphs began to play Morse signals of their own accord, as sometimes happened in the traffic office during storms; even the station-master's pigeons seemed to me to be cooing in unison, and at last the very horizon soared and blazed with the colours of fire. (pp. 74–5)

> Zaplavilo mne světlo, které neustále sílilo, pořád jsem kráčel nahoru, celá země se třásla, ozývalo se dunění a hřmění, měl jsem dojem, že to nevychází ani ze mne ani z těla Viktorky, ale zvenčí, že celá budova se zachvívá v základech, okna drnčí, slyšel jsem, že na počest tohohle mého slavného a úspěšného vjezdu do života se rozdrnčely i telefony, telegrafy samy od sebe začaly vyhrávat Morseovy značky, tak jako se to stávalo v dopravních kancelářích při bouřkách, zdálo se mi, že i ti holubi pana přednosty všichni do jednoho vrkají, dokonce i obzor se nadzvedává a zaplál barvami ohňů. (vol. 5, p. 102)

Here, then we need to consider the hero's motivation. The sexual urge is taken as read and drives him to despair and attempted suicide, and then to triumph and transcendental self-confidence. His decision to participate in the act of sabotage is more difficult to explain, but stems not so much from his hatred of the enemy or love of his country – these feelings are under-stated in him, to say the least; Miloš operates more on an emotional than on an intellectual level: his strongest outburst at the Germans ("swine" – prasata) comes when he sees how ill-treated are the livestock they are trans-porting (Czech text, vol. 5, p. 85; English text, p. 47); and his response to the SS men who he thinks are about to kill him is that they are "beautiful" (krásní) and that they should be writing poetry or playing tennis (Czech text, vol. 5, p. 73; English text, p. 30). One should note that "handsome" might be a more appropriate translation for the Czech adjective here, which can be applied equally to males and females, though we should never lose sight of Hrabal's stylistic idiosyncrasy. Miloš's act of heroism is more to do with his admiration for Mr Hubička as a philandering anti-authoritarian, whose stamping Zdena's buttocks equates to Švejk's immoderate drinking: both actions represent an affront to the establishment and stand as an emblem of the individual's authenticity. Such individual authenticity does not debar isolated acts of heroism in a broader political or historical context, but Miloš's diffidence, his sentimental education, his rites of passage are at least as important.

That ontology takes pride of place over historical or political considerations is borne out by the array of secondary characters, each of whom is motivated by matters other than the war, or conditioned by circumstances peripheral to it. The way in which the war is depicted, largely through Miloš's eyes, makes for confusion or at least ambivalence, while whether one dies or survives depends largely on arbitrary forces. We have already noted the way that the hero contemplates the crashed airplane; there is also the chaos in the photographic studio and on the street during the air raid. The refugees from Dresden Miloš first mistakes for escapees from a concentration camp, and he notes how he feels no pity for them, when he could shed tears over kid goats being slaughtered (Czech text, vol. 5, p. 107; English text, p. 82). Incidentally, the English text is slightly ambiguous here rendering as it does "kůzle" as simply "kid". Furthermore, Miloš's emotional responses to the German soldiers are unpredictable. He could feel out and out sorrow for calves being shipped in freight wagons (Czech text, p. 84; English text, pp. 46–7), but on seeing two transports of German soldiers – one going to the front, one in a hospital train coming in the opposite direction, the feelings are more complex (Czech text, vol. 5, p. 90; English text, p. 56). Those going to battle are "the same age" as him or "younger" (byli tak jako já, někteří ještě mladší), and the narrator records their shock when they see the strafed train, though, we are told, they must have seen worse things at home; the wounded soldiers are "sympatičtější" (Czech text, vol. 5, p. 90; English text, p. 56); "nicer" might be a more accurate translation than the literal published English version of this most common of Czech epithets.

In the war descriptions there is no sense of history. We are not told when the conflict started or when it will end. Instead we have an account of the hero's family history, going back to 1848. For Miloš the important thing is that the family seems to have acquired a reputation for skiving. Great-grandfather had a pension from the age of eighteen, after sustaining a knee injury in the rising of 1848; thus he indulged in rum and tobacco on the proceeds of a state pension, invariably in the presence of those who had to work. The subsequent beatings he received eventually killed him. Grandfather was a hypnotist, and as such was considered a layabout. Father retired at the age of forty-eight and is similarly regarded as an idler; and Miloš is afraid that his suicide attempt will be likewise construed as a bid to avoid work. So even if history does exist, the various members of the

Hrma family are widely perceived as being non-participants in it, their nationalist sentiments and Grandad's attempt to hypnotize the German tanks into retreat notwithstanding.

So in the absence of history or the ability to play a role in it, the individual comes into his own. All the characters in *Closely Observed Trains* have aspirations of a kind; and not a few of them are creative artists, not least the narrator, who has extraordinary powers of perception and description. In this we see an elaboration of the technique we noted at the outset, of moving from a detail to a broader plane.

A minor character, the engine driver of a goods train, gives us the clue. He tells the dispatcher that he is still painting, that he enlarges from postcards. If he painted from nature he would have to reduce everything (English text, pp. 44–5; Czech text, vol. 5, pp. 82–3); and he recounts how he only once worked from nature, using a stuffed vixen which a couple of dogs tore to pieces. The narrator realizes that the engineer only stopped at this station to see Hubička, having learned about his exploits with Zdena. The Station Master, bedecked with his pigeons, is also on the scene, and the engineer remarks that he should be in the circus. "In a potato puppet theatre," retorts the dispatcher (Czech text, vol. 5, p. 82; English text, p. 44). So the notion of performing, playing or play-acting, which we noted in *Pábitelé*, is underscored in this text too. Grandfather was a hypnotist, Máša's uncle a photographer. After Miloš and Viktorka have made love he imagines her flying on a horizontal bar (or more likely, trapeze – "na hrazdě"); and she confirms that she is an artiste, performing before the war in a show of "aerial attractions" (Czech text, vol. 5, p. 103; English text, p. 76).

In each creative act the performer achieves a triumph, perhaps only minor or temporary, over the horrors or tedium of life, and a triumph over the cliché. Mr Lánský's marriage is an inversion of the norm: she beats him, he berates her. His act of slaughtering his German breed of pigeons and replacing them with Polish ones as a protest against the Germans, for all its pettiness, asserts his freedom. His ornate office with its Persian carpet and Turkish stools, palm tree and Venetian armchair fit in neatly with his aspirations to be promoted to Inspector of State Railways and to acquire the title of "baron", having discovered that he has some blue blood. Even his hair forms a Gothic arch in the wind, and this links in with the Greek and Roman columns of Prince Kinský's grain storehouse. As a self-appointed custodian of morals and etiquette, a member of the S.O.S (Svaz obrodných snah, literally the "Union of Revivalist Efforts"), he bemoans all the sex in magazines and films, modern artists and sex education. With unwitting perspicacity he inadvertently illuminates Hrabal's artistic preoccupations:

That is what comes of it when there is nothing above folks anymore! Neither

God nor myth, neither allegory, nor symbol. We're on our own in this world, so everything's allowed. But not for me! For me there is a God! But for that grunting pig [i.e. Hubička] nothing exists but pork, dumplings and cabbage ... (p. 24)

Ale to je tím, že nic už nad lidma není. Ani Bůh, ani mýtus, ani alegorie, ani symbol. Jsme na světě sami, proto je dovolený všecko ..., ale ne pro mě! Pro mě je Bůh! Ale pro támhleto prase vepřový existuje jen vepřová, knedlík, zelí ... (vol. 5, pp. 68–9)

Hrabal might well subscribe to the view that there is nothing above man, other than man himself as a creative artist. There is a very clear echo of Ivan Karamazov's assertion that God no longer exists and all is permitted; this is particularly amusing, given the nature of Hubička's peccadillo and the scale of the evil exhibited in Dostoevsky's novel. There is irony in the Station Master's claim that God does exist for him, given that the Countess frequently upbraids him for being "lukewarm" (vlažný) in the faith, reminding him that "when the Catholic Church fell the whole world would fall" (English text, p. 28) (když padne katolická církev, tak padne i celý svět – vol. 5, p. 72). The last sentence quoted above is typically untranslatable: "grunting pig" (prase vepřový) is perhaps the best that can be done with of course a tautology which gives rise in the speaker's angry discourse to "vepřová, knedlík, zelí", forming an alliteration and using the commonest of Czech dishes, indeed the national dish – the equivalent of fish and chips – as a symbol for all the miscreant's self-indulgence. This rapid descent from the sublime to the commonplace is multiplied throughout the novel.

Hubička divides women into two categories according to their physical attributes and irrespective of class or status. So we have a similar scene of bathos when the countess spreads her legs as she leaps onto her horse, and the dispatcher declares: "To je pěkný prdeláč", a phrase which involves a not altogeher common diminutive of "prdel" (arse). Those women with beautiful breasts attract the epithet "ceckounek", again a personal coinage based on the vulgar "cecek" (stronger than the only available English rendition: "tit") (vol. 5, p. 71). The English translation here ("smashing bummie", "busters" – p. 27) is hardly felicitous.

Such linguistic eccentricities, which provide some of the humour, find echoes in the names of several of the characters. The Station Master's surname is perfectly common and stands in ironic contrast to his mild delusions of grandeur, his sartorial fastidiousness and so on. But "Hubička" means appropriately "little kiss", while Zdena's surname, "Svatá" (holy, sacred), is ironic in the extreme. Presumably the English translation was trying to capture this when it provided her with a different first name, Virginia. The ranting and despotic transport chief, who terrifies everyone except Hubička, is called Slušný, a common enough surname, but one which means "decent, "reasonable", or even "civil-tongued". The girl who delivers the bomb has a German surname, "Freie", while her first name, Viktorie – usually diminutivized to Viktorka – is quite appropriate given that she conquers the hero's sexual ineptitude and is instrumental in destroying the train. The best joke name must surely go to the hero himself: "hrma" means "Mount of Venus".

With certain authors (Dostoevsky, Gogol, Dickens) characters' names are charged with significance and often give a clue to their personalities or circumstances. This is only partially true for Hrabal. In *Closely Observed Trains* one feels that in selecting the names that he does, the author is simply indulging in some of the verbal play that his characters engage in.

Another aspect of the book, also present in *Pábitelé*, is the fusion of the lyrical and the horrific. This in fact works as a structural device in the novel. In addition to the narrator's account of the crashed airplane, which involves wonder and horror, there is Mrs Lánská, who does crochet work, but is adept at slaughtering rabbits and letting them bleed slowly to death, so that the meat will be tender. A "quietness" (English text, p. 20) (ticho, vol. 5, p. 66) is exuded from her needlework, as she creates flowers and birds (yet another example of a creative artist), but she has the same expression when she is killing rabbits. The hero's perceptions of the world can be beautiful and uplifting, or they can centre repeatedly on the carcasses of dead horses, rooks and other animal life, or on his bleeding wrists as he lies in the bath expecting death. The ambivalence is clinched in the last scenes where Miloš and the German die, side by side, and so many opposites meet.

The former has achieved manhood, whereas the latter, an older man, is calling out for "Mother". The narrator takes this at first to be a call for his own mother, only later realising that it is a call for his wife, the mother of his children. Two enemies are united, the hero clutching the German by the hand. The momentary and the eternal come together, while the sublime and the vulgar are fused in the darkly comic closing words of the novel which Miloš repeats to his companion: "You should have sat at home, on your arse." (English text, p. 91) (Měli jste sedět doma, na prdeli . . . – vol. 5, p. 113).

I Served the King of England – The Triumph of Aesthetics; *Too Loud a Solitude* – The Triumph of Culture

Arguably, *I Served the King of England* (*Obsluhoval jsem anglického krále*) and *Too Loud a Solitude* (*Příliš hlučná samota*) are Hrabal's two most accomplished and sophisticated works. Both of them, but in particular the latter, may be understood within the context of *pábení* and all its ramifications, as discussed above. Yet for a fuller appreciation, we need to consider the particular artistic movements which influenced Hrabal so profoundly and to which he has made his own special contribution, namely Dadaism and Surrealism.

Of the various explanations for the origin of the former movement's name, the most likely is that a group of rebellious artists and anti-war campaigners, meeting in Zurich in 1916 stuck a paper knife at random into a French–German dictionary and it lighted on the French word for hobbyhorse, *dada*. The term seemed most appropriately to stand for a rejection of artistic conventions, bourgeois values and straightforward thinking, all of which had, after all, led to the First World War. A truly international movement with centres in Zurich, Berlin and Cologne, in Paris and in New York, Dadaism initially was concerned with the visual arts, but it came to embrace all the arts. Its chief features were collage and montage, the first being the assembling of apparently unrelated images, the second term, more associated with cinema (especially the films of Eisenstein), involving the interruption or modification of a narrative line by introducing images which are ostensibly unconnected with the unfolding drama. The art of the dadaists often included an element of performance, staged "happenings" designed to shock and outrage. In Paris in particular the movement influenced creative writing, with André Breton, Louis Aragon and Paul Eluard being among the prime early practitioners. Photography played an important part, as did the use of ready-made artifacts of all sorts. The movement also took on a political aspect (see below).

It must be said that Dadaism's main preoccupations were with rejection and negation, and perhaps for this reason it was soon to inspire the more affirmative and far more influential movement of Surrealism. André Breton published *The Surrealist Manifesto* in 1924. The surrrealists sought to unite, or rather re-unite, the conscious and the subconscious. They rejected the rationalism of the nineteenth century, which in their view had led to the slaughter of the First World War. Dream and fantasy were to be joined with the rational, everyday world. Of course, a lot of this theorizing was borrowed or adapted from Sigmund Freud and his explorations of the subconscious and the dream. For the practising artist or writer, surrealism often meant juxtaposing perfectly ordinary, but quite unrelated, images, producing highly arresting, even disturbing, combinations of images and ideas, to create, in Breton's words "an absolute reality, a surreality".

Paul Eluard became the leading surrealist poet of the interwar years, and went on to even greater prominence in the newly expanded Soviet empire of the post-war period. His major collection *Une Rose Publique* was translated into Czech by Nezval and Bedřich Vaníček in 1936. Much later on, Milan Kundera could write in *The Book of Laughter and Forgetting* that Eluard did not respond to Breton's appeal in 1950 to help save their fellow surrealist Záviš Kalandra from the gallows, for "Eluard was too busy dancing in the gigantic ring encircling Paris, Moscow, Warsaw, Prague, Sofia and Athens; too busy reciting his beautiful poems about joy and brotherhood".[12] Surrealism was on the Left, and there were enough Leftist critics around to explain away its grotesque and fantastic productions as mirror-like reflections of the distortions wrought on the human spirit by the injustices of capitalism. For them, surrealism was serving the same function in the West as had Russian nineteenth-century "critical realism", when Socialist Realism was officially adopted at the First Soviet Writers' Congress in 1934. Surrealism would be superannuated once socialism was achieved.

One should also note that Surrealism was to an extent in conflict with the Cubism which so attracted Čapek. Čapek will sow the seeds of doubt, but still through the means of perfectly realistic characters and plots – even his science fictions have a logic to them once the rules of his brave new worlds are established. Cubism and Čapek are formulaic; Surrealism and Hrabal, by contrast, operate through the prism of poetry and dream.

In *Too Loud a Solitude* there are frequent references to Jackson Pollock (1912–56), the American abstract expressionist painter, who, like Hrabal, was extremely well read and intelligent, and who was at first appreciated only by a few, despite his widespread publicity. His abstract expressionism has generally been traced back to the surrealist and expressionist movements of Europe. One could well see affinities between his "active painting", involving the "drip technique" whereby he poured paint onto canvasses rather than using a brush, and Hrabal's unencumbered processing and utilization of the verbal material he surrounded himself with in smoky pubs and random workplaces. Indeed, in a Foreword to *The Little Town Where Time Stood Still*, he writes:

> I am attempting in this text something that I have been thinking about for several years now, how gradually to get from a realistic drawing to a deformation and eventually to go over to what is the essence of gesticulatory painting, as Jackson Pollock did. I am setting myself such a lofty aim that it disappears in the twinkling azure, because what I am attempting to do in order to combine consciousness with unconsciousness, vitality and existentiality, to annul an object as an external and internal model, requires a leap
> . . .
>
> Pokusím se v tomto textu o to, nač řadu let myslím, kterak z realistické kresby zvolna se dobrat deformace a nakonec přejít v to, co je podstatou gestické malby, tak jak to učinil Jackson Pollock. Stavím si laťku tak vysoko, až mi mizí v třpytivém azuru, protože to, oč budu usilovat, abych spojil vědomí a nevědomí, vitalitu a existencialitu, abych zrušil předmět jako vnější a vnitřní model, k tomu je zapotřebí skoku . . . [13]

Hrabal's catholic interests in all the arts and philosophy are instantly

recognized in the two major works under discussion here. The ready interaction of notions, images and changing guises is likewise taken up
ubiquitously in his oeuvre, as characters may adopt different personalities,
events, great or small, are recounted from unexpected angles and sense
perceptions overlap. Synaesthesia (see p. 35 on Čapek), the condition
where one sense is described in terms of another or is stimulated by another
(for instance, we speak of the "colours of an orchestra") can be highly
developed in Hrabal. Of course, such interchange of the five senses was
something discovered by the French and Russian Symbolists at the end of
the nineteenth century and erected into a quasi-religious outlook. In
Hrabal, it is more a celebration of life's richness. In addition to the very
title "Too Loud a Solitude", there are any number of examples in this and
other works: in *Cutting It Short* (*Postřižiny*) the female narrator (a rarity
in Hrabal) has hair which is likened to Pilsner beer and then her interlocutor goes back into the pub to "drink more of her hair" (dál popíjet ty
vaše zlaté vlasy).[14] Uncle Pepin, the foul-mouthed, loveable brawler and
raconteur, is momentarily transformed into an opera singer by the imagination and powers of expression of the brewery cooper (English text, p. 86;
Czech text, pp. 72–3). In the sequel to this book, *The Little Town Where
Time Stood Still*, we have a different narrator but many of the same characters; the narrator's father has an electric massage-machine, with which he
treats a female friend overly fond of drink:

> "You've got to see it," said Dad, and like a magician and hypnotist he
> continued with this instrument, drawing a purple violet cloud and perfume
> round the chest and heart of the butcher's wife, her breasts heaved not with
> indignation, but with delight, with astonishment. (pp. 216–17)

> "Máš ho vidět," řekl tatínek a dál jako kouzelník a hypnotizér obtahoval
> přístrojem fialové mračno a vůni kolem prsou a srdce paní řeznice, její prsy
> se vzdouvaly ne pobouřením, ale rozkoší, podivením.[15]

Hrabal's own term for his technique was "total realism" (totální real-
ismus), a method inspired in part by his friend, Egon Bondy. Originally
the term meant little more than not having any inhibitions when one wrote,
but it came to mean the art of creating "a whole world out of a square
metre" (vydupat z čtverečního metru celý svět),[16] fanning out from a small
detail into a wide realm of images and concepts. We noted the technique in
Closely Observed Trains. Yet one might, in the case of the two novels now
under discussion, see "total realism" in the manner in which any border
between any perceived or "objective" world and the inner, private world,
and even the subconscious, is abolished.

I Served The King of England had a will o' the wisp existence before the
fall of communism. Completed in 1975 it was deemed inappropriate by the

authorities for publication. Hrabal had partially ingratiated himself with the post-1968 regime in an interview in *Tvorba* in January 1975, but received what might be called only token publication in return. However, the work was widely known amongst intellectuals, and parts of it were dramatized. The text appeared in a "Petlice" edition, that is the illegal *samizdat* publishers, which did so much to keep Czech and some banned foreign literature alive during the years of "normalization". The book was eventually brought out in 1983 by the "Jazz Section" of the Czech Musicians' Union in a closed edition for their members only. This act of defiance was only one of several which finally led to the arrest of some of its members and their imprisonment in 1987. Earlier texts differed from the post-1989 version, and this explains some of the discrepancies between the English translation and what can now be regarded as the authorized text. One notes immediately the repeated phrases, omitted in the translation, which, with very slight variations, open and close each chapter: "Pay attention to what I'm going to tell you" (Dávejte pozor, co vám teďka řeknu) and "Is that enough for you? I'll finish with this today." (Stačí vám to? Tím dneska končím). The device points up the conversational tone, the element of *pábení*, which, given the extraordinary events and characters, the public and private history that we are taken through, might at times be overlooked.

Like the book's publication history, the hero is similarly vulnerable to waves of serendipity, bouts of opportunism and ultimate fulfilment. In vain would the reader try to attribute to him any consistency – he attracts and repulses, delights and infuriates. In flat contradiction to Radko Pytlík's assertion (p. 181), we might say he is a complete inversion of Robert Musil's "man without qualities", for he possesses all the qualities, adopting them and discarding them with little reference to circumstance. One of Hrabal's cardinal achievements in this novel is the manner in which he decouples human emotion from what the reader might view as external stimuli. Dítě survives the Second World War – and a lot more besides – as emotionally detached as Švejk survived the First. What shocks the reader, the hero takes in his stride; what the reader might shrug off, drives the hero to thoughts of suicide.

I Served the King of England is characterized by paradox, as epitomized at the very start of the novel when the boss of the Hotel Praha twigs the hero by his left ear and tells him that as a bell-hop he has seen nothing and heard nothing, and then twigs him by the right ear and tells him that he has seen all and heard all (Czech text, vol. 7, p. 9; English text, p. 1). One major paradox is in the hero himself. His name means "child", and in one sense he remains childlike throughout: small of stature, persistently surprised at the world around him, rarely taking responsibility for his actions, quick to forget past experiences or failing to mature through them; he is content with the non-explanation (because "I served the king of England") as to why his mentor, the head waiter Skřivánek at the Hotel Šroubek, knows everything; he adopts his own version, "I served the Emperor of Ethiopia", by way of explanation to himself and others, when circumstances seem to require an explanation. On the other hand Dítě, the child, can at times feel tall, and he leads a lengthy life, embraces a variety of lifestyles and contemplates death and his possible immortality with a kind of quietist wisdom that many would envy. Might he not stand as a metaphor for the Czech predicament?

The hero's life might be considered under various headings: his personal life, his career, his interaction with History and Culture. First, his personal life leaves us with little information as to where he came from, and his parentage seems vague. We have his father's injunction that he should have an aim and that then he will be "saved" and would have something to live for (vol. 7, p. 14). The word for "saved", attributed to his father, is "zachráněn". In the English translation it is rendered as "be all right"[17] (p. 9), but it might also mean "rescued" or "redeemed". Given that the hero's aim in life, at least at the opening of the novel, is to fiddle enough money by short-changing the train passengers who buy his sausages at the railway station in order to fund his visits to the brothel, the notion here is especially ironic and the comedy unmistakable. He has fuller recollections of his grandmother, with whom he lived for three years, and the outlandish manner in which she collects the personal linen from the travelling salesmen who use the public baths next door. All we learn of his mother is that she was single when he was born (English text, p. 39; Czech text, vol. 7, p. 36).

Dítě's personal life most frequently involves sensual pleasures, notably sexual encounters, but also his delight in fine clothes and wine. His materialism leads him to ambitions of becoming a millionaire and great hotelier; yet initially his real pleasures come in the brothel and with his wife; the sex act is nearly always associated with flowers and poetry, as he adorns the genitalia of his partners with posies. His concern with how he appears to others eventually gives way to a concern for how he appears to himself. Towards the end of the war, on his way to a new assignment he looks at himself in a mirror at a railway station, and sees himself as "a stranger" (p. 153) (jako cizího člověka – vol. 7, p. 121), as a member of the Sokol who let himself be examined by Nazi doctors so he could copulate with a German and sang German patriotic songs while the Germans declared war on the Russians, and "while people at home were suffering he was sitting pretty in hotels and inns, serving the German Army and the SS-Waffe" (p. 153) (zatímco doma lidé trpěli, tak já se mám dobře v německých hotelích a hotýlcích, kde posluhuji německé armádě a eseswaffe – vol. 7, p. 122). At the end of the story, unattached and alone, apart from some fellow drinkers in the pub and a retinue of domestic animals, he installs mirrors in his home; and he contemplates his life in a more penetrating manner than hitherto. The road he has to mend comes to resemble his life (English text, p. 225; Czech text, vol. 7, p. 176). He is unable to improve it but can make it passable, and he sets himself a modest goal in his road clearance (so different from the "goal" before him in the brothel at the start of the novel). "My life to this point seemed like a novel, a book written by someone else, even though I alone had the only key to this book of life" (p. 226) (celý můj život až sem byl román, kniha, kterou napsal někdo jiný, avšak k té knize života jsem měl jediný já klíč – vol. 7, p. 176). And shortly after this:

> As a matter of fact whenever I was in the pub I realized that the basic thing in life is questioning death, wanting to know how we'll act when our time comes, and that death, or rather this questioning of death, is a conversation that takes place between infinity and eternity, and how we deal with our own death is the beginning of what is beautiful, because the absurd things in our lives, which always end before we want them to anyway, fill us, when we contemplate death, with bitterness and therefore with beauty. (p. 228)

> Vlastně já jsem v tom hostinci vždycky zjistil, že podstata života je ve vyptávání se na smrt, jak já se budu chovat, až přijde ten můj čas, že vlastně smrt, ne, to vyptávání se sebe sama, je hovor pod zorným úhlem nekonečna a věčnosti, že už řešení té smrti je počátek myšlení v krásném a o krásném, protože vychutnávat si nesmyslnost té své cesty, která stejně končí předčasným odchodem, ten požitek a zážitek svého zmaru, to naplňuje člověka hořkostí, a tedy krásou. (vol. 7, p. 178)

Here we are a long way from the Dítě obsessed with bodily delights, but we are still dealing with the paradoxes. On the one hand there is the existential notion so prevalent in post-war fiction, and explored in Sartre and Camus, that the very knowledge of death invests life with meaning, despite the latter's apparent absurdities. Yet how are we to understand what would literally translate here as the "discourse from the viewpoint of infinity and eternity"? and how does "beauty" follow on from "bitterness"? Perhaps we should simply note the alogism and allow Dítě to proceed to his own contemplation of his death, his remains washed away both by the Danube and the Vltava, carried out to the Black Sea and the North Sea and eventually to the Atlantic Ocean, so that in death he will become a "citizen of the world" (světoobčan).

The hero's progression from sensualist to philosopher is far less surprising than some of the absurdities we encounter in the book. His career is no less deserving of the refrain "and then the unbelievable became true" (neuvěřitelné se stalo skutkem). The opening of the novel in the original full text: ("Dávejte pozor, co vám teďka řeknu. Když jsem přišel do hotelu Praha..." is slightly more obscure than the published English translation: "When I started to work at the Golden Prague Hotel … ". The original might imply that the hero could have worked somewhere else before; the vagueness about the start of his career matches the vagueness of his parentage. He goes on to change his job fluidly, from this first appointment he moves to another provincial hotel, the Tichota in Stráncice, but is sacked because he is blamed for the mix-up over the substitute bambino di Praga statue during the consecration ceremony. He gets another job, this time in Prague at the Hotel Paris (Hotel Paříž), probably his most important position, for it is here that he meets the head waiter Skřivánek and here that he serves the Emperor of Ethiopia, and thus acquires a sash and a medal. Soon after this high water mark in his career we learn that he is turned down three times for military service, because of his height, starts learning German and watching German films, meets Líza, and when the country is occupied gets a new job in a mountain retreat over Děčín, where the air is pure and so is the Nazi breeding. When he hears that the German soldiers there are learning Russian he states that he thinks this means there will be war with Russia. This incurs the wrath of the commander who calls him a Czech chauvinist, and though his prediction is proved true moments later, he is still fired, and forced to take up a new position in a country hotel in Košíček, where German officers and their partners spend their final days before the men are dispatched to the Eastern front. He then fetches up in the canteen at a military hospital attending the wounded whom, though he recognizes no one in particular, he knows are the same people he served at his last two postings.

Near the end of the war his career suffers an ostensible setback when he is arrested by the Germans, in a case of mistaken identity involving his old colleague Zdeněk. This turns out to be a blessing in disguise, because his collaboration with the Germans will now be obliterated. None the less, with the war over, he gets six months from the new Czech government for his German sympathies; then he buys his first hotel, quickly leaving it to build a really luxury establishment. With the communist seizure of power in February 1948 (one of the few dates, if the only one, in the text) millionaires are imprisoned, and he has to beg and plead to be treated accordingly. The extraordinarily lax regime in the prison and its eventual closure are followed by the hero's having to work in a forest brigade (comprising himself, a female juvenile delinquent and a professor of French literature), and later alone, as a road maintenance man. So ends his career.

The paradox thrown up by his personal life and his career is that there seems little emotional or philosophical co-ordination between the two: he has no qualms about cheating train passengers, but attempts suicide when unjustly accused of stealing a golden spoon after the Haile Selassie feast; he has no scruples over using the stamp collection that his wife stole from Jews to finance his business after the war, yet he is anxious to be punished as a

millionaire by the communist authorities. There is no emotional reaction
when his wife is killed in an air raid, and he simply abandons his idiot son
to an institution. The emotional "de-coupling" as we called it earlier is to
be found in other areas of the book too: the wood-cutting porter at the
Hotel Tichota is "gentle and sensitive" (p. 85) (jemný a citlivý – vol. 7, p.
69) yet attacks his wife, her lover, his cat and pretty much anything else
with his axe. The reader's emotions are similarly pushed in unexpected
directions, from laughter to horror, bewilderment to contentment, moral
outrage to compassion.

Dítě also interacts with Culture and History. Though for the most part
there is a timeless quality about the text, as in a dream, there are some
crooked signposts. Haile Selassie was the first Ethiopian Emperor to travel
abroad, visiting major European capitals in 1924. Tomáš Masaryk's
pronounced Victorian values come in for a vicious mauling when "The
President" frolics with the beautiful French lady at the Hotel Tichota. The
extraordinary story in the aftermath of the Nazi massacre at Lidice, when
one František Saidl, on completing a sentence for murder, returns to his
native village to discover it no longer exists, Hrabal incorporates into Dítě's
biography. Even the curious title of the novel can be construed as a tangential, wry reference to the abdication of Edward VIII in 1936, which was the
talk of Europe and the United States – continentals (not least, in his day,
General and President Charles de Gaulle of France) failing routinely to
distinguish between Great Britain and England.

It is, however, the aesthetic and cultural references which are more
important, and in fact give *I Served the King of England* its substance. The
history of the Czech Lands is hovering in the background: the free and easy
ways of the First Republic, the entrepreneurial spirit and the commercialism; similarly there is the repression of the Nazi period and its mirror
image with all the attendant absurdities under the communists. Yet the allusions to the aesthetic debates of the changing eras interlock more readily
with the characters and events of the book, providing a framework and, it
can be argued, ultimately upstaging the cultural polemics.

Early on in his sensual career the hero learns that "for money it is
possible to buy not just a beautiful girl, but poetry too" (p. 16) (za peníze
lze koupit nejen krásnou dívku, ale za peníze lze taky koupit poezii – vol.
7, pp. 19–20). At his next hotel, the general, on his second visit, brings some
girls "together with some fat poet" (p. 64) (s nějakým tlustým básníkem –
vol. 7, p. 55). We read that the two men argue furiously about poetry and
about a male and a female writer, and a little later we learn that they argue
specifically about the death of poetism and the new trend of surrealism,
now entering its second phase, and art and pure art (English text, p. 66;
Czech text, vol. 7, p. 56). The references and the debates will be tediously
familiar to anyone with a reasonable knowledge of twentieth-century

Czech literature, and our narrator provides no details – poetism, Czechoslovakia's own brand of surealism, is the most indigenous of the terms. The poet and painter Tonda Jódl, who published at his own expense *The Life of Jesus Christ* (English text, p. 37; Czech text, vol. 7, p. 34), used to live at Dítě's first hotel and insists that the job of the poet is to seek the "new man". There are several allusions to him later, as when the narrator recalls the literary debates he engendered leading to fights between the hotelier and his wife, about romanticism, realism, Smetana and Janáček (English text, p. 52; Czech text, vol. 7, p. 45), or when the headwaiters from the Prague and from the Paris appear to the hero like saints, like Tonda Jódl, and he wonders what kind of headwaiter he will make (English text, pp. 97–8; Czech text, vol. 7, p. 79). This episode occurs when the hero is first given the explanation by Skřivánek that he once served the King of England. So the equation between a headwaiter, a saint and a poet is made; indeed poetry is persistently associated with sex and with religion throughout the text.

The literary debate comes especially to the fore when the hero is in the work brigade and encounters the professor of French and the delinquent. The latter and the hero are eventually educated by the academic in the delights of Jarry, Desnos and the beautiful men and women of Paris (English text, pp. 213–14; Czech text, vol. 7, pp. 166–7) – there are specific references to *La rose publique* and *L'Histoire du Surréalisme*. Shortly after this we have the narrator implementing some of the chief techniques of the surrealists in an amalgam of collage and montage:

> I was emptying out of myself drawers and boxes full of old bills and useless letters and postcards, as if fragments of tattered posters were blowing out of my mouth, posters pasted one on top of the other, so that when you rip them away you create nonsense signs, where soccer matches blend into concerts or where art exhibitions get mixed up with brass-band tattoos ... (p. 221)

> Vysypávám ze sebe škatulky a zásuvky plné propadlých směnek a zbytečných dopisů a pohlednic, že ústy se mi odvávají útržky starých napolo roztrhaných, jeden druhým přelepených plakátů, které ve stržení tvoří nesmyslné texty, mísící oznámení fotbalových zápasů s oznámením koncertů, plakáty výstav se propojují s dechovkami. (p. 173)

The other strand of the cultural debate is closely associated with the party politics of the age – fascism and communism. In both camps there is talk of the New Man, the Nazis trying to achieve the phenomenon by science, the communists by education. At the breeding station the Nazi pictures extolling the glorious German past remind Dítě of Jirásek's *Old Czech Legends*. We need to recall that the poetry debate at the start of the novel also revolved around the New Man; and here Hrabal comes into his own, for his book must not be seen as merely a belated, dated repeat of the artistic experiments of the thirties, which in such folly might be equated with the crass political extremism the book so clearly castigates. It is rather a simultaneous genuflexion to the miracle of art and to the rejection of all dogma, even in the arts.

Thus we can view Hrabal as a surrealist taken to a commonsensical extreme, a writer who incorporates bits of surrealism, just as the traditional surrealists incorporated bits of realism. In *I Served the King of England* the arresting image becomes just as important as conventional narrative or character: tailored suits produced on airborne torsos, billowing laundry discarded by travelling salesmen, a gargantuan feast for the Emperor of Ethiopia, Jezulátko, the bambino di Praga, instrumental, as so many legends recount, in the survival of the Czech nation, a prostitute in a restaurant pouring grenadine over her head in defence of her humiliated client. And the images sometimes become motifs or are cross-referenced in ways that provide the book, no less than does the story-line, with its cohesion, or often they link obscurely to real historical events (as we have noted on occasion earlier): when Dítě has to plead to be imprisoned as a millionaire, the informed reader may well recall the "survivor" of Lidice asking, allegedly, the Gestapo to punish him too; Dítě's idiot son hammering nails into the floor curiously echoes the antics of Oscar, the dwarf-hero of Günter Grass's *The Tin Drum* of 1960; the unlikely image of the rich gypsies at the start of the book is balanced by the hero's encounter with the poor gypsies at the end; the hilarious attempt at suicide where Dítě's head bangs against the feet of someone who has beaten him to it finds a counterweight in the contemplation of death and immortality at the end; flowers, poetry, sex and religion are ubiquitously related, the sacred and profane intertwine.

A final point about Dítě: he is the manipulator *par excellence*. He cheats customers, he scatters coins just to watch passers-by scrabble for them, he cons Nazis and communists alike. Near the very end of the book the villagers in the pub kill his dog deliberately to get him to come back and converse with them because they cannot live without him and he is a better talker than their priest. So, one can surmise, Dítě, through the words he weaves, is a life-giver, a writer, who like his creator, has the power to make "the unbelievable come true".

Too Loud a Solitude could easily be seen as political allegory. Škvorecký called it a "poetic condemnation of the banning of books",[18] while the review of the English translation in *The New York Times* called it "a remarkable story about the indestructibility of books and knowledge".[19] Certainly the text suffered the same sort of vicissitudes that beset *I Served the King of England*. The work was completed in 1976, part of the text was published in the émigré journal *Svědectví* in 1978 (no. 57); in addition to various *samizdat* productions, an abbreviated text was issued by the *Mladá fronta* publishing house in Prague in 1981, the full text appearing in the author's homeland only after the Velvet Revolution. There are further complications, in that there have been three versions of the work, one in verse and two in prose. One can barely talk about a definitive text. A 1992 edition containing *The Little Town Where Time Stood Still* and *The Tender Barbarian* has a six-page appendage "Adagio lamentoso" in blank verse, which mixes eroticism with such forthright statements as "The future of humanity is a bookshop" (budoucnost lidstva je knihkupectví) and satirical barbs like "Lenin obtained Party card no. 1 signed by Leonid Brezhnev himself" (Lenin obdržel stranickou legitimaci číslo jedna podepsanou samotným Leonidem Brežněvem).[20] *Too Loud a Solitude* is thus a fine example of the author's contention that all his oeuvre represents "work in progress".

Set against Hrabal's other major fiction, this short novel is something of an exception, for there is in fact very little incident. The hero-narrator, Haňťa, having worked for thirty-five years in a paper-pulping plant in Prague and with five years to go to retirement, commits suicide by climbing into his hydraulic press. He is in despair at the new, mass-production pulping plant he has seen and at the fact that his boss, angered by his tardiness with the work, has arranged for him to be transferred to a factory where they process new paper.

Of course, it is possible to see a political message in the bare plot-line, and there are other expressions of a political nature: towards the end of Chapter Five the author tells us how he loved destroying Nazi propaganda after the war, especially pictures of Hitler. Nothing very risqué in this for a Czechoslovakia "normalized" – to use the Soviet parlance – by Soviet tanks, but Haňťa is regularly visited by a former professor of philosophy who used to work for *Theatre News* but was thrown out of work five years earlier (vol. 9, p. 39). (Incidentally, the Heim translation has (p. 44) "for political reasons". Either the translator is working from a different text or is, perhaps understandably, adding a gloss for foreign readers.).[21] Near the start of Chapter Three there is a passage which talks of intellectuals doing menial tasks in the sewers and elsewhere (a clear reference to post-1968). In Chapter Seven one detects some unmistakable anti-communist hints – when two members of the Socialist Work Brigade from the new plant come to visit the hero's workplace, he exclaims "Bravo, bravissimo, molodci" (vol. 9, p. 65; English text, p. 80), the last word here being the Russian term for "Fine lads", which usually translates as "Well done!" Perhaps understandably, the English text makes no attempt at translation here. Shortly afterwards, the narrator recalls how former property owners (English text has "the once wealthy", p. 83) (bývalí majitelé činžáků, vol. 9, p. 67) were pleased at the spectacle of workers turning to religion.

This most poetic of Hrabal's works is a celebration of the world of ideas. The hero, who has in his own words been educated "against his will" (proti své vůli – vol. 9, p. 9) (the Heim translation, rather eccentrically, has "unwittingly" . . . – p. 1), has amassed from the doomed books at work his own library at home, so many tomes they threaten to fall and crush him, and he makes each bail at work with loving care, putting in a favourite volume, opened at a favourite page. Quotations from literature and philosophy abound, bearing out the book's epigraph from Goethe, "Only the sun has the right to its spots" – the implication here being that humanity's overriding aim should be the pursuit of perfection, that philistinism and mediocrity are intolerable.

Yet the sublime can never be divorced from the sordid, and in *Too Loud a Solitude* we witness the familiar, yet peculiar, harmony of contrasts, so typical of Hrabal: slovenly, licentious gypsy women and saints; images of beautiful Prague churches and beneath, in the sewers, the never-ending battle between the two armies of rats, the victorious side itself breaking into two warring factions; the author's first love shunned and ridiculed because the ribbons in her hair have become besmirched with human faeces after a trip to the toilet, or later, on a luxury holiday, a turd on her ski. One of the narrator's close acquaintances, Frantík Šturm, used to delight in writing newspaper articles about drunken brawls, but has now become the sexton in a church; yet he still avidly collects books on aviation, convinced that "Icarus was Jesus' forerunner, the only difference being that Icarus fell from the sky into the sea, whereas Jesus was launched by an Atlas rocket" (p. 80) (Předchůdce Ježíše byl Ikaros, akorát s tím rozdílem, že Ikaros byl sražen z nebes do moře, zatímco Ježíš raketou Atlas [. . .] byl vynesen – vol. 1, pp. 65–6).

As in other texts, Hrabal makes judicious use of refrains to provide cohesion and rhythm. Each chapter, with the exception of 4 and 8, opens with the information that the hero has worked at the same job for thirty-five years; and, with slight variations, we are told repeatedly that "the heavens are not humane, nor any man" (nebesa nejsou vůbec humánní, a člověk také humánní není). Such verbal reprises match the to-and-fro movements of the hydraulic press, controlled by the green and red buttons. The overall effect is to create a conception of infinity and eternity. As the hero tells us at the end of the first chapter: "I am never abandoned, I am simply alone, so as to live in a solitude populated by thoughts, because I am a bit of a big head (furiant) of infinity and eternity and Infinity and Eternity have a liking for people like me" (translation R. P.) (já opuštěný nikdy nejsem, já jsem pouze sám, abych mohl žít v myšlenkami zalidněné samotě, protože já jsem tak trochu furiant nekonečna a věčnosti a Nekonečno a Věčnost mají asi zálibu v takových lidech, jako jsem já – vol. 9, p. 14). (The Heim translation here seems rather free: "I can be by myself because I'm never *"the hero becomes his book"*

lonely, living in my heavily populated solitude, a harum-scarum of infinity and eternity, and Infinity and Eternity seem to take a liking to the likes of me," p. 9). So the hero becomes his book; "In a sense, I am both artist and audience" (English text, p. 6) (já sám sobě jsem v jistém smyslu současně umělcem a divákem, vol. 9, p. 12), and the chosen manner of his suicide reinforces the point in a darkly comic way. One might note that the published translation here is slightly free, but manages splendidly to capture the alliteration and assonance of the original.

The visual arts play no less a part in the hero's psychological make-up than does the world of ideas. Thonet, the German inventor of bentwood furniture (he had factories all over the world, one of the largest being in Moravia) rates a mention, along with Rembrandt, Van Gogh, Picasso, Pollock and others. Hrabal's eclecticism contributes to the notion of "total realism" as well as amounting to a refusal to turn any philosophy or artistic credo into a cult.

role of the visual arts as well as ideas.

Yet, of all the cultural threads that make up the web, three predominate: the Hellenic world, Jesus Christ and Lao-tzu. The hero is struck by the youngsters who can afford to have holidays in Greece, and he ponders that his own travels there have been cerebral, but clearly what delights him are the cult of the human form and the clarity of Greek thought. Christ, as the most salient example of all the religious imagery in the book, stands quite simply for faith, but he is also an ardent revolutionary who wants to change the world (English text, p. 33; Czech text, vol. 9, p. 31); and Lao-tzu, legendary founder of Taoism and arguably the single most important influence in Chinese thought and religion before the coming of communism, is a wise old man who, we are reminded, advocated a way (the Tao) to learned ignorance. Here we should recall Hrabal's own definition of *pábení*, which we noted above (see p. 55).

3 other cultural threads
greek
krist
Lao tzu

The manner in which the hero finds a place for all of the most diverse of thinkers and artists – at one time or another they all seem to be his favourites, whether it is Goethe or Schiller, Seneca or Socrates, Kant, Nietsche or Erasmus, Sartre or Camus – echoes a more general aspect of Hrabal's fiction: the notion of clowning and trying on various masks; and of course there is a splendid example in this story of Hańta acting out the parts of the young, put-upon worker and the tyrannical boss for the benefit of the visiting professor, and making money out of both guises. As in *I Served the King of England*, it is manipulation, but it is also an exercise in identity-fixing.

In our discussion of *Closely Observed Trains*, we raised a small objection to a dead hero-narrator recounting his own story; it challenged the overall realism of the text. In *Too Loud a Solitude*, such are the poetics of the work that there is no such jarring, for Hańta has become so fused with immortal words that his end is more of a transition than a death – just like

Hańta as a "dead hero-narrator recounting his own story"

Dítě's. The novel can be read as a political tract, after all it was written just at a time when so many books were being banned or withdrawn from public libraries in Czechoslovakia; but it can also be read as the victory of culture over philistinism, unchecked mass-production and conformity anywhere or at any time.

Hrabal and his characters – his fellow yarn-spinners – have an unfailing genius for finding miracles in the commonplace and for emancipating the commoner to the rank of artist. Clearly, Hrabal was racked by the need to pursue his art while repeatedly having to reach a *modus vivendi* with odious, albeit changing, regimes. This explains in part Dítě's fixation with appearances. At the same time Hrabal, like so many writers operating under totalitarian oppression, found, and provided for others, freedom and joy through his linguistic virtuosity.

> the richness
> the facility of his language
> the long, complex sentences...!!

Josef Škvorecký
(1924–)
Fascism, Communism and all that jazz

_____

Josef Škvorecký has become one of the most prolific and popular Czech writers of the post-war period. In addition to producing his own creative works he has translated a great deal of English and American fiction, has produced a book about the Czech cinema, and written film scripts, criticism and politico-cultural commentary. It would be fair to say that some of his fictions are unashamedly lightweight, but the best of his novels and novellas represent very substantial achievements. At the same time he possesses a lightness of touch – even in his most penetrating works – that make him forever accessible and engaging. Like Graham Greene, he modestly describes some of his works as "entertainments". His sterling labours as an editor, particularly on the journal *World Literature* (*Světová literatura*), continued when he went into emigration in January 1969 hard on the heels of Jan Palach's self-immolation. Indeed, together with his wife, the writer Zdena Salivarová, he founded in 1972 the most successful of the Czech émigré publishing houses: Sixty-Eight Publishers, in Toronto.

For some twenty years this publishing firm did much to keep alive that literature which the neo-Stalinist regime in Prague found unacceptable. Modestly priced, good quality paperback editions in Czech ensured that the likes of Kundera, Kohout, Havel and Škvorecký himself were able to reach an audience throughout the Czech diaspora as well as, surreptitiously, back home. The logo on each volume depicted a little man using an opened book as an umbrella, and this illustrates something broader: the great Russian writers and many of the great anglophone writers have frequently sought over-arching philosophical truths, Isaiah Berlin's hedgehogs and foxes, F. R. Leavis's "great traditions" and "common pursuits". The Central European tradition has been different, and at times literature appears here more as a life-line or survival kit than as a key to life. Sixty-Eight Publishers' editions could at least keep the rain off, and Škvorecký, whether producing literature, writing about it, teaching it or translating it, always comes across as the antithesis of Clevinger, the "very serious, very earnest and very conscientious dope" in Joseph Heller's *Catch-22*, who "knew everything there was to know about literature except how to enjoy it". In *The Engineer of Human Souls* some of the lecturers at Edendale College seem dangerously similar to Clevinger. The citation from Heller's famous anti-militaristic novel is not fortuitous: his Czech colleague's writing contains similar recurrent motifs.

Such is the scope of Škvorecký fiction that it will be easier to deal with it in terms of general themes, concentrating on key works, rather than by offering an exegesis of each work. That said, the starting point must be his first novel *The Cowards* (*Zbabělci*), for the saga of its publication and its reception tell us a lot about the cultural politics of the time, while the substance of the book establishes the principal features of Škvorecký's art. To that extent, this novel can be regarded as seminal.

Some critics have likened the publication and then banning of *The Cowards* in 1958 to the appearance of Solzhenitsyn's *One Day in the Life of Ivan Denisovich* in the Soviet Union in 1962. The comparison is only partially valid – Škvorecký was not inundated with correspondence thanking him for revealing a hitherto undisclosed historical truth which questioned the very legitimacy of the government. Nonetheless, *The Cowards* offered an irreverent view of the Czech war effort which outraged the establishment and breached the tenets of socialist realism. The result was that for several years the author was under a cloud and had to survive by translation work and publishing under the name of his occasional co-authors. While *Ivan Denisovich* is a tragedy housing heroes and villains, *The Cowards* is a comedy populated largely by fools, and as such, and particularly since it involves the debunking of the war effort, it might be more usefully compared to Voinovich's *Life and Extraordinary Adventures of Private Ivan Chonkin*.

The novel is paradigmatic of so much of the author's life and work. It was written in 1948, when he was in his mid-twenties, and it made its brief debut only ten years later. The protagonist, Danny Smiřický is to remain the author's alter ego for several more books, as his fate is traced through the 1960s and the Prague Spring, and into emigration in Canada, or is elaborated on in "prequels" such as *The Bass Saxophone* (*Bassaxofon*) and *The Swell Season* (*Prima Sezóna*) which give us more material on his existence during the Nazi occupation. *The Republic of Whores* (*Tankový prapor* – literally, "Tank Corps/Battalion" – the published English title is based on a phrase in the novel) is a rarity for literature in the socialist era, in that it recounts the activities of Warsaw Pact troops in peace time. To that extent it is comparable with other works by the aforementioned Russian writer, Voinovich, notably *By Means of Mutual Correspondence* and several stories in the collection *In Plain Russian*. (Voinovich was stationed in

Poland for much of his national service in the 1950s, so time and geography provide a further link between the two writers); in *The Republic of Whores* Danny is spoken of in the third person, whereas elsewhere in what we might call "the Smiřický cycle" he is the hero-narrator.

Stemming from *The Cowards*, we can consider Škvorecký's major fiction under three headings: Politics and History; Lyricism; Foreign Influences and Emigration.

Politics and History

Many of the chief works are firmly grounded in a specific temporal setting. *The Cowards* consists of Danny's diary entries from the 4th to the 11th of May 1945. The work opens when Hitler is already dead (he committed suicide on 30th April) and the Germans are in retreat, on balance keener to surrender to the Western Allies that to the approaching Red Army. The action takes place in the town of Kostelec, the fictional version of Škvorecký's home town of Náchod on the Polish border north-west of Prague. The superficial details of the author's biography replicate that of his hero: both come from relatively comfortable middle-class, Catholic backgrounds, both were compelled to postpone higher education when the Nazis closed the universities, both did compulsory labour in the Messerschmidt factory, and both were wild about jazz and girls.

History is clearly at a critical juncture, and this generates awkward political configurations. Přema Skočdopole is anxious to mount an armed struggle against the Germans; the bourgeois establishment, open to charges of collaboration, is prepared to negotiate the Germans' peaceful departure (such mediation probably saves the hero's life early on in the book when he is marched off after telling a German soldier, in English, to "Shut up!" – "Šatap!").[1] The individuals who populate Danny's immediate circle, though keen to see the war at an end, are more concerned with their personal world (music, girls and the accompanying adolescent fantasies) than with party/partisan politics. The communists are assumed by Danny and his friends to want to engage the Germans, but they are regarded with some hostility by many of the locals. The very title of the novel is provocative, given the era of prescribed *heroes* – of the positive variety – in which it was written and eventually published.

Danny is motivated not by political conviction but by an urge to appear heroic in the eyes of others, most notably his would-be girlfriend, Irena. The best illustration of this comes when he is photographed carrying a submachine gun by his pal Berty (Bertík). He assumes his habitual Clark Gable smile for the pose and asks for extra copies to be made (Czech text, p. 101; English text, p. 113). Even his emotional attachment to the girl comes in for questioning: on the whole his thoughts are of lust rather than love, and on one occasion he admits to himself that he loves her because there is "nothing better" available (English text, p. 66). The Czech original here is tarter and more cynical than the translation can convey: "Miloval jsem ji z nedostatku lepšího zboží ("I loved her out of a deficiency of better goods" – p. 60). Elsewhere, when contemplating his death at the hands of the Germans he decides finally that he would prefer to attend her funeral rather than have her attending his (English text, pp. 75–6; Czech text, p. 68). He recalls lusting after her at her home while she is finishing her bath and noting the family book collection: *History of the Czech Nation*, František Palacký's monumental scholarly cornerstone of the Czech National Revival, and the collected works of Alois Jirásek, whose worthy if at times pedestrian novels charted the oppression and then revitalisation of the Czech people, plus an autographed photo of Doctor Karel Kramář, a leading industrialist, nationalist and later first Prime Minister of Czechoslovakia under the presidency of Tomáš Masaryk (English text, pp. 95–6; Czech text, pp. 86–7). Such stalwart symbols of the Czech nation-alist establishment are utterly downgraded by the hero's erotic ponderings. There is also some mild disdain for the local aristocracy, as evinced when Danny visits the "castle" (zámek – "château" or "country mansion" might be a more accurate translation – English text, pp. 262–5; Czech text, pp. 237–40). For a brief time Danny does emerge as a conventional hero, shooting dead an SS man and, together with Přema, knocking out a German tank. Is he acting out of character here or is he a more complex individual than we have hitherto been led to believe?

The Cowards sketches out many of the political and historical issues that subsequent novels investigate more fully. The well-heeled and intelligent Danny tells one of the English ex-POWs he has accommodated that he would prefer to have been liberated by the English rather than the Russians (English text, p. 404; p. Czech text, p. 362), and such seems to be the case with most of his circle. Danny reflects at one point that he has "nothing against communism", and that he "does not know anything about it" (p. 392) (Neměl jsem nic proti komunismu. Nic jsem o něm nevěděl – p. 352), and he is struck by the strange and wild appearance of the Russians, referred to as "Scythians", with even an allusion to Alexander Blok's poem of that name. The arrival of the Russian liberators brings far greater crowds out on to the streets, and Danny and his friends' well-meaning but exhausting patrolling is quite overshadowed. There are farcical skirmishes between the middle-class militia and the communists; at one point Danny and his associates waylay an "innocent" philanderer on his way home to his marital bed after a clandestine tryst. While Danny's commander dies of a stroke, the communists take full charge of the situation. Towards the end of the novel Danny draws uncomfortable parallels between the speech of the liberating Russian commander and a speech he heard earlier from a Nazi calling on all Czech citizens to contribute to *Winterhilfswerk*, "voluntary" work to aid the war-effort (English text, p. 399; Czech text, pp. 358–9).

Affection for the English, sympathy for all the other ex-POWs and even for individual retreating German soldiers, guarded enthusiasm for the Russians (one incident buttresses the rumours that they have been looting – in particular, wrist watches), all these spontaneous emotions sit awkwardly alongside crude ideological positions propounded by both extremes of the political spectrum. Danny's pal Lexa recalls his obsession with a beautiful eighteen-year-old German girl who shocks him by spouting racist theories and is physically repulsed and flees when he lies to her that he is half-Jewish (English text, pp. 168–9; Czech text, pp. 152–3). The entry for 9th May has Danny recalling a communist pamphlet Přema had shown him declaring that "the uprising against the Germans would have to be transformed into a social revolution that would bring down the bourgeoisie" (p. 279) (ozbrojené povstání proti Němcům musí být přeměněno v sociální revoluci, která má svrhnout panství buržoazie – p. 252).

Such political constructions, even leaving aside any inherent faults of logic they may contain, are wholly at variance with the hero's system of values. In Danny's fluctuating love for Irena, his interest in other girls, his dreams of the night-life of Prague and girls there, his fixation with jazz and the Western world (he speaks fluent English and no Russian), in all his self-proclaimed contradictions and self-centredness there is one cardinal quality: his candour with the reader. This condones the one value in the novel which overrides all others, the need to explore the self. Danny's deliberate fantasizing about Irena is somewhat ousted by lengthy passages which draw together his broader perceptions and preoccupations. These essentially lyrical flights will be examined under the appropriate heading below.

The Miracle Game (Mirákl) and *The Engineer of Human* Souls (*Příběh inženýra lidských duší*) are generally regarded as Škvorecký's finest achievements. This is, at least in part, because they address head-on the two major historical and political events that followed on from the historical juncture described in *The Cowards*, namely the 1948 communist takeover and the 1968 Prague Spring.

The Miracle Game is based on a real incident, as well as – like the bulk of Škvorecký's fiction – on his own biography. In 1949 a Catholic priest, one father Josef Toufar, was accused by the communist authorities of fabricating a miracle in his church, in the village of Číhošť, whereby a statue of St Joseph in his church was apparently made to move of its own accord.

This was an officially inspired attempt to discredit the Catholic Church in this brand-new atheist state. The priest was arrested and, apparently, died as a result of fierce interrogation and even torture in a vain effort to get him to confess to his fraud. During 1968 these and more allegations came to light, in which it emerged that in all likelihood the police themselves had engineered the "moving statue".[2] Yet the overriding point must be, as far as the novel is concerned, that nothing is absolutely clear.

The opening section of the novel shows us the hero-narrator Danny Smiřický handling the statue in 1968 and ascertaining a minor ambiguity about it – that the peg by which it fits into the pedestal is not part of the artifact, but is itself glued in. This small discovery and the real-life occurrence outlined above serve to illustrate some of the ambiguity of the post-1948 political situation. On the one hand, the Czech communists had all the powerful backing of Stalin's Soviet Union, which after all had smashed the greatest war machine in history; on the other, they felt they had to resort to petty subterfuges and violence against essentially passive individuals to consolidate their hold. On the one hand, they were convinced of the inevitability of their victory, as predicted by the "scientific thinking" of Karl Marx, and exemplified by the victory over fascism; on the other, they were unnerved by the support that "obscurantist" religion seemed to enjoy.

In investigating this political ambiguity, Škvorecký indulges his predeliction for the detective story, a predeliction exhibited in his Lieutenant Borůvka cycle of stories somewhat reminiscent of Čapek's *Tales from Two Pockets*, and in the novel he wrote immediately prior to *The Miracle Game* and his last to appear in Czechoslovakia before the Velvet Revolution, *Miss Silver's Past* (*Lvíče* – literally, "The Lion Cub"). Danny Smiřický is by now, in 1968, a successful writer of, among other things, popular libretti. He was present when the statue moved, but unfortunately was asleep during the service. He and his friend, Jůzl, an investigative journalist and the recipient of various letters regarding "the miracle", expend much energy on solving the mystery: was it a genuine "miracle"? – after all, the priest was unshakeable in his faith; or did he cynically rig it? or did the police rig it? – in which case it would have made the priest unshakeable in his faith and therefore able to withstand torture. Jůzl the believer and Danny the sceptic are eventually upstaged by Dr Hrzán the worldly-wise cynic who treated Danny for his virulent attack of gonorrhoea and who, it transpires, engineered the miracle as no more than a practical joke.

The insecurities, dilemmas and absurdities of the 1948 coup d'état and its aftermath are all replayed in the heady days of 1968. It was Danny's scepticism about the new political platforms and some of the people who mounted them to call for "Socialism with a human face" or whatever that angered the novel's opponents when it appeared in Toronto in 1972. Like *Miss Silver's Past*, *The Miracle Game* is to a degree a *roman à clef*. As with all works of this genre, an initiated reader will delight in the bonus of some undemanding detective work – even if offence is taken at the depiction of any individuals identified; the uninitiated reader will miss a little, but if the book is any good, not much. The purpose of the genre is traditionally satirical, though not necessarily hostile. What exercised Škvorecký, and several of the other leading writers of his generation, was that it appeared that not much had been learned between 1948 and 1968 about the dangers of political euphoria and extremism. Moreover, some of the most vocal champions of the new liberalism had twenty years before been the most uncompromising advocates of the very non-liberal socialism. Paul Trensky makes some uncompromising equations in the case of the most prominent of the characters: Vrchcoláb is Pavel Kohout, the playwright and vociferous supporter of Dubček, who in the early years of the 1948 "revolution" was a staunch supporter of Stalinism. Hejl can only be Václav Havel (the only playwright in Czechoslovakia at the time to enjoy an international reputation). Bukavec is, of course Luděk Pachman, the chess master and dissident of the 1960s and '70s. Some political figures are cheekily "disguised": the minister of justice of the day Čepička (little cap) becomes Klobouček (little hat).[3] In the original Dubček is referred to only as the "First Secretary", but in the English translation his name is, understandably, restored. The best way of responding to such pseudo-discretions might be to reflect on the hero-narrator himself. Škvorecký's Danny, like most literary *alter egos*, is a debased but affectionate version of his creator. In addition to the satirical function, the thin disguising serves to generalize and universalize. And it might well be that several of the characters are best understood as composites. For example, in his Preface to the French language edition, Kundera writes: "Ivana the Terrible, the headmistress who picked out the least bad quotations from Karl Marx, is a real *heroïne de modération*: I knew dozens of her sort."[4] *The Miracle Game* doubtless provided a lot of entertainment for literary sleuths, and at least in this work the sleuthing was justified.The Soviet poet and liberal editor of *Novy mir* (the Soviet Union's leading literary journal) Alexander Tvardovsky wrote a poem (naturally, unpublished but circulated clandestinely) which contrasted the reception of the Red Army by the Czechoslovak population in 1948 and 1968. (He, along with a good many other liberals within the Soviet literary establishment, might provide a model for the Russian writer Arashidov in *The Miracle Game*.)

So the embryonic ambiguous feelings on display in *The Cowards* to the Soviet Union are vindicated and elaborated by the real-life events of 1968 and the relentlessly realistic narrative of Škvorecký's novel. The Czechoslovak army offered no resistance to the Warsaw Pact invasion (in essence the Red Army invasion, with token contingents of troops from the other member states), and the numbers of Czechoslovak casualties (several hundred deaths, and a similar number wounded) miniscule in comparison with those suffered in the Second World War. So the banality of the historical events described in *The Cowards* is further enhanced in *The Miracle Game*. Marx's adage to the effect that history repeats itself first as tragedy and then as farce (he was adding to a comment by Hegel) is the one bit of Marxism that Škvorecký's novel endorses. The Soviet sledge-hammer's crushing of the Czechoslovak walnut resulted in countless scenes like the one in the novel where Danny, Sylva and her children are stranded in their car in a Soviet tank column and the bemused soldiers rummage through the thoroughly unSocialist underwear in her suitcase.[5]

As so often in Škvorecký, the individual elements that make up the history, be they personalities or events, are comic, while the overall historical picture is grim tragedy. Post-1948 Czechoslovakia, as revealed in *The Miracle Game*, is a land of tyrants, petty and otherwise, and victims, great and small; the provincial school in which the young Danny teaches is a microcosm for the whole society, where ideology swamps personality, individualism and common sense. Half-decent-minded characters have to resort to all manner of strategems. The same process of ubiquitous comic pettiness adding up to grand tragedy is seen in 1968. Danny is anxious to retrieve the manuscript of his novel satirizing the Czechoslovak army (a transparent reference to *The Republic of Whores*), since, with the reimposition of Brezhnevite socialism, it will deeply compromise him. The real tragedy of the 1968 débâcle resided in precisely the cultural and intellectual sphere. The politicians who had headed the Prague Spring were variously sacked and pensioned off, the blue and white collar workers were bought off materially; and leading writers and intellectuals went abroad or underground.

Danny's scepticism as regards the political debates at home is carried over to his sojourn in the United States. Here we have a foretaste of the life of the émigré which is explored in full in *The Engineer of Human Souls*. The Czech expatriates offer quick-fix solutions or offer opinions on what should have been done to avoid the Soviet occupation. The Czechs abroad in some official capacity, Danny being one of them, are cautious in what they say. The hero himself is dismayed at the crude political thinking especially to be found among young radicals, *mutatis mutandis* as crass as the ideology that the teachers in Danny's school in 1949 had to spout. To take one uncomfortable parallel: the poet Vrchcoláb back in the Stalinist 1950s makes a speech urging the prohibition of mutes on musical instruments because they "deform the optimistic tone of the brass instruments" (p. 304) (optimistický tón žesťových nástrojů deformují – pp. 371–2) and he calls for the banning of the saxophone altogether. At a meeting of student radicals in Connington, some twenty years later, Danny hears chairman denounce the Beatles as "profoundly reactionary [. . .] 'I content of their songs is banal and bourgeois – mostly about love – ar their music is based on a suggestive rhythm that stimulates the passions Thus they distract the attention of our youth away from the only serious problem confronting society – how to wage class war" (p. 349) (hluboce reakční [. . .] je obsah jejich písní banálně buržoazní, většinou o lásce [. . .] jsou to písně založené na vyzývavém rytmu, jenž rozněcuje vášně. Tím se pozornost mládeže odvádí od jediného vážného problému naší společnosti, kterým je třídní boj – p. 422).

The satire here may be a bit heavy-handed, but it points to the main thrust of Škvorecký's credo, what we call below his "lyricism". Before addressing this, we should consider one last political issue – the title of *The Miracle Game*. After all, "zázrak" is the usual term for "miracle". "Mirákl" does not feature in Czech dictionaries and in Russian the term is used exclusively to mean "a miracle play". In one of the anonymous letters that the Catholic journalist Jůzl receives arguing that the miracle in the church was contrived by the secret police, we learn that the operation was code-named "miracle", a Russian term (English text, p. 87; Czech text, p. 109). Incidentally, this would partially explain the published English translation of the title. The ironic connotations of the title are manifold: the "miracle" is either a shoddy trick, or an innocent joke that has tragic consequences, rather like the joke in Milan Kundera's novel of that name which backfires because of the unremitting seriousness of the age. The "miracle" must refer to the euphoric naivity of the Prague Spring, when the Czechs and Slovaks convinced themselves at least for a few months that the Soviet system would allow them their alternative socialist path. Then, the "miracle play" might also refer to the clear-cut moralizing of the medieval church, now transferred to the new religion of Marxist doctrine; and finally, there is the miracle of the events in the few weeks after 21 August 1968, the day when the Warsaw Pact troops poured into Czechoslovakia expecting to find armed counter-revolutionaries and a grateful populace, and instead met massive, yet essentially passive, civilian resistance. There was indeed something of a surreal miracle about the spectacle: Soviet tanks side by side with Western tourists, many locals going about their everyday business, others engaged in heated political debate on street corners, students and others heckling, jeering, occasionally and futilely attacking nonplussed Red Army men (many of them non-Russian, none too sure which country they were in), shops and restaurants open, machine-gun fire strafing (whatever for?) the façade of the National Museum at the top of Wenceslas Square. If nothing else, Škvorecký's book captures with utter realism the absurdity and dislocation of those days.

Lyricism

The Cowards opens with Danny and his friends playing jazz. It closes with
the hero seeing that Irena is reunited with Zdeněk (the boy she really loves)
and playing a sad tune on his saxophone that draws together nearly all the
main themes of the book:

> I got up, gravely raised my sax to my lips and sobbed out a melody, an impro-
> visation in honour of victory and the end of the war, in honour of this town
> and all its pretty girls, and in honour of a great, abysmal, eternal, foolish,
> lovely love. And I sobbed about everything, about my own life, about the SS
> men they'd executed [. . .] about youth which had ended and the break-up
> that had already begun, about our band which wouldn't even get together
> again like this [. . .] about the world that lay ahead of us [. . .] and about the
> sun. And out of the orange and saffron sunset clouds in the west a new and
> equally pointless life bent towards me, but it was good, and I raised my glit-
> tering saxophone to face it and sang and spoke to that life out of its gilded
> throat, telling it that I'd accept it, that I'd accept everything that came my
> way because that was all I could do, and out of that flood of gold and sunlight,
> the girl bent towards me again, the girl I had yet to meet. (p. 412)

> Vstal jsem, pozdvihl jsem slavnostně saxofon a rozvzlykal jsem se na počest
> vítězství a konce války, na počest tohohle města a všech jeho krásných dívek
> a na počest veliké, bezedné, věčné, pitomé, krásné lásky. A vzlykal jsem nad
> tím vším, nad svým životem, nad esesáky, které popravili [. . .] nad tím časem
> mládí, který skončil, a nad rozchodem, který začínal, nad orchestrem, který
> se už nikdy takhle nesejde [. . .] na svět, který přijde [. . .] nad sluncem, a z
> oranžových šafránových červánků na západě se ke mně skláněl nějaký nový
> a nově marný život, ale byl hezký a já jsem pozvedl třpytící se saxofon k
> němu a zpíval jsem a mluvil jsem z jeho pozlaceného korpusu, že ho
> přijímám, a že přijímám všechno, cokoliv přijde, protože nemohu nic dělat,
> a odněkud z té záplavy zlata a slunce se ke mně zase naklonila ta holka, co ji
> teprve potkám. (p. 370)

Lyricism denotes primarily the expressing of a poet's emotions and
thoughts per se, and as such implies the absence or at least reduction of
narrative, or "message" or ideational content. In Škvorecký, as of course
with a good many Romantic poets, lyricism becomes a credo, yet as so
often, the intrinsic aesthetic qualities of the writing cannot be divorced
from its broader context, social, political, ideological. Škvorecký's books
are all concerned with specific politics and history and ideas. His lyricism
is in conscious opposition to these; it becomes not escapism but defiance,
and points towards existentialist considerations of self. In *The Cowards*
Danny and his pal Benno find a few moments of quiet respite, and lying
on the grass, they stare at the sky:

Looking up at the sun and with the big white building looming behind me and in that stillness which was like the quiet in a country where the people have all died, I felt very far away and an awful feeling of futility spread into every pore and cell of my body and everything, everything except me, seemed worlds away. (pp. 301–2)

A jak jsem hleděl vzhůru ke slunci a veliká bílá budova stála za mnou a ticho bylo jako v zemi, kde všichni lidé vymřeli, mohlo to být kdekoliv, a na mě padla veliká marnost, rozlila se do mě do všech pórů a buněk v těle a bylo mi všechno, všechno kromě mě samého, nesmírně vzdálené. (p. 272)

He goes on to reflect that all revolutions and what kind of a society they will be living in after the war are irrelevant to him, since he cannot win Irena's love. Such individualism alone, leaving aside the unheroic depiction of the Czechoslovak war effort, would have been sufficient to put the novel under an ideological cloud.

The most eloquent expression of Škvorecký's lyrical stance is to be found in his splendid novella *The Bass Saxophone*, which is usually published together with the apologetic essay "Red Music", and the most evocative of his love stories *Emöke* (*Legenda Emöke*) . For Škvorecký the cornerstone of lyricism is, of course, jazz, but it manifests itself in other ways too.

The Bass Saxophone is the densest of the author's texts. First published in 1967 this prequel to *The Cowards* contains references to Benno and Lexa, and though the hero-narrator is never named, he is clearly Danny Smiřický, given his age and his obsession with jazz and girls, and the fact that we are in Kostelec at an unspecified period during the occupation. Indeed, the timeless quality of the text leads Paul Trensky to suggest that the time-setting is really the 1960s,[6] but this can only be true in the sense that this is the time when the narrator chooses to recall the wartime experience. The story involves just one brief incident, when Danny is persuaded by a travelling band of German musicians to stand in for their indisposed bass sax-player. He does so, in disguise, so as not to be deemed a collaborator. The sick musician hauls Danny off-stage before the end of the performance and takes over. Yet into this simple story Škvorecký injects an extraordinary range of resonances, and in a word, without a trace of didacticism, fleshes out his commitment to art and his view that it transcends all else, especially political considerations. The essay "Red Music" forcefully makes the point that jazz was frowned on by the Nazis because it was deemed to be the product of an inferior race, the negroes; and under the communists it was under a cloud, because it was viewed as a symbol of Western, capitalist decadence.

Of course, the whole ethos of jazz insists on individual liberty, spontaneity, and improvisation. The saxophone (if we except synthesizers, the electric guitar and the like, the most modern of musical instruments – it was patented in 1846) is the jazz instrument *par excellence*. Thus Škvorecký's musical passion – he was an amateur saxophonist in his youth – is ready-made for the creation of a celebration of artistic freedom.

Where is the drama in a work that relies so heavily on atmospherics and so little on action? Primarily it is in the mystery and excitement of genuinely creative music on the one hand and drab routine on the other. Two Russian words are particularly useful here: *Byt* which might be translated as humdrum, everyday life/routine, the quality which Maiakovskii railed against in his last poem before committing suicide; and *poshlost'*, which might be rendered as petty bourgeois vulgarity, kitsch, triteness, banality. The obvious enemies of Danny's music are fascists and communists, but there is a third:

> They honour common sense in Kostelec, not hallucination, they have a saying there, a sort of trade mark of the sensible: " . . . in Kostelec. They didn't like it in Kostelec, they don't believe it in Kostelec, they had no patience with it in Kostelec"; with that you can take care of the opinion of the whole world and anybody (I can still hear it from the lips of my aunt – on a concert of the Chamber Harmony Ensemble, on an exhibition of abstract painters, on Allen Ginsberg).

> V Kostelci ctí rozum, ne fantasmagorii; je tam taková fráze, trademark rozumnosti: *v Kostelci se to nelíbilo, v Kostelci tomu lidé nevěří, v Kostelci to obecenstvo odsoudilo*, dá se tím vyřídit mínění celého světa a kohokoliv (dodnes ji slyším užívat, z úst své tety: o koncertu Komorní harmonie, o výstavě abstraktních malířů, o Ginsbergovi).[7]

And the complacent decorum of Kostelec – surely the Czech equivalent of Southern England's Tunbridge Wells – is alluded to again when Danny is performing:

> Something [. . .] the broader Kostelecs of our world will never understand: it is that treacherous moment when the gate to life appears to open, yet on to a life that is unfortunately outside this world and outside the things praised by this world – not the gate to art, but to sensation, to euphoria, perhaps to an optical, accoustical illusion but certainly the gate to that being's essence, that creature who is childish, naive, superficial, lacking profundity or exalted emotion, primitive, helpless [. . .] the old mythical illusion of something that will destroy us, because it is the anchor of youth [. . .] I played [. . .] I wailed like a musical clown on a borrowed alto sax, tears ran down my cheeks, I didn't know why, one never knows – sorrow perhaps that one has to die just when one is beginning, that age-old Alpha-Omega. (pp. 119–20)

> Něco [. . .] ten velký Kostelec našeho světa; ta zrádná chvíle, kdy se jako by otevře brána do života, který však naneštěstí je mimo tento svět a věci jím chválené; ne do umění: k pocitu; k euforii; snad k optickému, akustickému

klamu, ale k podstatě bytosti: taková je: malá, dětská, naivní, povrchní, neschopná větších hloubek, vyšších citů; primitivní; bezmocná [. . .] dávná, mýtická iluze čehosi, co nás nakonec zničí, protože je to kotva mládí [. . .] hrál jsem [. . .] lkal jsem jak hudební komik na vypůčenou altku, po tvářích mi tekly slzy; nevěděl jsem proč; to člověk nikdy neví; lítost že člověk musí umřít, právě když začíná; ta prastará alfaomega. (pp. 166–7)

The clear traces of nineteenth-century Romanticism here, the quasi-religious ecstatic outpourings and the reason-free wonderment would be all too easy to dismiss, were it not for the wider picture in which they are set. First, one notes that Danny is playing not on the bass sax, whose very appearance first enthralled him and persuaded him to abandon his Czech nationalist sympathies. But much more than this, there is the grotesque irony of the band itself and the music they play.

Only the vocalist, the girl with Swedish hair is normal, beautiful even. The others are all deformed: the leader and violinist, Lothar Kinze, is haggard and bald (the casualty of a flamethrower attack), the old man who first engages Danny is a decrepit road manager of sorts, and he has creaking limbs and one eye down on his cheek; the female pianist has a sad clown's face and an enormous nose, while the trumpeter has legs amputated at the knees and the percussionist is a blind hunchback; finally, the accordionist is a one-eyed giant. There is nothing contrived or artificial in this spectacle, given that at this stage in the war no fit and healthy human being would be exempt from active service. Furthermore, the music that they play, though ostensibly "jazz", is very much of the anodyne variety, as truncated and impaired as the members of the band. Yet even in this, the free spirit of creativity will make an attempt at self-assertion. In spirit Danny is with them, even though they fall far short of his ideal. In this one notes Škvorecký's affection for the middlebrow, along with his admiration for high artistry.

The conflicting demands between art and life are maintained throughout the work, with the hero caught in the middle, having to resort to disguise but also transported to a realm far beyond the here and now. The duality is established in the very first words of the story: "Twilight. Honey and blood. Indifferent to the historical situation of nation and town, it spoke to me, aged eighteen, on the leeshore of a land-locked lea in Europe, where death was less extravagant, more modest" (p. 73) (Podvečer. Medový a krvavý. Nezávislý na historické situaci národa a města, hovořící ke mně, starému osmnáct let, v závětří závětrného koutku Evropy, kde smrt byla milosrdnější, skromnější – p. 103). Incidentally, "more merciful" might be a better rendition than "less extravagant". The hideous physical appearance of the ensemble and their mediocre playing are matched by the lengthy descriptions of the rundown hotel, the time-battered case the saxophone is kept in, and the harsh conditions of foreign occupation, personified by the local Nazi tyrant, Horst Hermann Kühl. His harsh German cadences form a definite juxtaposition to the frequent references to the foreign jazzers Danny so admires: his favourites bands and players/singers are named, the English words to their songs cited.

The ideal of high artistry is established in the passage where Danny is invited by the old man to take the bass saxophone out and even try it:

> I reached inside the case and raised it the way I would help a sick friend to sit up. And it rose in front of me. A mechanism of strong, silver-plated wires, the gears, the levers, like the mechanism of some huge and absolutely nonsensical apparatus, the fantasy of some crazy mixed up inventor. It stood in my hand like the tower of Babel, a conical shape, the valves reflecting my face full of respect, hope and love – and faith (it was ridiculous, I know, but love is always ridiculous, like faith: the mechanism interested me more than any philosophy ever had, and I admired it more than any Venus possible – certainly more than the Venuses of Kostelec's town square, and certainly more than any other, say the Venus de Milo [. . .] the thing was beautiful. It stood like a blind silver tower, submerged in a golden sea, in a beige and gold room in a town hotel, touched by timid fingers, and behind it Rollini's ghost at the other end of the world in Chicago. (p. 82)

> Sáhl jsem do pouzdra, pozdvihl jsem ho, jako bych pomáhal nemocnému sednout. A on se přede mnou vztyčil. Strojek ze silných, postříbřených drátů, jejich pletivo, převody, páky jako strojoví nějaké obrovské a zcela nesmyslné mašinérie, patent pomateného vynálezce. Tyčil se mi v rukou jako věž babylónská, kónický, zužující se vzhůru, v zašlých klapkách se tisíckrát zrcadlil můj vlastní obličej úcty, naděje a lásky; a víry (je to absurdní, já vím; láska je ale vždycky absurdní; a víra; zajímal mě víc než kdy jaká filosofie; obdivoval jsem se mu víc než možné Venuši, jistě než venuším kosteleckého náměstí, ale jistě i víc než každé jiné, třeba milósské; [. . .]) ale byl krásný. Pnul se jako slepá stříbrná věž, oblitá zlatavým mořem, v béžovozlatém pokoji městského hotelu, dotýkán bázlivými prsty, a za ním přízrak Rolliniho na druhém konci světa v Chicagu. (pp. 115–16)

The imagery here could scarcely be more condensed. The instrument defies reason or common sense, yet it is to Danny like a sick person to be helped – the translation even makes it into a "sick friend"; it is likened to the Old Testament challenge to God while simultaneously recalling the various languages at play in the story (notably Czech, German and American English). It outdoes in attraction all Danny's would-be loves among the local girls (the town square Venuses), and even the Venus de Milo. Shortly after this passage, the hero recalls Kühl roaring in hatred at Danny when the latter once smuggled some jazz record into a public performance ("Hate, unfortunately, is always much more observant than love", p. 85; vždycky, bohužel, je pozornější nenávist než lhostejnost – p. 119).

Incidentally, the translation here is a little misleading: "Indifference" would be a closer rendition than "love". In the allusion to the Venus de Milo we have a clear statement of Danny's chosen path to high artistry. Boris Thompson's discussion of the nature of art with particular reference to Russian literature in the twentieth century unashamedly emphasizes its personal and subjective qualities. He highlights what he regards as the central contradiction in Marxist thinking: that art is "the finest creation of humanity", but that it is "not quite reliable, partly because of its questionable origins". He postulates simply: "It could be that the main function of the arts is to serve as a living disproof of all systems."[8]

The Bass Saxophone offers us two more points about art: first, that it is a mystery and secondly that it is a painful struggle. The bass saxophonist transcends all the others' mechanical playing:

> Like a dancing male gorilla, like a hairy bird of legend slowly beating its black wings, the voice of the broad metal throat screamed the bound strength of bamboo vocal chords, the tone of the bass saxophone, not in three-quarter time but beyond it, in four heavy beats through which it slid with an immense secret yet emotive strength, in septolets [. . .] as if it were shaking off not only all the laws of music but also the cramping weight of something even more immense; a polyrhythmical phoenix, black, ominous, tragic, rising to the red sun of that evening from some horrible moment, from all fearful days, the Adrian Rollini of that child's dream come true, personified, struggling – yes! [. . .] The man was struggling with the bass saxophone; he was not playing, he was overpowering it." (pp. 122–3)

> Jako tančící gorilí samec, jako kosmatý pták Noh pomalu mávající černými křídly hlas širokého kovového hrdla, řvoucí, spoutaná síla bambusových hlasivek, tón bassaxofonu; ale ne ve tříčtvrtečním taktu; mimo něj; ve čtyřech těžkých dobách, přes něž lehce a s nesmírnou, tajenou, a přece cítěnou silou klouzal v septuolách [. . .] jako by ze sebe setřásal nejen veškerou zákonitost hudby, ale také tísnivou tíži něčeho ještě obrovitějšího, polyrytmický Fénix, černý, zlověstný, tragický, vznášející se k rudému slunci tohoto večera z nějaké příšerné chvíle, ze všech příšerných dnů, adrian rollini toho dětského snu zpřítomnělý, zosobněný, zápasící – ano [. . .] muž se saxofonem zápasil; nehrál; zmocňoval se ho. (p. 171)

"Noh", featuring in several Czech fairy tales, is the equivalent of the Griffin, the legendary animal in Greek mythology with the head of an eagle and the body of a lion.

The saxophonist's physical description is similarly anomalous, for he resembles a Sicilian, he is about forty and is large, "wild" (divoký), "hulking" (rozložitý – p. 121) – in his appearance and his art he is clearly a cut above the rest; and we never learn what his affliction was. When Danny is so unceremoniously whisked off the stage and returns to the hotel room, he notices a trail of blood there: the saxophonist had to fight with himself before taking on the instrument, and his art came at a price; yet it delights the other players and enrages Kühl.

The Bass Saxophone is about the lyrical self and the essence of true art. Yet it is also about the real and sordid world, where disguise and subterfuge are necessary to survive and where the natural beauties of a sunset or a pretty girl can be overshadowed by the grotesque. The references to the metaphysical or to the greatest jazz performers of the day (Rollini, Fitzgerald etc.) are countered by a brief catalogue of concentration camp names (Treblinka, Auschwitz, Majdanek) and allusions to Nosferatu (the silent movie precursor to the Dracula films) and Bosch and Brueghel, famed for their depictions of Hades. The strong nostalgic element, the references to the Austro-Hungarian Empire and to the fact that the bass saxophone is no longer manufactured anymore (it is indeed a rare instrument) might best be understood as contributing to the timeless quality of the story and to the eternal qualities of true art rather than as the narrator's mere longing for some elusive yesteryear. Such ethereal reflections on the nature of art are buttressed by the mellifluent aspects of Škvorecký's prose in this story. Paragraphs are intentionally of inordinate length and syntax is at times lax, as images and impressions assume more importance than hard lexical meaning; and this is surely the hallmark of lyricism.

The lyrical is, not unsurprisingly, also to be found in the love relationships in Škvorecký's fictions. In the more mature ones we find an advance on the puerile fantasies that permeated *The Cowards*. *Emöke*, often published together with *The Bass Saxophone* is a love story, where the musical motifs are certainly present but where there is hardly a trace of comedy, even of the darker variety. Long, languid paragraphs again feature prominently. The lyrical is in the eponymous heroine, a young and beautiful single mother, at one time much abused by her now deceased partner. She attempts to reside in a spiritual enclave, depriving herself of the material world, especially of its carnality. The hero makes some headway in breaching her emotional defences and convinces himself and her that he loves her – yet he is thwarted by his uncouth rival, a school teacher, who tells her of the hero's amorous attachment in Prague. However, for the hero she will always remain a "legend": "But perhaps somewhere an impression is left, at least a trace of the tear, the beauty, the loveliness of the person, the legend, Emöke" (p. 70) (Ale snad někde přece zůstává alespoň otisk, alespoň stopa slzy, té krásy, té líbeznosti, toho člověka, toho snu, té legendy, Emöke – p. 99). It is not without significance that *líbezný* is an epithet often applied to music and might translate as "melodious". The haunting quality of the story is enhanced by the nature of the heroine herself, for she remains an enigma, clearly able to strike up relationships with those around her, but expressing ideas that are an admixture of

Catholicism and out-and-out superstition, with the emphasis on parapsychology. All this sits uneasily with the hero, who is a rationalist and intellectual. His own intellectual searches are overtaken by his emotions, and the closing words of the story, set out as a separate paragraph, are simply the thrice repeated "Nevím" (p. 99) (I do not know). The published English translation has a less determinate rendition: "I wonder" – p. 70). This story is not typical Škvorecký, for more often than not the tenderness of the love affairs is offset by some bleak misunderstandings and some self-deception, laced with explicit sexual comedy (*The Swell Season*, another prequel to *The Cowards*, is a case in point).

It is in literature itself that the lyrical reaches its most sophisticated. It is easy for writers like Škvorecký to mock ersatz *belles-lettres*. In *The Republic of Whores* some of the belly laughs surely come from the military-inspired doggerel that recruits are compelled to produce, or worse still, feel genuinely moved to write. The obscene graffiti and parodies of official works are more arresting for being more inventive and heart-felt. It is more difficult to make out a positive case for literature, yet this is what Škvorecký does in *The Engineer of Human Souls*, as cogently as he makes out a case for jazz in *The Bass Saxophone*.

As the author acknowledges in the book's preamble the title is a phrase generally attributed to Stalin,[9] and the words display all the dictator's talent for accessible, practical turns of phrase, while masking any accompanying constricting policies and repression. In Škvorecký's novel the phrase is heavily ironic. In a sense the hero is employed as an engineer of human souls, having to teach literature in a college in Toronto in the 1970s. One should recall that Škvorecký has always had a love–hate relationship with the teaching profession and Danny often recalls his time as a tutor. There is a parallel between ersatz literature and the ersatz teaching that is brought about by bureaucratic directives and cynical staff members. In *The Miracle Game* the young Danny manages to get all his pupils through asinine tests on ideology without any textbooks or curriculum; Danny in the tank corps in *The Republic of Whores* similarly gets his very reluctant charges to impress the examining board and have them awarded the Julius Fučík medal, when they have read none of the material. Danny in his Toronto college by and large keeps his reservations about his students to himself, indulges them and patiently tries to broaden them, while quietly despairing at their limited horizons. In *Emöke* the schoolmaster is painted in the blackest colours, not just for his vulgar philandering, but for intellectual and pedagogical shortcomings. In a passage where the moralising and social concern are clear-cut enough to engender echoes of socialist realism (the story was published twice legally – in 1963 and 1965) the hero berates the school teacher for despising the untutored parents of his charges: "He never considered that it is just as hard, if not harder, and just as worthy, if not worthier, and probably far more beautiful to be able to control the delicate mechanism of a precision lathe" (p. 50) (neuvažoval nikdy [. . .] že je stejně těžké, ne-li těžší, a stejně záslužné, ne-li záslužnější, a pravděpodobně mnohem krásnější ovládat jemný mechanismus frézy nebo soustruhu – p. 70). Incidentally, the translation omits a phrase that puts the teacher in an even more unsavoury light: v mozku stiženém učitelským slavomamem (in a brain overburdened with a schoolteacher's megalomania) and makes no mention of the *fréza* (milling machine).

The lyricism in *The Engineer of Human Souls* represents the most skilful of structural devices, for it counterbalances episodes in the book which might otherwise be taken as political bias, while binding together the various narrative lines and linking in with the other areas that we identify as predominant in Škvorecký's fiction, namely foreign influences and emigration. In alluding to all manner of literature, citing from a wide variety of works and lobbing in disparaging asides about literary critics, Škvorecký's Danny throws into greater relief his own assertions on the true essence of literature. In our discussion of *The Engineer of Human Souls* we are entering the workshop of a master craftsman.

In his penetrating essay on Škvorecký, Stanislaw Baranczak argues that literature might be a surer path to an understanding of life in the old Eastern Bloc than eye witness accounts:

> Attempts to penetrate the inscrutable East from outside usually stop at the first banquet table with a generous supply of caviar [. . .] What I am saying amounts to a praise of the cognitive potential of literature, which here, in this hemisphere swarming with deconstructivists, is a rather contemptible opinion to hold. Yet, at the risk of sounding hopelessly backward, I hereby admit that I indeed believe in literature's power to name reality – or, to put it differently, to let us hear and comprehend reality's many-voiced hubbub more subtly and fully than any other kind of account [. . .] As witnesses go, literary fiction nearly always beats both being on the safe ground of supposedly hard facts and being in the clouds of ideological dogmas.[10]

In *The Engineer of Human Souls* the lyrical element is persistently tied in with perfectly plausible stories – many of them based on fact – which demonstrate Baranczak's contention precisely. The novel represents a dramatic departure from *The Cowards* and a further development on *The Bass Saxophone* and *Emöke* in that its lyricism lends substance to the narrative rather than the other way round.

Each of the seven chapters bears the title of a writer: Poe, Hawthorne, Twain, Crane, Fitzgerald, Conrad and Lovecraft. Six of these are American, Conrad being the odd one out. The essence of each of these writers is explored in and beyond the relevant chapter, through the current narrative taking place in Toronto in the mid-1970s, through flashbacks to the Nazi occupation of Czechoslovakia, the communist era and the Prague Spring and through a good many letters that the narrator and some of the other characters receive. Over and above this "naive" structure, the novel rests on two recondite ironies or jokes. One concerns Conrad, and this will be dealt with below; the other is to be found in the fact that, in this novel more than any other, the author subscribes to Stalin's notion that the writer is a teacher. The only difference is Škvorecký wants to teach about the "many-voiced hubbub" of reality that Baranczak speaks of, whereas Stalin's engineers of the human soul were handed on a plate a monotone "reality" by their political masters and ordered to teach it, despite anything to the contrary that their consciences, common sense or sensibilities might have directed them to. Hence Škvorecký's impatience with readers and teachers of literature who make little or no attempt, no matter how difficult it may be, to grasp the kernel of any piece of serious literature and instead take refuge in formalism or ideology. As the narrator tells us in the second chapter: "I despaired for those legions of students who are taught American Literature by someone from Harvard who, lecturing on the function of colour in *The Scarlet Letter*, deals only with the function of colour in *The Scarlet Letter*. I suppose for them, for all of them it will always be just a movie. Until the fall of the Western world" (Zazoufal jsem v duchu nad zástupy studentů, kteří nemají profesorem americké literatury člověka odtamtud, ale někoho z Harvardu, jenž v hodinách věnovaných funkci barev v *Šarlatovém písmenu* skutečně probírá funkci barev v *Šarlatovém písmenu*. Asi to pro ně pro všechny navždy zůstane biograf. Ne navždy. Do pádu Západního světa).[11] Elsewhere Danny has to listen to Hakim's crudely one-dimensional and ideological interpretations of texts that have engaged the subtlest of minds and the most diverse readerships. Some of the verbal jousting is not so dissimilar from the literary "debates" endured in Danny's tank corps in the 1950s.

The essence of Edgar Allen Poe (1809–49) is of course to be found in his Gothic horror stories and the sheer mystery of his verse. For a time Poe was not taken seriously as a writer – and indeed his reputation may have been widened, but was hardly deepened, by the gory film versions of works like *The Fall of the House of Usher* and *The Pit and the Pendulum*. Yet for Danny the magic and resonances of Poe's most famous poem "The Raven" are what count. The novel opens with a seminar on the work in which the narrator reads the version, or rather adaptation, of the poem by the Russian dissident writer Alexander Esenin-Volpin. Danny is adding to the mystery (at least for readers with some knowledge of Russian literature) by using this version rather than the far better known and more accurate translation by Konstantin Balmont. His student Irene (Irena) has dismissed the poem as a "A worthless, sentimental piece of tripe" (p. 5) (bezcenný, sentimentální kýč – p. 16), though only in revenge for his having castigated her for plagiarising an essay the previous term. Danny succumbs to his "foolish but probably irrepressible desire to explain the inexplicable (p. 5)" (hloupé, jenže snad nezlikvidovatelné tendenci vysvětlit nevysvětlitelné – p. 16). He also cites to his readers Hemingway's contention that "something written well can have many meanings" (p. 6) (je-li něco napsáno dobře, může to mít mnoho významů – vol. 1, p. 18). Esenin-Volpin's version of the work, though magnificently executed, is far more politically loaded than the original (or Balmont's translation), and therefore it makes the poem all that more accessible to naive, young minds seeking "messages" in their literature. Having read the Russian version with as much gusto as he can manage and been moved by it practically to tears, Danny then recites his own translation of it:

> The translation murdered everything, the rumbling Russian *r*'s, Poe's "O", the saddest of all vowels, far, far sadder in Russian than in the language of the Stratford genius, that court lickspittle, but I could still hear the Russian verses rumbling in my ears, interpreting E.A.P. with immeasurably greater understanding than the literary critics possess, despite a long century and a great ocean between them, displaying a knowledge of life that Poe, through some secret twist of fate and despite what Krutch said, did have – a knowledge that Joseph Wood Krutch does not possess. (p. 9)

> Překlad [. . .] všechno zavraždil: rachotivá ruská r, Poeovu nejsmutnější samohlásku o, daleko, daleko smutnější v ruštině než v jazyce génia avonského, toho dvorního patolízala – ale mně v uších drnčela dál ruština a přes absurdní vzdálenost dlouhého století a velikého oceánu vykládala EAP s nesrovnatelně obrovštější znalostí než profesoři – s životní znalostí, již Poe nějakým tajemstvím osudu a navzdory Krutchovi měl, – ne že neměl – se znalostí kterou nemá Joseph Wood Krutch. (vol. 1, p. 20)

Krutch is the critic of Poe that another of his students, Sharon, is mindlessly regurgitating for her seminar paper (English text, p. 7; Czech text, vol. 1, p. 19).

Thus in the very first pages of the novel the author establishes the fundamental poetic and ineffable qualities of great literature, but at the same time forges a link between great literature and reality or the real world. Moreover, he exhibits a sympathy and enthusiasm for the Russian language and even Russian culture, which represents a massive shift from that attitude to the Russians displayed in *The Cowards* and *The Miracle Game*. At this stage the narrator is admitting his inability to articulate his appreciation of the true essence of literature, but he acknowledges its capability to surmount political barriers. Moreover, Danny, anglophile extraordinary, is prepared to denigrate even Shakespeare to make the point. All this ties in with the lynchpin, penultimate chapter, "Conrad" (see below).

The most famous work of Nathaniel Hawthorne (1804–64), in the minds of many the only one really worth reading, is *The Scarlet Letter*. This tale of adultery in a Puritan community is concerned primarily with the iniquities, hypocrisy and indeed evil that a rigidly applied, simplistic moral code, more preoccupied with social *mores* than inner conscience, can lead to. For Danny, discussions about the colour imagery in the work seem beside the point, when the moral questions it raises are so relevant to the society he has known in Eastern Europe. So, throughout the chapter we have illustrations of how Hawthorne still applies today, while Danny's students in their class papers argue the work's shortcomings and irrelevance. At the same time, the mystery of true literature, established in the first chapter, is maintained, while other episodes relate more directly to the various cardinal principles embodied in the other chapter headings. The complexity and polish of the finished product is combined, as in the work of any good engineer, with easy access to the working parts.

One can isolate at least four stories, among many, in "Hawthorne" which *The Scarlet Letter*'s main thrust anticipates: 1. Jana Honzlová, a Czech singer on an official visit to Moscow, is castigated for her attire by a staunchly communist member of the quartet, who, it turns out, merely mimes into the microphone, since her voice is so bad. One notes that anecdotes like this were legion in the communist era and more than a few were certainly based on fact. Danny recalls the words of one of Hawthorne's characters, an ugly and pitiless woman, ranting about Hester, the adulteress: "This woman has brought shame on us all, and ought to die. Is there no law for it?" (p. 70) "Měla by viset" (she ought to hang – vol. 1, p. 101) is all we have in the published Czech text here.[12] 2. In emigration in Canada Danny supports a fellow countryman, Milan Fikejz, in his attempt to gain political asylum, and at the hearing one of the magistrates "looked like one of Hawthorne's shrieking women" (p. 73) (vyhlížela jako volající žena z Hawthorna – vol. 1 p. 106). Finding the applicant's calls for "freedom" rather abstract and old-fashioned, the court decides that he knowingly violated the *law* of his country, so therefore his fate on his return will be "prosecution" not, "persecution". 3. Danny's plotting with Nadia during the Nazi occupation to sabotage the planes they are building raises questions of the morality of implicating friends in a dangerous act of heroism. Later, when they are both being compelled, along with other workers, to sign a petition denouncing the assassination of Heydrich, she pretends to faint, rather than sign. Is this an act of deception rather than heroism or cowardice? And how relevant might it be to the situation Hester's seducer, Dimmesdale, is in? Another of Danny's Canadian students, W. W. Bellissimo writes off *The Scarlet Letter* as a product of its own time, criticising it for not condemning Dimmesdale unilaterally "for his moral weakness nor for his male chauvinism" (pp. 112–13) (za morální slabost ani za *male chauvinism* – vol.1 p. 106). 4. Danny recalls another passage from Hawthorne on the finery the ruling elite are obliged to wear by convention and which would be frowned upon if worn by the lower orders; he lists examples of similar image-building that surrounded Stalin on his 70th birthday, culminating in press reports of the dictator's bathtub with its three gold taps: "I see Stalin as naked as a waterbaby, splashing about in lukewarm perfumed water. Oh, Hawthorne, have you any idea what you wrote?" (p. 112) (vidím STALINA nahatého jako plaváček, jak se šplouchá ve VLAŽNÉ PARFUMOVANÉ vodě . . . ach Hawthorne, víš, cos napsal? – vol. 1 p. 160).

All of these stories, and others, can to varying degrees, be related to other chapter headings. For example, Danny's heroics in the Messerschmidt factory tie in closely with the "Crane" chapter. But the burden of the Hawthorne chapter is that Puritan religious conviction is no more than another ideology, just like the two ideologies of the twentieth century which claimed so much purity and wrought so much evil.

Mark Twain (1835–1910) is probably America's greatest satirist and humorist, and his best known works concern youthful innocence and its gradual loss. Danny Smiřický is hardly Tom Sawyer or Huckleberry Finn, but there is in Škvorecký the same fixation with youth. If Twain's moral awareness was enhanced by the rigours of life on the Mississippi and the evils of slavery, how much more so was Škvorecký's by the swift shock of Nazi occupation, quickly followed by Communist dictatorship?

The "Twain" chapter opens with a seminar on *The Mysterious Stranger*, not one of Twain's best known works, but one that, significantly, only came to light after his death. It was published in 1916. This, plus the fact that Twain is a pseudonym, echoes Škvorecký's penchant for the *alter ego* and contains a mild submission that great literature will outlive its author. Another reference to *The Mysterious Stranger* is linked to a lengthy letter from Danny's writer friend Jan back in Czechoslovakia. Jan is an honest and talented writer, perhaps not in the first league; but persistently, what he says about literature and his own difficult circumstances help to define Danny's own literary approach, and as we shall see, it is Jan who gets closest to a real definition of true literature. At a party in Toronto Veronika is listening to some new musical recordings from Prague. They have something of Danny's former world about them, but the literary world in Czechoslovakia has gone (English text, p. 142; Czech text, p. 201). The interjection "Poor Jan" (Ubohý Jene – "Jene" being a slightly old-fashioned version of the vocative) and the reference to *The Mysterious Stranger* hint at Škvorecký's respect for the middlebrow and for work achieved in good faith which may yet fall short.

The real stuff of the chapter though runs close to the notions of the futile attempts at recapturing one's youth. Invited to join a Marxist discussion group in Edenvale College, Danny replies with the final words of *Huckleberry Finn*: "I been there before" (p. 140). The Czech original retains the English words here (vol. p. 199). An earthier Czech phrase, and one that, one suspects Mark Twain would have approved of, would have been: "Děkuji, už jsem blil" (Thanks, but I've already puked). The chapter develops Veronika's impossible nostalgia for her former life in Czechoslovakia and charts further the relationship between Danny and Nadia. These two are now no less fugitives than Jim and Huck – Danny contemplates by turns becoming a priest, joining the German army or running away to join the Czech partisans in order to escape the Gestapo now that his pathetic attempt at industrial sabotage has been discovered by the foreman. But as it turns out, both he and Nadia are more on the run from his parents, after their love-making in his apartment, love-making remarkably innocent and in clear contrast to his wild fantasies about the other girls he chases.

As with the other chapters, all manner of stories feed into the title: While Vicky mindlessly reproduces a critic's view that the river is the unifying principle of the *Huckleberry Finn* and later that Jim and Huck are in fact gay (English text, p.172–3; Czech text, pp. 24–3), Danny recalls one Mr Pytlík who worked first as a Gestapo informer and later became a communist official, largely responsible for incarcerating Danny's father. So, we might ask, isn't Twain's novel more about friendship and loyalty than about homosexuality? Margitka, Danny's casual lover, and her invalid husband, we learn, endured ten years without physical relations while he was in prison ("I was a Catholic and he was a sea-scout" – p. 187; Já katolická, von vodní [skaut] – vol. 1, p. 263), and there is a grim account of how the scouting movement was suppressed by the communists. This, together with the stories that Préma Skočdopole's father tells Danny about his bloody career as a legionnaire during the Russian Civil War, represent the dry land with all its problems and evil that Huck and Jim have to endure; while Danny's equivalent of a liberating, carefree and innocent Mississippi is little more than an intermittent stream, a brief moment of love with a down-at-heel girl who will later die of consumption.

Stephen Crane (1871–1900) has been ranked with Tolstoy in his depiction of war and the ambiguous nature of bravery. *The Red Badge of Courage* was an instant critical and popular success. Its relevance to *The Engineer of Human Souls* is readily apparent for any reader with a sense of irony. It is not clear from Crane's text which side his hero is fighting on in the American Civil war. He is wounded while fleeing his first engagement, but later throws all caution to the winds and is hailed as a hero. Crane spares us little in detailing the horrors of war. Danny's student, Higgins, rather irritates his tutor in offering an interpretation of the book, culled from a standard critic, which eschews these prime features: the book for him is not about war, but about "the emotional and intellectual maturing of a young man" (p. 213) (o citovém a myšlenkovém zrání mladého muže – vol. 1, p. 299). Danny is wearied by the clichés on war that his students offer, and even cites with some sympathy a remark he attributes to Stalin regarding "just and unjust wars " (p. 215) (spravedlivé a nespravedlivé války – vol. 1, p. 302).[13]

The "Crane" chapter has a number of stories, some containing more humour than *The Red Badge of Courage*, which quietly debunk, as does Crane, the standard notion of heroism. Danny, during the war, is now a terrified adolescent and his act of sabotage seen as no more than stupidity. Yet he still finds time for philandering and moments of happiness. He is roughed up not by the Gestapo but by Nadia's boyfriend (English text, p. 268; Czech text, vol. 1, p. 373). In another episode, just after the communist takeover Danny is dragooned by his pals into composing a propaganda leaflet for an anti-government group, though, as he tells us, at this stage he is not entirely out of sympathy with the new government (English text, p. 234; Czech text, vol. 1, p. 327). Moreover, he is afraid, but co-operates because "some things are stronger than fear" (p. 219) (Pořád jsem z některých věcí měl strach větší než ze strachu – vol. 1, p. 307), the Czech original here having more irony than the translation can capture. In the Toronto scenes we have more of Mr Pohorský's ludicrous schemes for overthrowing the post-1968 regime in Prague: this time one Mr Levene (who appears in the English text as "Egon Bondy"!) and he contemplate founding the Czechoslovak National Liberation Army Limited, and Levene/Bondy proudly displays an automatic rifle (English text, p. 245; Czech text, vol. 1, pp. 341–2). At the same émigré event, which involves some hilariously accented folk-singing (sadly lost in English despite the commendable translation – English text, p. 243; Czech text, vol. 1, p. 339), a recording is played of Tomáš Masaryk making a speech, but only after technical difficulties produce the voices of Mickey Mouse and King Kong (English text, p. 254; Czech text, p. 354). Mr Pelikán tells how he escaped in 1948, squeezed into the roof compartment of a train. His bladder gave out and the Communist functionary seated beneath him tasted the liquid dribbling onto his table. Safely on the other side of the border, Pelikán is released and is mocked by the communist for urinating out of fear; Pelikán counters that one day the communist will "shit himself" with fear and will have nowhere to run to – and indeed, four years later the communist functionary is hanged (English text, p. 258; Czech text, p. 358). There is even a reference in this anecdote to Tycho Brahe, the Danish astronomer of the 16th century, buried in the Tyn Church in Prague, who allegedly let his bladder burst during an official function, so the comedy here is hardly contrived.[14] The "Crane" chapter concludes with the closing days of the war, Danny and his resistance-fighter friends now fearing the Soviet calls for the liquidation of "the bourgeois so-called anti-German resistance groups directed from London" (p. 273) (měšťácké t. zv. skupiny proti-německého odboje dirigované z Londýna – vol. 1, p. 379). So Crane's device of not stating which side his hero is fighting on receives further endorsement.

Scott Fitzgerald would of course earn a special place in Škvorecký's Hall of Fame, for he typifies more than any other writer the jazz age, the 1920s. The very titles of such collections as *Tales of the Jazz Age* and *All the Sad Young Men* relate readily to the Czech author's creative forays into the world of the adolescent. Moreover, Fitzgerald's ambivalent attitude to the American society of the day would draw Škvorecký. The American writer constantly strove for the "American Dream", while all the time recognizing and abhorring the vulgarity and commercialism of the roaring twenties. Affluence, anguished love and mental breakdown form some of the major themes in his novels like *The Great Gatsby* and *Tender is The Night*. Danny Smiřický can revel in the relative social and economic security which Canada extends to him, but he can never shake off his exasperation at the superficial values on display, not least among his own students. The Fitzgerald Chapter opens with a party on board Irene Svensson's father's yacht; the alcohol- and marijuana-induced befuddlement might well recall Fitzgerald's own repeated struggles against alcoholism.

Again we have a number of romantic encounters shot through with ironies: Irene (as ever there is emphasis on her expensive clothes and coiffure) offers herself to Danny on the yacht and, being more than twice her age and her tutor, he turns her down this time. In war-torn Czechoslovakia he gets to spend the night with the down-at-heel and God-fearing Nadia, only to be beaten up by her fiancé, not as he thinks, because he has seduced the girl, but because he has put her at risk by implicating her in his misguided attempts at sabotage. Years later he looks up an old flame, Marie, but the sexual chemistry this time is between him and her daughter, Dana (named after him – he is her "spiritual father", he informs us). The decadence and degeneration that Fitzgerald catalogued is never far away even in Smiřický's Toronto.

By now, the lyricism, as evidenced in the chapter titles, is seriously loosening our grip on reality. The Conrad Chapter will bring us back, but before considering this section, we shall peer, with a light-hearted and comic invitation from the author, into the abyss of insanity with the final chapter.

Why Howard Phillips Lovecraft to round off a novel as much about literature itself as about anything else, and to conclude an erudite series of discourses on some of the greatest of writers? Lovecraft's books of the fantastic and macabre are rarely in print these days; Irene can, for once, be forgiven for her ignorance, confusing him as she does with the American chain of sex shops, from which she has equipped herself for her trip to Paris with Danny; Danny even seems to have a little difficulty getting hold of Lovecraft's most successful work *At the Mountains of Madness* to read to her (English text, p. 549; Czech text, vol. 2, p. 383). She rightly complains that Lovecraft soon starts to get repetitive (English text, p. 552; Czech text, vol. 2, p. 386), and Danny admits the writer's limitations.

Yet there is some gruesome entertainment value in Lovecraft and he provides a neat link to the opening of the novel, which, we recall, addresses Poe. The stomach-turning and grisly tortures recounted by Voženil in the toilet at the factory where Danny works, represent a debased version of Poe (at one point, English text, p. 500; Czech text, vol. 2, p. 313) there is even talk of a sharpened pendulum used to slice at a victim's abdomen – cf. *The Pit and the Pendulum*). These are largely dismissed by the storyteller's audience. Stories, as told by artists, carry more weight, and the final chapter of *The Engineer of Human Souls* is peppered with some grim incidents: the deaths of Benno and Nadia, the suicide of the poet Prouza, Veronika returning to communist Czechoslovakia, Milan Kundera (in a fleeting appearance in the novel) telling Danny in 1968 that he hopes he doesn't live long, the reappearance of Uher, the turncoat, Skočdopole killed in a hurricane in Darwin, Pohorský blown up with his own home-made bomb. Two really comic developments in plot simply celebrate the madness of the world in which the characters live: the first concerns the black barman, Booker, who has been writing rabidly pro-communist letters to a lady in Czechoslovakia – on the instructions of his expatriate Czech employer Dotty he has been so doing to in order to get Dotty's friend out to the West; in fact the plot misfires because the letters are so well-researched and committed that the (of course) cynical authorities in Prague see right through them; moreover, Booker has travelled to Prague to meet "his love" and bring her out, but they have genuinely fallen in love and she is not allowed to leave. The second is Lojza's final letter to the author – typically illiterate yet genuine and heart-felt, it recounts how good life is in normalized, post-1968 invasion Czechoslovakia and reflects on the fact that now both Lojza and Danny are professional writers . . .

When Danny tells Irene that he is taking her to the Mountains of Madness he is offering her Lovecraft as a metaphor for what he tells Hakim when this radical student accuses him of being "irrational":

> You have to take that into account. What we feel is obviously more important than what we know. That's what we live for. We may think we live for wisdom, but in fact we're living for the pleasure that wisdom brings us. Perhaps our feelings do guide us to the most reasonable solution [. . .] Maybe our greatness lies in our irrationality. In the way we sometimes go against reason in order to achieve rationality. (p. 506)

Musí se s tím počítat. Co cítíme, je zřejmě důležitější, než co víme. Žijeme pro to. Pokud se nám zdá, že žijeme pro moudrost, žijeme vlastně jen pro radost z moudrosti. Náš cit možná opravdu poukazuje k nejrozumnějším řešením [. . .] V naší irracionalitě je snad naše velikost. [. . .] V tom, jak irracionálně někdy jdeme proti rozumu, abychom naplnili rozum. (vol. 2, p. 322)

The interview with Hakim closes with the words that Danny recalls when he was teaching Poe at the start of the novel: Raven. *Havran. Voron.* Poetics will always win out over intellect and even the gaudy, overblown prose of a Lovecraft can play its part in this.

Finally, to Conrad. He is deliberately the odd one out, the only non-American, but as a Polish exile and Anglophile, he is closest to Škvorecký's heart. *Heart of Darkness*, a novel which inspired the film *Apocalypse Now*, is arguably his most read work and certainly is the one to generate most interpretations. It forms the centrepiece of this penultimate chapter and indeed the centrepiece of the whole novel. One of the chapter's epigraph's, "The merely poetic destroys poetry" (p. 365) (To jenom poetické ničí poezii . . . – vol. 2, p. 129), forewarns against the excesses of lyricism that the final chapter comically takes us into. Professor Smiřický, like any good teacher, is forced to oversimplify as he attempts to explain Conrad to his students; he also indulges, as Conrad occasionally does, particularly in *Under Western Eyes*, in some unremitting anti-Russian sentiment. For Danny, *Heart of Darkness* is a "prophecy [. . .] about the Soviet Union" (p. 369) (proroctví [. . .] o Sovětském svazu – vol. 2, p. 136). He sets out the notion that Kurtz, though not without science and knowledge, is driven predominantly by faith, which leads him straight to dictatorship and ultimately to "the horror" and the conviction that all those who cannot obey must be exterminated. The Russian harlequin in Conrad's story epitomizes for Danny the willingness of Russians to trust in dictators. Incidentally, in modern Russian literature the same idea is put forward most eloquently by Vasilii Grossman in his brilliant short novel *Forever Flowing . . .* , so Škvorecký's analysis of the Russian psyche – his piece of "light-hearted charlatanism, which may not be charlatanism at all" (p. 369) (zábavné šarlatánství, které možná není žádné šarlatánství – vol. 2, p. 136), as Danny confesses to himself – is not unique and is hardly xenophobic.

Of course, Škvorecký is more than aware that Conrad's text has been the topic of countless discussions over the years (a barefaced example of White imperialism in Africa, a psychological journey into the human mind, or the id, or whatever), and his truer appreciation of the work must reside in its universal magic, its poetry, which yet has applicability to the stuff of real life. He spells this out in two ways in the Conrad chapter: first, in one of the letters that Danny periodically receives from his writer friend Jan back in Czechoslovakia:

The snobs treat us like charlatans, if not outright criminals, when our work is not successful. Except that it usually seems to me they can't hear.

What I mean is, they do not have good ears. They cannot hear what literature has in common with music and what makes it art. It is no problem to define the technical procedures, to analyse and praise them; stream of consciousness, achronology, the narrative point of view and consistency in the categories of narrative forms. But what is all that without the ancient and unacquirable talent of *mimesis*? That secret ability, unaccessible to the reason, to awaken in the reader the joy of recognition [. . .]

In the end, every art is a mystery. And also, there is not just great art and non-art, with nothing in between; there is also minor and not at all *dishonourable* art [. . .]

Faulkner once said that all novels are shipwrecks. Derelicts. And he was right. There is something that falls short of perfection in every book, without exception, something influenced by the age, even something ridiculous; just like everyone, without exception, has his weaknesses and is trapped in his age and environment, and may even be ridiculous. But if he is an honourable man and if it is an honourable book, no one has the right to ridicule it or heap contempt on it. Genuine lovers of literature will instead feel sorry that the author was not up to some things, and will look for the remains of the golden treasure in that shipwreck on the bottom of the sea of criticism. (pp. 392–3)

Snobi zacházejí s námi jako s podvodníky, ne-li zločinci. Jenomže mně se obyčejně zdá, že neslyší.

Nemají sluch, myslím si. Pro to, co má literatura společného s hudbou a co z ní právě dělá umění. Technické postupy není problém definovat, rozebrat a pochválit: proud vědomí, achronologie, vypravěčské hledisko a důslednost v kategoriích vypravěčských forem. Co to však všechno je bez starodávného neosvojitelného talentu k *mimesis*? K té tajemné a rozumem nedosažitelné schopnosti probudit v čtenáři radost z poznání [. . .]

Nakonec je každé umění tajemství. A také: není jen velké umění, a pak jen neumění, nic mezi tím. Je také malé, ale *nikoli nečestné* umění [. . .]

Faulkner jednou řekl, že všechny romány jsou ztroskotané lodi. Vraky. A tak to je. V každé knize, žádnou nevyjímaje, se najde něco nedokonalého, dobou podmíněného, i směšného, stejně jako každý člověk, žádného nevyjímaje, je v něčem nedokonalý, zajatec své doby a prostředí, i směšný. Ale je-li čestný člověk a je-li to poctivá kniha, nikdo nemá právo na posměch, nebo dokonce na opovržení. Kdo má literaturu rád, spíš lituje, že autor na něco nestačil. Spíš se ve vraku na dně kritického moře snaží objevit zbytek zlatého pokladu. (vol. 2, pp. 167–8)

The remark here on the "joy of recognition" recalls Melville's words that "Genius, all over the world, stands hand in hand, and one shock of recognition runs the whole circle round." Škvorecký at his best is a prime example of this.

Secondly, at the close of the chapter and of the extended seminar on Conrad, when Danny has infuriated Hakim, we read:

Beyond the panoramic windows a sad expanse of flat land, and on it, through
a pre-spring mist, the Edenvale raven struts and frets towards Lake Ontario.
Voron. Havran. Raven. Once upon a time Manitou stumbled here, held out
his arm to break his fall and the palm of his hand made that vast watery plain,
and the five fingers of his hand made those five long lakes with the lovely
names: Canandaigua, Keuka, Seneca, Cayuga, Owasco . . . (p. 483)

Za panoramatickými okny přesmutná prérie. Po ní předjarní mlhou kráčí k
jezeru Ontarijskému veliký edenvaleský havran. *Voron. Raven.* Manitou tu
kdysi zakopl, natáhl dlan do krajiny. Z dlaně vznikla tahle veliká vodní plán,
z pěti Manitouových prstů dlouhá jezera s krásnými jmény Canadaigua,
Keuka, Seneca, Cayuga, Owasco . . . (vol. 2, p. 287)

We are pulled back to Danny's first seminar, on Poe, and thus given a gentle
corrective to the anti-Russian tenor of the chapter; and the Russian, Czech
and English words for "raven" in three gigantic linguistic steps, greater
than Manitou's, take us from East to West right round the world. The
haunting, mysterious quality of the Indian lake names extend no lexical
meaning to Danny (elsewhere he shows an extraordinary range of
languages, classical and modern), and their appeal is solely in their lyricism.
But that lyricism has to have a context, as the quotation from Holan at the
start of the "Conrad" chapter suggests. The context is exile.

Conrad is the exiled writer *par excellence.* A Pole, exiled by the Russians
at the age of four to Vologda in northern Russia (a journey which nearly
killed him), he returned to Poland, then later went abroad, serving in the
French and then the British merchant navies; utterly devoted to England
and writing his novels in English, he was eventually granted British nationality. He is an anomaly among the American writers that Škvorecký
chooses for his chapter titles, as anomalous as a Russian harlequin in Africa,
as anomalous as a Czech writer teaching (mainly) American literature to
Canadian students. And beneath the surface the students nearly all turn out
themselves to be exiles of one sort or another: Sharon McCaffrey is Irish,
Irene Svensson is Swedish, William Wilson Bellissimmo is the son of a
Neopolitan labourer, Veronika Prst is a fellow Czech, Larry Hakim is a
draft-dodging American of Arab extraction . . . As Danny tells the students
at the start of his exegesis of *Heart of Darkness,* "Nothing is what it seems"
(p. 368) (Je to všechno jinak – vol. 2, p. 135).

Foreign Influences and Emigration

The Engineer of Human Souls can be considered as much a Canadian novel
as a Czech novel. The translator, Paul Wilson, makes a fine attempt at
capturing the competing linguistic registers which spice the work's

comedy: standard Czech alternates with communist jargon, plain illiteracies run neck-and-neck with the similarly excruciating second-generation Czech of the would-be sophisticated émigré community. The text is in any case liberally laced with snippets of English. Or consider the first few pages of the book where common Czech terms, some of a more recent era, are eschewed in favour of certain canadianisms ("Familyhauz, interval, skájlajn, development" – vol. 1, p. 14). The polyglot Škvorecký/Smiřický merely notes non-judgementally these cultural phenomena, possibly deriving some amusement from them, but hardly condemning. Perhaps there is a joke in the name of Danny's publisher, Santner (clearly an oblique reference to Škvorecký's wife, Zdena Salivarová – though we should note that Danny is not married), to whom the book is dedicated. She it is who with practical advice, much experience and common sense will keep the anarchic business of literary creation and its practitioners on an even keel, and maybe even balance the books.[15]

Such linguistic quirks are a small price to pay for the cosmopolitan riches that are on offer. The epigraphs to the whole novel and to each chapter set the tone. The six openers are from Anatole France, Ezra Pound, Albert Camus, Viktor Dyk, William Blake and Aristophanes, i.e. two French writers of left-wing persuasion, an American fascist-sympathizer who went insane, a Czech, a Briton and an ancient Greek satirist, representing between them the classical world and the eighteenth through to the twentieth centuries. Each of the chapters has two epigraphs: "Poe" is prefaced by Poe and Huxley, "Hawthorne" by Josef Kainar and Colin Wilson,"Twain" by Vladimír Holan and Madame de Staël, "Crane" by Kainar again and Walter Sorrell, "Fitzgerald" by František Zavřel and again Colin Wilson, "Conrad" by Holan again and by Ardengo (Argento in Škvorecký's text) Soffici, and "Lovecraft" by Poe again and Shakespeare. The diligent reader could spend hours relating the various quotes to the text proper; they are, after all, part of the fine mesh of cross-references throughout the text. To take one of the most obvious examples, the last epigraph ("We are such stuff as dreams are made on . . . ") prefixes the middle-aged Danny's sojourn in Paris with his rich and beautiful student Irene, whose name, we are reminded early on in the novel, is particularly close to the narrator's heart (cf. Irena in *The Cowards*). There are, to be sure, less light-hearted inferences to be drawn. To take one of the least obvious examples: Soffici (1879–1964) was a leading Futurist painter and writer, who became an ardent supporter of fascism. Škvorecký's quote (Czech text, vol. 2, p. 129; English text, p. 365) from him when he was Mussolini's ideologist during the war, illustrates superbly the author's contention that there is nothing to choose between fascism and communism. One should also note, moreover, that Soffici published in 1914 a collection of essays under the title *Harlequin*; and it was the presence of the Russian harlequin in Conrad's story that first puzzled the students and thus set in motion their teacher's masterly and provocative explanation of the work.

The overriding significance of the epigraphs (and the other multiple quotations in the novel) might usefully be characterized as the author's endeavour to seek out the essential validity in literature, no matter what its source or even context, to identify what we might call, in the light of our discussion in the previous section, the "hard" lyricism. Such a truth might come from anywhere, from writers great or mediocre, or even in one epigraph here, from a fascist politician. As we have seen, Jan provides the most poignant comment on what constitutes real literature, and he remains on the whole consistent, guided primarily by considerations of art and literature.

His letters to the hero and those of the playwright Vratislav Čenkovič complement each other; the former are literary and reflective while the latter are marked by a jocular, earthy sprinkling of dialect and substandard forms and feature some knockabout comedy, not least at the expense of Jan Vrchcoláb (with his echoes of Pavel Kohout). It would not be difficult to confuse the two correspondents, especially in the Czech text, where none of the letters are dated or given a place of origin. Yet there are clear differences. The playwright signs himself off in various ways: Vraťa, Vratislav, Vratislav Čenkovič, Vratislávek, krajan, and Zarückheil Glücker – this last being his own translation into German now he is in exile. Vratislav starts out a communist (English text, p. 79; Czech text, vol. 1, p. 116) and ends up a notional Christian (English text, p. 547; Czech text, vol. 2, p. 383), signing himself off "Uratilaus, a redeemed sinner" (polepčenej říšník). Jan, by contrast starts out insisting that he is not a Communist Party member (English text, p. 66; Czech text, vol. 1, p. 96), when hauled over the coals by the "comrades" for his article in praise of Churchill. He consistently uses a literary style and always signs himself unaffectedly "Jan". Like his communist colleague he is subject to villification, and could the reference to his *Monologues* (*Samomluvy*) English text, p. 212; Czech text, vol. 1, p. 297) in fact be an allusion to Milan Kundera's last collection of poetry *Monology*? His abiding regard for artistry saves him from any of the charges of flippancy and hypocrisy that his communist colleague is open to.

To this reader's mind, Jan is at his best when he is citing Faulkner (see above); Jan himself notes how one homespun source (Stanislav Neumann (1875–1947), a talented but staunchly communist writer) lets him down (English text, pp. 105, 139–40; Czech text, vol. 1, pp. 149 and 198), but then Jan seems to graduate to Jiří Kolář (1914–), the poet, theoretician and graphic artist: "Neumann is abstraction. Kolar is concreteness" (p. 286) (Neumann je abstrakce. Kolář je konkrétnost – vol. 2, p. 22). Finally, Jan comes to Vladimír Holan (1905–80), generally regarded as the most accomplished of modern Czech poets, especially in the post-war era (English text, pp. 497–8; Czech text, vol. 2, p. 310). The Russian émigré writer Zinovy Zinik has written of "emigration as a literary device",[16] and this is certainly the case in Škvorecký. The best writers use their own cultural baggage to engage foreign cultures. Danny has been more successful than his literary friend in mobilising world literature to escape the "age and environment" that Jan refers to.

It is natural that in his last two major novels *Dvořák in Love* and *The Bride of Texas* Škvorecký should explore further the Czech émigré scene in North America. It has to be said that the author has become a compulsive storyteller, and in his major works, such as *The Miracle Game* and *The Engineer of Human Souls*, the reader seeking and admiring the wood, can at times feel lost in the trees. Moreover, some of the discussions on topical issues and scandals (Angela Davis, the black activist jailed in the early seventies, Eldridge Cleaver, the Black Panther leader and fugitive, American engagement in Vietnam, let alone the essentially Czech topics, not least Dubček and the Prague Spring) have become remote for younger generations.

Dvořák and The American Civil War are sufficiently historical to have solved the problem of dating. *Dvořák in Love: A Light-Hearted Dream* (*Scherzo Capriccioso: Veselý sen o Dvořákovi*) celebrates in the main the composer's time in America, but as in all that Škvorecký's writes, it attempts to de-mythologize without denying the metaphysical. Dvořák comes across as very much the human being, the happy family man and, in his early years, the gauche and injured suitor, as well as one of the world's greatest composers, fêted throughout the world. In the opening chapter, when Adèle Margulies visits him in his Bohemian village to cajole him into taking the post of Director of the National Conservatory of Music in New York, she is persuaded that "Dvořák, however godlike, was sitting on two stools, one in heaven and the other on earth" (Božský Dvořák sedí na dvou židlích: jedna je na nebesích a druhá na zemi).[17] The dichotomy is maintained throughout, as we witness the composer's prodigious drinking bouts, his rage if the beer is brought from the tavern without a decent head on it, his love of simple Czech food; and then there is the chapter "The Mystery of the Cadenza" (Záhada konce),[18] where Dvořák forbids his friend the cellist Hanoušek Wihan to perform his own cadenza – the piece turns out to be too derivative of a song the composer himself has created. Yet the most ethereal motif must be the repeated vision of Rusalka, which in Škvorecký's account turns out to be based on Dvořák's falling asleep while fishing and accidentally catching sight of the delectable Rosemary Vandevilt bathing in the nude at night.

The ladder that Škvorecký thus constructs between earth and heaven also serves as a paradigm for the organic development of music from the late nineteenth to the twentieth century and also for the general contribution that the Czech emigration has made to the America that we know today. The author records Dvořák's fascination with popular song at home and abroad and with negro spirituals. These feed into *The New World Symphony*, and this in turn is not so far away from the sounds of Scott Joplin, Tommy Dorsey and George Gershwin. Musicologists have debated at length the vying influences that have been brought to bear on Dvořák's greatest symphony. Is the work a celebration of the bustle and energy of America as she approached the twentieth century or is the clearly Slavonic element in the composition a nostalgic gesture to the old country? There is an understated contrast between, on the one hand, Dvořák's excursion to the States, involving wealth and status, followed by his return to the Czech Lands, and on the other hand, the harrowing one-way trip of the early immigrants (notably the Kovařík family), cheated and exploited at every turn until they establish their own Czech community in Spillville in Iowa. Elsewhere we have glimpses of Tomáš Masaryk's in-laws, the Garrigues, and the aristocratic Kounic family that the hero's sister-in-law marries into. Again we note a muted contrast here with Dvořák's own humble origins (his father was a butcher and pub landlord).

Although this is the author's first attempt at a historical novel, there are familiar stylistic devices (also present in *The Bride of Texas*): plots are fragmented by a series of flashbacks, usually denoted by italic script, or by forays into the future; towards the end of the novel Czech participants in the Civil War are mentioned and these become major players in *The Bride of Texas*); and in Spillville we are regaled with lurid stories from the Civil War that are reminiscent of the horror stories recounted in the men's room at the Messerschmidt factory in *The Engineer of Human Souls*. Finally, Škvorecký will intrigue the reader with the occasional haunting fantasy, half-suggestive of the book's main themes, yet at the same time comprehensible as a piece of freestanding lyricism: at the age of ninety-five (from sources other than the novel we can establish that the year is 1945–6[19]), Dvořák's patron Mrs Thurber recalls, among much else, the hero's displeasure at Chief Sitting Bull, the vanquisher of General Custer, featuring in a Wild West Show – such humiliation! The chapter closes: "When she woke up the next day, there was the Master sitting next to her bed in a waistcoat, with his sleeves rolled up, and he was playing a saxophone" (p. 271) (Když se druhý den probudila, seděl u postele Mistr, jen ve vestě, rukávy vyhrnuté, a hral na saxofon – p. 206).

It might be argued that in the case of *The Bride of Texas* (*Nevěsta z Texasu*) the work is of more interest as a historical and social footnote than as serious fiction at its best, and as accomplished by the author elsewhere. That said, the work has considerable merits, not least as a "sort of memorial", to use Škvorecký's own term in his Postscript to the English-language edition (this is quite different from the Autorova poznámka in the Czech text). Perhaps the real value of this novel (and *Dvořák in Love*) resides in the fact that it is almost entirely liberated from the anguish of emigration, as evinced by the author in *The Engineer of Human Souls*. There is little of the wonderment, bewilderment, disorientation and homesickness that Veronika or Danny himself experiences. Moreover, in the numerous political debates running throughout *The Bride of Texas* there is none of the totalitarian ideology that generates so much absurdity and moral ambiguity in Škvorecký's earlier works. Politics without ideology is perfectly possible within the compass of this novel. Characters will disagree over whether to abolish slavery, over whether the press should be free, or over what one's national allegiance should be – and of course such disagreements lead to gory conflict – but in a curious way, all the characters are convinced that they are masters of their own destiny; they make their way in the world and experience success or failure. The forces ranged against them are sometimes formidable, but they are never blind, incomprehensible and sinister. In this, as much as in the historical setting, *The Bride of Texas*, its fragmented plots and the four "Writer's Intermezzos" apart, owes much to the nineteenth-century novel.

Škvorecký tells us also in the Afterword to the English-language version that in addition to describing the little known aspect of the Civil War, to wit, the role played in it by Czech and other European émigrés, he was anxious to correct the simplistic Marxist view of the war which he had been fed back home; he rejects also what he refers to as a "popular recent opinion" that sees Sherman as the conceiver of "total" war – he remembers only too well the Nazis marching into Eastern Europe – and deliberately tries to portray both him and General Ambrose Burnside in a sympathetic light.

Yet the author will never abandon his predilection for recording life's inanities. Is there a pun in the Czech title (Nevěsta/Nevěstka, Bride/Whore), understandable given the heroine's promiscuity and occasional profession? There are Czechs fighting for the Confederates as well as for the Union[20] and Lída/Linda Toupelíková is reunited with her Vítek only when he has died fighting for the other, Confederate, side. Indeed the novel opens with both sides in retreat (English text, p. 3; Czech text, p. 11). In a fashion that Crane would applaud, blunders become acts of heroism, as when Zinkule bayonets an enemy (English text, p. 75; Czech text, p. 80) or Shake jumps down from a tree on to an enemy rider and captures him (in fact the branch broke). In words blatantly reminiscent of Crane we read of "the red badge of ardour" (pp. 404–5) (rudý odznak nelhostejnosti – p. 412); and there are faint glimpses of *The Good Soldier Švejk* in the figure of the fat blacksmith called Baloun (Czech text, p. 150; English text, p. 150) and the general berating Colonel Shryock with the words "You don't know me, but you will!" (p. 311) (Vy mě neznáte! Ale až vy mě poznáte! – p. 318). This particular exchange contains an untranslatable joke, as the stammering Pepek (Pepík) keeps repeating "Sir, Sir" (Ser, Ser – the familiar imperative from *srát* (to shit)) to his superior.

Škvorecký makes it clear that his novel is a celebration of the Czech contribution to the Unionist war effort and in non-combat scenes he will record the inventiveness and resourcefulness of the new immigrants: Jan Amos Shake (a.k.a Schweik, the only Czech character whom Škvorecký wholly invents, starts a reading circle and brings erudition to the soldiers' discourse where the others are more likely to bring obscenity. Cyril Toupelík introduces cottonseed mash into the North American farming methods (Czech text, p. 158; English text, pp. 158–9). At the same time the memories of the bloody débâcle of 1848 back in Prague and the brutality of the Austrian rule as epitomized by Captain Hanzlitschek are never far away. The book abounds in fugitive slaves and Slavs. The most colourful of the former, Uncle Habakuk, is clandestinely educated, an accomplished malingerer and acquires a reputation for his culinary skills with insects. Thus it would seem that the Czechs would naturally side with the Union and the Abolitionists. However, we have noted that there were some Czechs on the other side, and anyway towards the close of the novel we learn that their degree of commitment is less than whole-hearted.

The formation of Lincoln's Slavonic Rifles has something of *The Cowards* about it. Should they be prepared to fight the Indians as well as the Confederates, if called on to do so? And as Shake says: "Only fourteen of us marched onto the field of honour, and two were Hungarian, one was a Czechified German, and one a Jew. All the rest decided to forego the glory. They had family, livelihoods, rheumatism." (p. 507) (Těch vytáhlo na pole cti čtrnáct a z toho ještě dva byli uherského jazyka, jeden přečeštělej Němec a jeden žid. Ostatní se slávy vzdali. Měli rodiny, živnosti, revma – p. 506). One notes here a recurrent theme in Škvorecký – that truth lies in the particular not in the generalized picture. Despite all the blundering, bawdiness and self-seeking, the individual Czechs, Kakuška, Kapsa, Zinkule, Stejskal and so on display as much courage and commitment as the Americans, but the author is not in the business of creating a general myth. This point is buttressed by the figure of Lorraine Tracy, whose *nom de plume* is Laura Lee, authoress of many frothy stereotyped romances. Her one attempt at serious writing – Poe is always on her mind, notably his notions about consistency of tone and that poetry is close to music – gives her inordinate trouble. Her professor husband derides her literary efforts, but his own are deemed abysmal by the reviewers. Neither he nor she could be described as "dishonourable" to use the writer Jan's term from *The Engineer of Human Souls*, and years later his novel appears in a scholarly edition, while her lightweight works will, she conjectures, be viewed one day as prototype feminism. As she says herself: "Literary criticism is, I sometimes feel, the art of seeing ghosts" (p. 530) (Literární věda, mám někdy dojem, je umění, jak vidět duchy – p. 531).

Finally, *The Bride of Texas* helps to put the whole question of emigration in perspective. The generational and political differences between the Czechs, Germans, Poles, Hungarians and others in the nineteenth century mirror exactly the twentieth century frictions and conflicts that Škvorecký has depicted elsewhere. Utterly aware of the trauma of emigration, he has more than many other exiles acclimatized and integrated. *The Bride of Texas* is worthy testament to that.

Ota Pavel
(1930–1973)
Laughter in the dark

For most people with a serious interest in Czech literature, the 1970s, especially the early 1970s, presented a miserable time. By 1970 the old liberal-minded (though of course still communist) Union of Writers had been disbanded and a new one, thoroughly loyal to President Gustav Husák and therefore to Brezhnev's Soviet Union was established. The new membership's chief characteristic was artistic mediocrity, underpinned by careerism and opportunism. Alexej Pludek produced a "novel" called *Vabank* (*Going for Broke*), which was a thinly veiled attack on all the leading writers associated with the Prague Spring. Jiří Hájek, the critic, (not to be confused with his namesake, the erstwhile Minister of Education and then Foreign Affairs, who became a dissident activist after 1968) produced a volume called *Konfrontace* (*Confrontation*) which attempted a literary indictment of the leading liberal writers of the day, not least Milan Kundera.

The vast majority of the big names in Czech literature were now totally proscribed, some living abroad, others internal émigrés: Kundera, Arnošt Lustig, Škvorecký, Pavel Kohout, Ivan Klíma, LudvíkVaculík; and it might be said that where they had achieved some kind of international reputation (which might offer them a little protection), this was more for the political construction that was placed on their work than for its intrinsic qualities. This led Kundera for instance, later on, to declare wearily in his Preface to the restored English-language edition of his first novel *Žert* (*The Joke*) that it was a "love story", not as had been suggested to him, an indictment of Stalinism.

Thus when the slim volumes by Ota Pavel appeared, they were a breath of fresh air. Not that their author was unknown. As a sports reporter for many years, he had published several collections of his coverage of national and international events and the people they featured. Rather in the manner that the English writers Harold Pinter and Alan Ross combined literary activity with a passion for cricket, while the cricket commentator John Arlott occasionally wrote poetry, Pavel developed his passion for describing sport to a degree where he could turn to pure literature. His two major collections of stories *Smrt krásných srnců* (*Death of the Beautiful Roebucks*) and *Jak jsem potkal ryby* (*How I Met the Fish*) came out in 1971 and 1974 respectively and were collected under the title *Fialový poustevník* (*The Purple Recluse*) in 1977.[1]

Ota Pavel's biography is of interest, because it is largely one of personal rather than one of public or political hardship, in the way that might be more typical of his generation. He was born in 1930, Ota Popper, the third son of a Jewish father. During the war he and his family lived in the area of Kladno, some 15 miles North-West of Prague. His father and two brothers were dispatched to various concentration camps, and all were, miraculously, to return. But young Ota was spared, only to find himself working as a miner in 1943. From an early age he had a passion for sport, especially football and hockey. He was able to continue his education after the war, and from 1949–56, with a two-year break (1951–3) for military service, he was a radio sports editor. By the early 1960s he was accompanying the national sports teams abroad. However, while covering the Winter Olympics in Innsbruck in 1964, he succumbed to severe mental illness, manic depression, and found himself in and out of institutions for the next five years, having to give up his reporting career completely in 1966. He died of sudden heart failure in 1973.

Fiction

The two collections of stories are highly autobiographical, and on the surface disarmingly simple. Yet their appeal can be explained in several ways. First, there is an unblemished honesty and lack of affectation about them. Secondly, they sketch the life of a reasonably well off family during the First Republic, before the miseries of Nazism and then Communism struck. There is a strong emphasis on the country idyll in the 1930s, and this contrasts with the social stress and turmoil of the post-war period. For those with a knowledge of Russian literature one might point to Konstantin Paustovskii as a comparison. There is the same simple, straightforward style (the only linguistic difficulties that either writer presents to the foreign reader is the delight in the precise naming of flora and fauna, in the case of Pavel, this being pretty much restricted to freshwater, and occasionally seawater, fish). There is also the sheer love of the natural world, coupled with not a little nostalgia. Here too, a sense of tradition and history, especially local history, play a part. This detritus of Romanticism contributed to the "Village Prose" movement in Russia, which lasted from the late 1950s for some thirty years, developing moral and nationalistic traits.

In English literature, one might find affinities with Pavel in Laurie Lee. Along with the same celebration of the countryside, one detects the occasional primordial thrill at the challenge that the natural world can present to man; and, as in Laurie Lee, while simple, individual lives and everyday concerns hold centre stage, politics will eventually force an entry into the idyll. And tucked away in the undulations of the countryside there are ironies and abiding comedy, which frequently militate against the excesses of wishful remembering and nationalism. (In the case of Russian village prose such nationalistic sentiments at times seem uncompromising and unsavoury.)

This type of writing might seem decidedly passé, yet in the circumstances of Czechoslovakia in the early 1970s it achieved a number of goals. It was a reminder, directed at nationalist sympathies, of the beauty and precious nature of the Czech Lands. It was unashamedly nostalgic, with just a hint of escapism. It was also a subtle indication that previous foreign occupations had come and gone. When the narrator's father arrives at his friend Prošek's cottage to persuade him to help poach some venison (a capital offence under the Nazis), we read: "To see that cottage meant to know that that it was still standing, and would probably still be standing when the Germans had gone, and that Karel Prošek and maybe we too, we Jews, semi-Jews and quarter-Jews would still be here too" (A pak vidět tu chalupu znamenalo vědět, že ještě stojí a bude asi stát, až tu Němci nebudou, a že tu bude pak i Karel Prošek a možná také my, židi, položidi a čtvrtžidi – p. 33).

The seven stories that make up *The Death of the Beautiful Roebucks* take us through the immediate pre-war years, through the Occupation and just beyond. Dates do not matter; of far more importance is the geographical setting. A similar approach is adopted in the second collection, where, in effect, we are taken back over the same temporal territory, while the rivers, forests and folk, many familiar from the first collection, are the main centre of our attention.

The celebration of the natural setting is not mere window-dressing, though of course the area to the north and west of Prague has always been a favourite place for hunting, fishing and holiday homes. Take the opening of the title story of the first collection:

We three boys took enormous delight in making trips to the region beyond the castle of Křivoklát. At the time I didn't know why, but I do today. Even back then my dad understood that one day I would be able to see the boulevards of Paris and the skyscrapers of New York, but never would I be able to live for weeks in a cottage, where there was the smell of bread in the oven and there butter was being churned in the dairy, because one day there would be Škoda MBs parking outside those cottages, inside there would be television sets flickering away, and you'd be given rotten black coffee and pale bread.

My tři kluci jsme do toho kraje za hrad Křivoklát ohromně rádi jezdili. Tenkrát jsem nevěděl proč, ale dnes to vím. Můj tatínek pochopil už tenkrát, že jednou můžu uvidět bulváry Paříže a mrakodrapy New Yorku, ale už nikdy nebudu moci týdny bydlet v chalupě, kde voní v peci chleba a v máselnici se tluče máslo, protože u těch chalup budou jednou zastavovat embéčka, uvnitř budou blikat televizory, podají vám špatnou černou kávu a vybledlý chleba. (p. 28)

When the narrator addresses the natural environment there are some controlled flights of lyricism, buttressed by darker, yet life-affirming, considerations. When he catches a river barbel its body "looks like melted silver or a pewter vessel with which you serve wine from royal vineyards. A courageous fish. Fought no end for its life and still wanted to get into the current" (Bylo jak stříbro anebo jak cínová konev, s jakou se nalévá víno z královských vinic. Statečná ryba. Nesmírně bojovala o život a stále chtěla jít do proudu – p. 77). He stabs it through the head, since "the brave sometimes pay for their mistakes with their lives" (neboť i stateční platí někdy za chybu smrtí), and the body "which resembled long-haul aeroplanes" (se podobalo krásným stříbrným letadlům na dálkových tratích) became extinguished") (vyhaslo). In the story "White Mushrooms" (Bílé hřiby) there is a graphic description of the fungus, with each mushroom seemingly different as if painted and as if they had been growing there a hundred years. Mother promptly bursts into tears and reminds father and son of the old wives' tale that this means there will be war. The narrator tells us that the Germans seized the country the following year and "WE NEVER WILL COME HERE AGAIN/THE CHILDREN'S CARNIVAL IS OVER" (UŽ SEM NIKDY NEPŘIJEDEM/ SKONČIL DĚTSKÝ KARNEVAL – p. 82).

The village and small town place names, the named rivers and pools, the named castles and woods generate a notion of familiarity and tradition, of community and history. The Berounka River, which flows due west of Prague, Branov, Buštěhrad, Luh, Dlouhá míle, Palouk, Vlkovice and Šímovic Cliff all acquire in the text the same resonances as do Lee's settings in and around his home village of Slad in Gloucestershire. In the narrator's childhood imagination, legend and adventure are never too far away, yet they are filtered comically through the perceptions of an older, wiser and sadder man. "I am from Luh by Branov. They call me shortarse" [or possibly "scaredy cat"] (jsem z Luhu pod Branovem. Prdelka mi říkají – p. 80) is as succinct an example as to feature in a variant form on the cover of Věra Pavlová's 1993 book of memoirs about her husband. This declaration is preceded by a brief paragraph about the Křivoklát woods, which some people are afraid of, so we are told. "At any moment archers on horseback from Týřov might appear. Most likely we could encounter valiant Czech kings with their retinues" (Každým okamžikem se mohou objevit na koních s luky zbojníci z Týřova. Hlavně tady jsme mohli potkat české udatné krále s jejich družinami – p. 81). Such fancies contrast grimly with the thoroughly realistic scenes the hero later experiences with the occupying Germans, and his lucky escapes.

Particularly as the vicissitudes of war are felt, the surrounding countryside, and especially the Berounka and other waterways, takes on a primeval aspect – nature becomes the life-giver. But her bounty will only be extracted at a price. On at least two occasions in *How I Met the Fish* the hero's life is at risk in his quest for meat or fish. In "How Dad and I Served Eels" (Jak jsme s tatínkem servírovali úhořům) the dangers of nature become apparent when the hero nearly drowns on a fishing trip with his father – and this before the war. On the second occasion, in "They Can Even Kill You" (Můžou tě i zabít), with his two brothers and his father in camps, and other members of the family dead, young Ota embarks on a life-threatening career as a carp poacher. In one of those ubiquitous ironies that Czech literature throws up, he is saved by the very person he thinks is his enemy, the gamekeeper Záruba, who, in a charade put on for the benefit of the watching Germans, pretends to beat him when he catches him; he also advises him where it is safer and better to fish, and asks after his family. Of course, in the title story of the first collection, the account of the life-and-death quest for meat displays all the finely honed aspects of Pavel's craft.

Father reaches the conclusion that if his two elder sons are going to have any chance of surviving the camps, he must provide them with a good meat diet before they go. Both, as it turns out, do survive. "The lads stuffed themselves for the coming years, so as to survive Terezín, Auschwitz, Mauthausen and death marches in thirty degree frosts and carrying rocks uphill at Mauthausen in thirty degrees of heat and all the other lovely little things which the Germans had prepared for them" (Kluci se cpali na příští léta, aby vydrželi Terezín, Osvětim, Mauthausen a pochody smrti v třicetistupňových mrazech a nošení kamenů do mauthausenských schodů v třicetistupňových vedrech a všechny ty krásné věcičky, které pro ně připravili Němci – p. 39). Jirka, we are told, did not talk about his experiences very much, but just once mentions to the narrator, "Perhaps that roebuck saved my life . Perhaps those last pieces of proper meat were sufficient for me to see it out just to the end" (Možná že ten srnec mi zachránil zrovna život. Možná že ty poslední kusy pořádného masa mi vystačily akorát do konce – p. 39). One notes here an attenuated existentialist theme, which was so prevalent in earlier post-war years and which comes through time and time again in the writings of say, Lustig (in works like *Diamonds of the Night* [*Démanty noci*]), and in the grim, yet restrained novel by Jiří Weil *Living with a Star* (*Život s hvězdou*), in which, as in Pavel, we never see the camps, but where existence is reduced and concentrated on items, which in normal life would be trivial, but which are now vital. In Weil's novel, the (illegally held) cat, which the hero takes in, assumes all the importance of a loved one or a family. In Pavel, a few cuts of meat, obtained by risking life, sustain a life.

The death motifs in the story induce a degree of ironic black comedy. First of all, father tries to catch eels for his sons, but the moonlit nights mean the eels do not bite; and now the forest is so quiet that even a squirrel will not stir in it, let alone a roebuck. "Tears of fatigue and anger flowed from his reddened eyes. Nature had conspired against the Jew" (ze zarudlých očí mu vytékaly slzy únavy a vzteku. Příroda se proti židovi spikla – p. 35). Father has obtained a spurious sick note from a doctor friend in order to embark on this illegal errand, and now is the last day, the last chance, for his sons to live. There is an implicit contrast between the innocence and even justice of the law of the jungle as presented in the story and the evil of the man-made regime which has been visited on the protagonists. Karel Prošek (whose moustache – again a grim irony – resembles Adolf Hitler's), is father's close friend and the narrator's adopted "uncle"; understandably he refuses to risk his own life and the well-being of his six children to help father directly, but he agrees to lend him his hunting dog, Holan.

Holan is an Alsatian, which has become, we are told, something of a wolf, and he has been trained to kill the deer, thus shielding his master even in peace time from charges of poaching. The lengthy description of Holan is more than tinged with the epic, primordial qualities which we noted above. Moreover, the relationship between master and dog denotes total, primitive compatibility. The peasant who supplies the pup is glad to get rid of him, because even as a pup he killed hens. "Plucking and jerking [i.e. in order to break the prey's neck] and DEATH" (škub a trh a SMRT – p. 30). The friendship between them grows, the like of which the author has never seen among people, but Prošek, especially in his cups, will swear and throw stones at Holan. When Prošek sleeps off his drunkenness under the stars Holan thinks his master is dying and whines and howls. Yet above all Holan is a hunter. On spotting a deer on the hillside (parkland, that might better be called "The death of the beautiful roebucks", we are informed) Prošek only has to take the dog's head in his hands, order him to run, and:

> Holan, only yesterday a puppy, dashed off, as if he had been hunting since time immemorial. He caught the direction of the wind, so that the roebuck couldn't catch his scent, and ran along, taking it easy, like an Indian summer.

To start with he bounded along as if on air cushions rather than on his paws, then he ran the last ten meters hunched up, and finally he stalked. He struck, and unlike the roebuck, he had a flying start, such an important start, but more than this, the momentary advantage of surprise. The roebuck cried out, took off, but too late. Holan dashed along at his side for a few meters, leapt at his throat and and with double his weight brought him to the ground and usually broke his neck. He would also bite through the jugular with his powerful jaws. Before Prosek got to the roebuck it was all over.

A Holan, včera ještě štěně, vyrazil, jako by lovil odpradávna. Chytil vítr, aby ho srnec neucítil, a běžel lehce, podoben babímu létu. Nejdřív skákal, místo tlapek vzduchové polštáře, poslední desítky metrů přikrčen, a nakonec se plížil. Vyrazil a měl proti srnci letmý, tak důležitý start, a hlavně moment překvapení. Srnec bekl, odrazil se, a pozdě. Holan se řítil pár metrů po jeho boku, skočil mu na krk a dvojnásobnou vahou ho srazil k zemi a obvykle mu zlomil vaz. Mohutnou mordou mu ještě prokousl tepnu na krku. Než došel Prošek k srnci, byl konec. (p. 31)

This scene is replayed when, with some cliff-hanging difficulty, the narrator's father persuades Holan to hunt with him, and when there is much more at stake than the life of the roebuck. As in several of the other stories in the two collections, the elliptical allusions to the Nazi atrocities somehow make their evil all the more poignant when set against the innocent violence Pavel discovers in nature. The title of the story might be construed as an ironic metaphor for the death of so many innocent human beings at the hands of their own species. The narrative concludes with two natural deaths, Prošek and Holan, which also denote the death of the narrator's childhood. One final detail underlines the distinction which is made between the innocence of the hunt and the evil of the holocaust: Prošek, *against his principles* (proti jeho zásadám – p. 39) (my italics. R.P.), has displayed the head and antlers over the door of his cottage, telling the foresters that they came from the Alps, and never fulfilling a promise to his children and grandchildren to explain how the hunting of that deer was so much more dangerous than hunting predators in Africa.

It can be argued that some of the later stories in the second collection do not possess the same power as the best of Pavel's fiction, but taken as a whole the stories exhibit a number of other qualities which are worthy of consideration. There is a curious joke at the heart of the texts, namely that we have a Jewish hero engaged in some very unconventional activities for a Jew. While the anti-semitism is paraded (in the title story of the first collection the words "JEW" and "DEATH" are printed in block capitals) and there are all manner of narratives concerned with the father's business ventures, one feels that these are always second to his interaction with nature. Russian literature provides a more concentrated version of the Jew involved in unJewish things in Isaac Babel's stories of the Russian Civil War *Red Cavalry*. Here we have a Jewish intellectual, in a singularly brutalized army of ostensible atheists (though, by background, Russian Orthodox), fighting in Catholic Poland. Ota Pavel's Jews are nowhere near as anomalous as Babel's narrator-hero. Indeed, the bonds between the Jews and Gentiles – the narrator's mother is Christian – rather points up the banality of the evil.

Father's business ventures provide some of the lighter comedy and portray a First Republic that is reasonably prosperous, yet relaxed and enterprising, and very much part of a modern Europe. All of which has little to do with the real stuff of the narratives. Pavel's main business is with existence, not primarily with social and political life. The economic activities in fact work as a moral and even metaphysical foil to several of the other most moving stories from the Protectorate period, for example "Carp for the Wehrmacht" (Kapři pro wehrmacht) and "Long Mile" (Dlouhá míle). In the first of these, father has his carp pool confiscated by the occupiers, yet still tries to feed the fish, on one occasion proudly refusing a carp that the Germans offer "the Jew". On being summoned to go to the camp himself, oblivious to the dangers, he takes all the carp to eat at home, having spoken to them and caressed them. In "Long Mile" the narrator tries to catch a carp that his brother has deliberately hidden and been feeding in a pool near a mill. The miller callously takes it from the boy when he catches it, leaving him only with the fish's scales. The boy reflects that "the peasants were right when they said that the trees are as alive and as powerless as children and timid animals" (Sedláci měli pravdu, že stromy jsou živé a bezmocné stejně jako děti a plachá zvěř – p. 96). This latter story's references to the Lidice massacre, with potatoes and flowers growing over the graves of the victims make it the most sombre of Pavel's narratives.

Father's great ambition has been to own his own pool of carp, and working very successfully as a travelling salesman for the Swedish firm Electrolux, he is soon in a position to buy. His wife has always wanted a holiday in Italy. It turns out that the pool, once bought, contains no carp to speak of, Father has been duped and the vendor, Dr Václavík, has taken his wife on holiday to Italy. Father later gets revenge by selling the doctor a refrigerator that has no motor. Father can sell vacuum cleaners to peasants who live in areas where there is no electricity, promising them that he will help get it installed for them (p. 16). He sold two fridges to Dr Eduard Beneš, and acted as a go-between, unsuccessfully as it turns out, for his boss, who wants his wife's portrait painted, and the famous artist Vratislav Nechleba. After the war he is persuaded to sell a new brand of fly-paper an acquaintance has invented, only to have the products returned in bulk because they did not adhere properly; and later father learns that the invention has been successfully developed in Holland under the brand name "Sly

Killer". The son would have loved to tell his father that what he had been trying to sell was not itself of poor quality, but father is already dead. The narrator's unbridled love for his father seems to be well founded, given the latter's ability to win the affections of both the élite of the land and the simplest country folk. "Můj povedený otec" (my priceless or possibly, "very funny" father) becomes something of a refrain in the texts.

Father tries to instil his winsome ways in his son by packing him off to Brno to sell the doomed fly-papers, armed with nothing but a copy of *How to Win Friends and Influence People*, Dale Carnegie's international bestseller of 1936. But father's sales technique (he himself has never read the book) is based primarily on his earthiness, his lack of affectation, all summed up in the word "pumprdentlich", the title of one story. On catching a five-kilo sheat fish, he is at first pleased and then disappointed, dismissing it as "pumprdentlich". "Dad never knew precisely what this word meant, but he enjoyed using it. He used to say it was a bit like when a beautiful lady in evening dress or wearing a fabulous fur coat, totally stunning everyone who's looking at her, steps in some shit"(Tatínek nikdy přesně nevěděl, co tohle slovo znamená, ale s oblibou ho používal. Prý je to, asi jako když jde krásná dáma v plesových šatech anebo v báječném kožichu, všichni přihlížející jsou paf, a ona přitom šlápne do hovna – p. 131). Apparently based on the common Czech equivalent of "arse" (prdel) and with a German adjectival ending, the endearing quaintness of the term echoes not just father's qualities, but those of so many of his associates.

Several of the stories set in the post-war period are naturally concerned with the return to normalcy after the Occupation; here one detects yet another reason why Pavel should have proved so popular at this time, for Czechoslovakia was undergoing its own "normalization" programme after the 1968 invasion. This meant of course an enforced return to the restrictions, repression and absurdities of Soviet communism. The narrator, his family and friends, are free to engage in trade, to travel, to debate, to pursue careers, just when all these activities were especially difficult for the books' readers to undertake. At the same time Pavel is at pains to play down any heroism. "Fishing with a Submarine" (S ponorkou na ryby) describes with nicely balanced irony how the author is persuaded to talk to a Polish submarine commander, who expresses great interest in the Church at Kutná Hora and whom the author has down as a rabbit-breeder, about his post-war military service. Only later does he find out that the "rabbit-breeder" is an outstanding war hero.

The fishing trips that the author and his brothers and friends take assume a metaphysical edge, as the protagonists seek to make up for the loss of youth in the war years. In "Lanky Honza" (Dlouhý Honza) the canoe excursion which the narrator and Honza embark on is redolent of Huckleberry Finn's river odyssey – all is innocence and freedom while they are on the move, yet they can be mildly tainted by the corruption of man once they moor. Honza and the narrator inveigle their way into a couple's tent to shelter for the night, and Honza ends up courting the girl. Pavel's characters are for the most part caught between peccadilloes and decencies, between successes and failures, between infirmity and the therapeutic properties of the natural world. In "Lanky Honza" we read that "the sun is [. . .] a yellow bath towel, which rubs us down by itself, and it's like a hair-dryer that dries us. The sun also leaps into our heart and warms it for us, when it feels as cold as a dog's nose" (Slunce je [. . .] žlutý froté ručník, který nás sám utře, a jako fén, který nás vysuší. Slunce nám také skočí do srdce a ohřeje nám ho, když ho máme studené jak psí čumák- p. 117). At the end of the "Fishing-Rod Thief" (Zloděj prutů) the author tells us, underlining the trauma as it were, by using italics:

> *And then for a long time I didn't go fishing with my brothers. The horoscope was right* [see p. 141 of Pavel's text where he recalls a horoscope saying that one of the family would go mad R.P.]. *I went mad and I spent five years in an institution for the mentally ill.*
> *There are no fish there.*
> *Only kings, emperors, Napoleons, Christs, Aphrodites, Princesses Libuše and Joans of Arc.*
>
> *A pak už takhle na ryby s brášky dlouho nejel. Horoskop vyšel. Zbláznil jsem se já a pět let jsem strávil v ústavu pro duševně choré.*
> *Ryby tam nejsou.*
> *Jen králové, císaři, Napoleoni, Kristové, Afrodity, kněžny Libuše a Panny Orleánské.* (p. 142)

Health and infirmity hound the hero no less than decency and evil. In peace time the evils are nearly always redeemable. Mrs Frank can gently rebuke him for giving her a fish that should have been allowed to grow. His father will set aside eels, a specially prepared delicacy, because they have been oversalted, and then invite his son for eels for years afterwards to pay off the emotional debt.

Conclusion

Pavel's other writings will largely appeal to the sports enthusiast, yet critics have rightly noted that there is a clear link with his more creative works. At times his reportage does indeed take on all the vigour of fiction, and in this area, no less than in his autobiographical based fictions, one notes that in much contemporary writing anywhere, the divisions between fact and fiction have become decidedly porous.

It is interesting to consider Pavel's sports reportage in the general context of the political circumstances within which he was obliged to operate. In the communist countries, technically speaking there were no professional sportsmen and women, and a general impression was created for foreign, capitalist-country consumption that sports stars did all their training in their spare time, their "day job" being involved rather with the more mundane building of socialism. At the same time, during the communist era a great deal of political and ideological prestige was to be gained by international success, and the communist establishment would often go to extraordinary lengths to ensure high ratings. Since the collapse of communism disturbing stories have emerged concerning the use of performance-enhancing drugs and the like. Moreover, sport provided one of the very few ways in which young people were able to travel abroad – and at the state's expense.

Another point: sport, by its very nature, sets positive social examples, and as such, in communist countries, enables writers on the subject to be so easily categorized in terms of socialist realism. No doubt Pavel, and a great many of his colleagues, would have cringed at such pigeon-holing. Yet consider this gloss by Bohumil Svozil on "Climbing the Eiger" (Výstup na Eiger), the lightly fictionalized account of how Radan Kuchař and Zdeno Zibrin made it to the summit of Switzerland's most notorious peak in 1961:

> Here the mountaineers overcome the fatigue and weakness of the body, feelings of fear, they put themselves at risk, they conquer the consequences of misfortunes which make more difficult an already difficult ascent. Their greatest rival is the taciturn, dangerous mountain itself, and from the start of their ascent they are reminded of the recent death of the Austrian climber and the possibility of their own death: this prose is concrete in its view of the situation of two concrete individuals, however in it there is played out the age-old contest of man with the might of nature and with the danger of death.

> Horolezci zde překonávají únavu a slabost těla, pocity strachu, vystavují se riziku, zdolávají důsledky nešťastných náhod, které jim ztěžují i tak dost obtížný výstup. Největším jejich soupeřem je sama mlčenlivá, nebezpečná hora a navíc se jim od počátku výstupu připomíná nedávná smrt rakouského horolezce a tedy i možnost jejich smrti: tato próza je konkrétní v pohledu na situaci dvou konkrétních individuí, přesto však jako by se v ní odehrával odvěky zápas člověka s mohutností přírody a nebezpečím smrti.[2]

All but the last two lines of this quotation could be taken from any amount of conformist criticism; its closing sentiment touches on the broader aspects of Pavel's best writing. Many of his sports pieces are prefixed with quotations from great minds outside the world of sport: the collection *The Price of Victory*[3] has as an epigraph Alexander Fleming's assertion that the best way to understand human behaviour is through sports, especially team sports; and individual pieces in the collection have epigraphs, not just from sports participants and commentators, but from Socrates, Eisenstein, Maiakovskii, Camus, Hemingway, Slutskii, and the Czech writers Kohout and Lustig, both of whom were still *persona grata* until 1968 when the volume first appeared.

"When You Just Can't Do It" (Když ti to nejede) gives a poignant insight into the pressures that a sports star comes under, particularly when s/he is state-sponsored. Jan (Honza) Veselý tells his own story of how, after twenty years of competition cycling, he is persuaded to make one last bid in the tenth world championship. Interesting questions of motivation are raised as we read that the hero would issue a Švejk-like exhortation "for the Emperor" (ZA CÍSAŘE PÁNA) when they were being urged to win "for the homeland" (za vlast – p. 136), but they really wanted to win for themselves and for the ordinary people that supported them. Veselý is captain and he persuades his friend Honza Kubr to continue, when he can barely do so himself. They both give up in exhaustion, not helped by a hostile press and accusations of betraying the working class, and it is decided to send them straight home from Berlin. The hero is no longer referred to by his affectionate diminutive, but as "comrade" and the "vy" form of address is used – almost a comic contradiction in terms, given that at this time communists were actively encouraged to use the familiar form of address amongst themselves (p. 139). At five in the morning they are to be moved to a different (presumably cheaper) hotel. "WE HAD SIMPLY CEASED TO EXIST. No manager who might have had a heart-to-heart talk with us, no doctor who might have checked what state we were in physically and mentally. Just two tickets for the night train home" (PROSTĚ JSME PŘESTALI EXISTOVAT. Žádný vedoucí, který by s námi promluvil, žádný lékař, který by nás prohlídl, jak jsme na tom tělesně a duševně. Jenom dvě jízdenky na noční vlak domů – p. 139). Back home the Czechoslovak Union of Physical Education stripped him of his title of "Merited Master of Sport" and issued a two-year ban. He responded by returning all his awards and titles. Pavel ends the account with his witnessing Veselý and Kubr having their awards returned to them and their taking a lap of honour.

The most prominent and familiar straight reportage would be Pavel's piece about Emil Zátopek ("How Zátopek Ran on that Occasion" – Jak to tenkrát běžel Zátopek) , while the most fictionalized sports writing would be "The Fairy Tale about Raška" (Pohádka o Raškovi).[4] The first of these makes interesting reading simply because it is about the most famous Czech athlete ever, who won the 10000 meters Gold Medal in the London Olympics in 1948 and three Gold Medals in Helsinki in 1952. For the British, especially those of a certain vintage, there are interesting references to some of his contemporaries: Jim Peters, Gordon Pirie and Chris

Chataway. "The Fairy Tale about Raška" recounts in the manner of a fairy story how Jiří Raška won the Gold for ski jumping at the Grenoble Olympics. His father was a cobbler, who then became a grave-digger rather than make boots for the Germans to march all over Europe (pp. 4–5). One of four children, from humble origins, Jiří becomes a folk hero, returning to his native town Frenštát in triumph and presenting his aunt with a small bottle of Chanel no. 5 and a recording of Frank Sinatra singing *I Love Paris*. Her simple dwelling is thus transformed into the Paris she always dreamed of visiting. There is more than a touch of originality in the way that Pavel takes the simple facts of a successful career (no doubt duplicated ad infinitum in the world of sport) and injects them with a degree of magic and simple morality. The work is at once a children's story and, like so many of the other sporting stories Pavel wrote, an adventure for adults. The spirit of the book is exemplified by the illustrations – photographs of Raška and his family and associates coupled with cartoon-style line drawings by Adolf Born, in the best traditions of Czech children's book illustrations.

Ivan Klíma
(1931–)
Conscience and moral conundrums

The Kafka Connection: *Love and Garbage* and *Judge on Trial*

The publication in March 1990, hard on the heels of the Velvet Revolution, of the English translation of Klíma's *Love and* Garbage (*Láska a smeti*)[1] coincided with an article on Czech literature abroad in the weekly journal *Tvorba*, that commented on Klíma's recent prose. One English reviewer spoke of the novel's "somewhat uncontrolled and self-indulgent lyrical effusions" and suggested that "some of the loving superfluity" on display in the English translation "could surely have gone in the waste-paper bin".[2] The *Tvorba* commentator wrote:

> In Klíma's new novel there are excellently written passages, a series of truthful reflections on our recent past and on the situation of culture in present-day Prague, and we are given in allusive outline an agonizing love relationship, but about half-way through the book we realize that we are to expect nothing more than a new version of the old love triangle, emotion drowning in quarrels and mutual bitterness, and we are really rather disappointed. I perceive the weakness of the novel in its lack of a supporting conflict, the monotony of a single theme . . . [3]

Another English reviewer without the advantage, one suspects, of knowing the Czech original wrote: "It is rare that one meets a new literary voice of such originality and mastery in both structure and content. This, indubitably, is one."[4] First impressions of a lot of Klíma's prose might lead to comments as disparaging as the remarks by the first two reviewers quoted here. On a superficial level Klíma can seem sentimental, introspective and whimsical. He appears repetitive – there is frequent allusion to his childhood spent in Terezín, to his period of teaching in America and his voluntary return to Czechoslovakia in the spring of 1970, to his circumstances as a proscribed writer, a stoic witness to violations of human rights. The age-old theme of a man caught between love for his wife and love for his mistress is not confined just to *Love and Garbage*. It is central to *A Summer Affair (Milostné léto)*,[5] *Judge on Trial* (literally, *Judge out of Mercy*; original *Soudce z milosti*)[6] and plays a significant part in the short story collections *My Merry Mornings (Má veselá jitra)*[7] and *My First Loves (Moje první lásky)*.[8] It perhaps reaches its apotheosis in *The Ultimate Intimacy (Poslední stupeň důvěrnosti)*.Yet these criticisms have to be weighed against the comedy, the irony and the persistent sense of reality that are not far off ubiquitous in Klíma. One way of accommodating the sentimentality to the realism is to allude to the author's unquestionable moral stance, to fall back on the simplistic attitude of the well-meaning outside observer and assume that because the author is a good man he must be a good writer. However, Klíma deserves more than the benefit of the doubt.

One of the puzzles about Klíma's career as a prose writer is that it seems to have gone in reverse. From the grotesque fantasy of *A Ship Named Hope (Loď jménem Naděje)* with its doubts and uncertainties, we come to the relatively familiar territory of love triangles and persecuted Czech intellectuals. Yet the author's abiding interest in Kafka has grown more insistent, while his characters and situations have become more everyday. Very near the end of *Love and Garbage* the hero-narrator tells us:

> What used to fascinate me most about literature at one time was that fantasy knows no frontiers, that it is as infinite as the universe into which we may fall. I used to think that this was what fascinated and attracted me in Kafka. For him a human would be transformed into an animal and an animal into a human, dream seemed to be reality for him and, simultaneously, reality was a dream. From his books there spoke a mystery which excited me.
>
> Later I was to understand that there is nothing more mysterious, nothing more fantastic, than life itself. (pp. 212–13)

> Kdysi mě na literatuře snad nejvíc oklouzovalo, že fantazie v ní nemá hranic, je nekonečná jako vesmír, do něhož se lze propadat. Domníval jsem se, že i proto mě oklouzuje a vábí Kafka. Člověk se mu změnil ve zvíře a zvíře v člověka, sen, jak mi připadalo, byl pro něho skutečností i skutečnost snem, z jeho knih ke mně promlouvalo tajemno, které mě vzrušovalo.
>
> Později jsem pochopil, že není nic tajemnější ho, nic fantastičtějšího než sám život. (pp. 248–9)

For the time being, let us set aside the emotional turmoil that the hero of *Love and Garbage* experiences in his tortured relationship with his wife Lída and his mistress Daria, and concentrate on his other passions. First, there is his regard for Kafka. For the hero, Kafka's chief quality is his honesty *(opravdovost,* "truthfulness", "authenticity", "intellectual honesty" might be more precise, though pedantic, English renditions):

> Kafka endeavoured to be honest in his writing, in his profession and in his love. At the same time he realised, or at least suspected, that a person who wants to live honestly chooses torture and renunciation, a monastic life devoted to a single God, and sacrifices everything for it. He could not, at the same time, be an honest writer and an honest lover, let alone husband, though he longed to be both. (p. 182)

> Kafka usiloval být opravdovým ve svém psaní, ve svém povolání i své lásce. Zároven věděl anebo aspon tušil, že člověk, který chce žít opravdově, volí si trýzeň a odříkání, mnišství, jež se rozhodlo sloužit jedinému Bohu a tomu vše obětovat. Nemohl být zároven opravdovým spisovatelem i opravdovým milencem či dokonce manželem, i když toužil být obojím. (p. 214)

The Judaic tradition, which is at the back of a good deal of Kafka's writing, is also, in muted form, to be found in Klíma. *The Trial* can be read in terms of the Day of Atonement, Yom Kippur, when man is expected to recognize his guilt. On that day, according to Jewish law, a man must desist from work, eating, drinking, anointing his body, indulging in sexual intercourse or wearing leather shoes. *Love and Garbage* is, of course, about cleaning. The hero is a disaffected intellectual who takes on a temporary job sweeping the streets of Prague.

However, it soon becomes apparent that the real cleaning is going on in his conscience and in his soul, as he interlaces his account of his menial occupation and his colourful workmates with reflections on God, history, language and the anguished tale of his triangular love affair. The novel's opening paragraph talks of the people who "were supposed to look after our cleanliness. The cleanliness of our streets, of course, not the purity of our souls" (p. 1; omitted from Czech text). The English text of the novel concludes:

> But Paradise cannot be fixed in an image, for paradise is the state of meeting. With God, and also with humans. What matters, of course, is that the meeting should take place in cleanliness. Paradise is, above all else, the state in which the soul feels clean. (p. 217)

> Ale ráj se nedá zobrazit, neboť ráj je stav setkání. S Bohem, také s člověkem. Záleží ovšem na tom, zda se setkání událo v čistotě.
> Ráj je především stav, v němž se duše cítí čistá. (p. 253)

To this extent the spirit of the novel accords well with themes that one encounters in Kafka. Yet the fabric of the novel is made up of the very things which are, by Judaic law, forbidden on the Day of Atonement; if we except the wearing of leather shoes and anointing oneself, all the other prohibitions are infringed. The hero *elects* to work; the street-cleaning gang, the somewhat abstemious hero included, punctuates its shift with sessions in the pub; and the hero, without going into too much detail, candidly reports to us the extent of his sexual activities.

The hero is also attracted by Kafka's shyness (*plachost*) (Czech text, p. 168; English text, p. 141). Though the term is used only rarely – in stark contrast to the numerous references to "honesty"- we can use it here as a shorthand for the fixation that Kafka had with his self, with his personal world. As the hero reflects, after a meeting with a rather naive foreign journalist (in the Czech text she is American (p. 60), in the English translation French (p. 42)), who has questioned him as to why Kafka is more or less banned in Czechoslovakia:

> I think it would be difficult to find, in our century, many writers who were less interested in politics or public affairs than Kafka. There is no mention in his work of war or revolution, or of the ideas which may have helped to bring them about, just as there is nothing in his work which directly points to his Jewishness. (p. 43)

> Myslím si, že by se v našem století našlo jen nemnoho autorů, kteří by se tak málo zajímali o politiku a o veřejné dění, také nic, co by přímo připomínalo jeho židovství se v jeho díle neobjevuje. (p. 62)[9]

Later we read:

> In his questioning Kafka stopped at the very first step, at himself, because even here he'd entered an impenetrable depth. In a world in which the intellect predominates more and more, the intellect which believes that it knows everything about the world and even more about itself, Kafka rediscovered the mysterious. (p. 111)

> Kafka se při svém tázání zastavil hned na prvním kroku, sám u sebe, neboť již tady vstoupil do neproniknutelné hlubiny.Ve světě, kde stále více převládá rozum, který si myslí, že o světě, tím spíše o sobě, všechno ví, Kafka znovu objevil tajemství. (pp.135–6)

Klíma's, or at least the hero's, perception of Kafka here is important, for it suggests a clear distinction between arguably the most influential prose writer of the twentieth century and a great deal of literature in the same period which has concerned itself with mystification. Klíma's hero asserts that Kafka presents his paradoxes, enigmas and incongruities in good faith; they are to be taken at face value; there is no attempt to tease or mislead the reader. Another unusual slant on Kafka emerges shortly after the passage just quoted:

> I still believe that literature has something in common with hope, with a free life outside the fortress walls which, often unnoticed by us, surround us, with which moreover we surround ourselves. I am not greatly attracted to books whose authors merely portray the hopelessness of our existence, despairing of man, of our conditions, despairing over poverty and riches, over the finite-

ness of life and the transience of feelings. A writer who doesn't know anything else had better keep silent.

Kafka was desperate in nearly every situation of his life, and yet he was always looking for hope. When it seemed out of reach he'd put his manuscript aside and not return to it again. (p. 117)

Dosud si myslím, že literatura má cosi společného s nadějí, se svobodným životem za pevnostními zdmi, které nás, aniž to často tušíme, obklopují, jimiž se dokonce sami obklopujeme. Mě aspoň málo lákají knihy, v nichž jejich autoři jen popisují beznadějnost naší existence a zoufají si nad člověkem, nad poměry, nad bídou i nad bohatstvím, nad konečností života a přechodností citů. Spisovatel, který neví víc, měl by raději mlčet. (p. 141)[10]

On another occasion the hero views Kafka in an utterly conventional way, "as a sacrificial victim by his own decision". And he "certainly anticipated the fate of the Jews in our age of upheaval" (p. 130) (se stal beránkem, jenž se určil za oběť sám [. . .] předjímal židovský osud v převratném věku – p. 155). However, the hero feels a close affinity with Kafka in a very personal way, in the way that the two writers create images: "What tied me most firmly to life was my writing: anything I experienced would become images for me" (p. 47) (Nejvíc mě k životu poutalo moje psaní – všechno, co jsem žil, se mi proměňovalo v obrazy – p. 65). Of Kafka, the hero tells us: "Although he mostly speaks of himself and although his heroes are, even in their names, avowedly himself, he yet concealed the true nature of his struggles. He was not only shy, he was so much an artist that he expressed everything he experienced in images" (p. 133) (povětšině mluví o sobě a za sebe, se hlásí dokonce i jmény svých hrdinů, pravou podstatu svých pří však skrýval. Byl nejen plachý, ale umělec tak bytostně, že vše, čím žil, vyjadřoval v obrazech – p. 159). Thus it would be unseemly to consider *Love and Garbage* an autobiographical work, even though there may well be, in the minutiae, a strong autobiographical element. (However, a cautionary note: in an interview in the Slovak weekly *Literárny týždenník*,[11] Klíma recalls how people, having read his "conspiratorial story" from *My Merry Mornings*, refused to believe that he in fact had not sold carp at Christmas – and that when they did believe him, they were disappointed!)

There is of course nothing new in the spectacle of Czech writers claiming inspiration from Kafka, but in Klíma's case there is perhaps more justification, since in broad outline, as opposed to the minutiae, there are biographical affinities. Kafka was a Czech Jew, writing in German, under the hegemony of an alien Austro-Hungarian Empire. His sympathy for Czech nationalism is well attested, as are his shyness, decorum, politeness and sense of social responsibility. Klíma has displayed similar urbanity and decorum, despite all the harassment during the years of "normalization". (On one occasion in *Love and Garbage* the hero is thanked for his good work as a street-cleaner.) Klíma's patriotism has been unswerving yet unostentatious, and his regard for civil rights unquestionable. He has been writing in Czech in a country which has permitted, to use his hero's term, only "Jerkish", a language of 225 words "developed in Atlanta for mutual communication between humans and chimpanzees" (p. 42) ("jerksky" [. . .] jazyk [. . .] vyvinutý v Atlantě pro vzájemné dorozumívání lidí a šimpanzů – p. 61).

Another of Klíma's passions, much on display in *Love and Garbage*, is religion. In his recent prose this feature has become increasingly salient, and it presents something of a puzzle. On one level it could be taken as straightforward conviction on the author's part. It is not unusual for rationalists – even left-wing rationalists – to develop quasi-religious tendencies when revolutions turn sour, or, as in Klíma's case, when all intelligent thought, common decency and even common sense are rebuffed by the powers that be. If rational argument gets you at best nowhere, and at worst a prison sentence, religious conviction can become a very attractive alternative, even if that too invites persecution. Yet it would be difficult to square Klíma's sense of irony and scepticism, or his earlier interest in the fantastic and grotesque with any unqualified attachment to an established religion.

The lengthy novel, *Judge on Trial*, written between 1972 and 1985, examines many of the personal and public considerations that have confronted the population of Czechoslovakia in the decades since the war. The hero, Adam Kindl, a high court judge, after many years in the legal profession, finds himself trapped by all manner of conflicting loyalties – not least, and perhaps somewhat surprisingly, by the pressure exerted by his own conscience. The narrative is broken up by a number of flashbacks, all entitled, as the English translation has it, "Before we taste the waters of Lethe" (Než se napijeme z řeky Léthé) and in these we see that in the past Kindl, though able to distinguish truth and lies, was able to suppress his own urges towards human decency in order to survive. He and his family suffered under the Nazi occupation. Then under communist rule his father was unjustly imprisoned for two years. The son is now supposed to make things better, but this proves impossible when he is given his first "political" case. He sentences a shopkeeper to three and a half years for hoarding his stock – his own stock. He acts according to directives and not as a result of his own investigations and judgement. The inhabitants of the provincial town where this occurs are more aware of the true situation and stone his car as he leaves.

Yet years later, when the novel opens, the hero is confronted with a very different kind of case. Karel Kozlík is being tried for murder. He has a proven record of violence and crime. He is uneducated and has had medical problems. He has made a full confession (which he later retracts) that he gassed his landlady after a row with her, accidentally killing her granddaughter as well. In addition to being a perfect husband and family man – at least at the start of the story – Kindl is keen to see the abolition of capital punishment. His unpublished article on the subject eventually costs him his job. Kozlík is eventually sentenced to death. Kindl's professional problems are compounded by the fact that his brother lives in Britain, though he does return to Czechoslovakia towards the end of the novel.

This very brief outline of part of the plot demonstrates that moral considerations are persistently overridden by the prevailing political climate and there is no scope for personal conscience. Of course, to a large extent there is nothing new in the portrayal of this all-pervasive corruption of the individual. Yet Klíma's treatment of the theme is all the more poignant for its analysis of a man whose profession should damn him from the start in the eyes of the outside observer, yet gains him the reader's sympathy. His professional problems go hand in hand with complications in his personal life, and all this leads into considerations of emigration, patriotism and – especially for the hero's wife – religion.

The religious dimension frequently insinuates itself into Klíma's prose, and it is an open question as to whether we should accept it purely for what it is, or whether we should attach a subtle element of irony to it. There may well be authorial support and compassion for Alena Kindlová as she "prayed every night, for herself that she should at last find the strength to be humble and manage to be good [. . .] for Adam [. . .] for her children [. . .] for her former lover [. . .] for her long-lost friend Maruška [. . .] and for the murderer [Kozlík], whom she had never set eyes on" (p. 537) (se každý večer modlila [. . .] za sebe, aby konečně nalezla sílu k pokoře a dovedla být dobrá [. . .] za Adama [. . .] za své děti [. . .] za svého bývalého milence [. . .] za svou dávnou přítelkyni Maruš [. . .] za toho vraha, jehož nikdy nespatřila – pp. 626–7). However, Klíma's business is as much with self-deception as it is with establishing a spiritual and morally coherent dimension.

Three hundred years before, the hero's family had been evangelical, but had converted to the Jewish faith in the wake of Bílá Hora, in the hope of securing their future. Consequently, the family is sent to Terezín during the war. As a young man he is approached by the church and he reads the Bible. However, he has a special predilection for Rita Hayworth's bust, and only when he falls desperately in love does he read the Bible with avid enthusiasm (Czech text, pp.138–41; English text, pp. 112–15).

A number of the other characters in *Judge on Trial* also have firm convictions of one kind or another, not least the hero's father who is a communist. His "only friend" (p. 166) (jediný přítel – p. 200) defects after the war to West Germany, leaving behind an edition of Plato in which he has left a slip of paper. It reads: "What is required for human welfare and happiness? According to Socrates it is intellectual activity, good memory, straight thinking and truthful judgement" (p. 166) (V čem záleží dobro a štěstí pro člověka? Podle Sókrata v rozumové činnosti, v pamatování, v správném myšlení a pravdivých úsudcích – p. 201). Adam's father's left-wing views prove tragically naive, and his friend's admiration of Greek philosophers would appear to beg a number of questions. "Straight thinking" (*správné myšlení*) might be more literally rendered as "correct thinking" and the phrase has a whiff of the central committee about it.

His brother's letters and phone calls from abroad are presented to the reader as frivolous and misplaced, given the pressures that the hero finds himself under, but ultimately the brother returns to his homeland, despite all manner of warnings not to. However, when Adam writes to his brother, he highlights what he sees as the two kinds of exile: "One kind is when you are banished from your home and have no chance of returning. The other is when you abandon yourself and are unable to return" (p. 481) (můžeš se ocitnout mimo domov a ztratíš možnost se vrátit. Ale můžeš také opustit sám sebe a nedokážeš se vrátit – p. 562). Ivan Klíma's career has shown that he is not an exile in either of these senses.

Towards the end of the novel Adam, his brother Hanuš and friend Matěj bike to a church reputed to have been built by one man in just two and a half years. Such is the emphasis on this achievement that it can only be taken to stand as a summary of the repeated hints throughout the work that the only real key to life is within oneself, not within a given system. Undoubtedly the author's preferences are for religious and cultural values. Retelling the stories of *Tom Sawyer* and *The Pickwick Papers*, or listening to others talking about books while he was in Terezín as a boy, these are experiences that stay with the hero more vividly than do the horrors of the war period. Yet the muted ironies running throughout the novel militate against the advocacy of any prescribed value system, and rather point to the integrity of the self, with all its contradictions. In *Judge on Trial* there is a good deal of evil, but there are precious few villains.

The religious question is similarly pronounced in *Love and Garbage*, but a close examination of it reveals that, once again, it should not necessarily be taken at face value. One of the hero's workmates is Rada, a man who has had a variety of jobs over the years, but who in fact trained as a priest. At one point he shows the hero a book concerned with the cult of personality; he quotes from it briefly and attention is drawn to the cover design. The implication of the passage is clearly that man is nothing more than garbage, and the book is a reminder of how "we used to deify ourselves and physical matter" (p. 71) (jak jsme zbožnili sebe i hmotu – p. 92). Later on Rada confides to the hero that he attended a religious festival at Svatá Hora that attracted some 30,000 people, mainly youngsters

(English text, pp.102–3; Czech text, pp.126–7).[12] Though this strikes a chord with the hero, his attention is momentarily switched to an exhibit in an artist's window – there is a figure which at first he takes to be Don Quixote and then realizes it is the fourth horseman of the Apocalypse, and he reflects:

> man can behave arrogantly not only by deifying his own ego and proclaiming himself as the finest flower of matter and life, but equally when he proudly believes that he has correctly comprehended the incomprehensible or uttered the unutterable, or when he thinks up infallible dogmas and with his intellect, which wants to believe, reaches out into regions before which he should lower his eyes and stand in silence. (p. 105)

> člověk se může chovat zpupně, když nejen zbožní své já a prohlásí se za výkvět hmoty a života, ale také když sebevědomě uvěří, že správně pochopil nepochopitelné a vyjádřil nevyjádřitelné, když vymýšlí neomylná dogmata a rozumem, který chce věřit, se sápe do prostor, před nimiž by měl leda sklopit zrak a stanout v tichosti. (p. 129)

Thus, for all his sincerity and sensitivity, Rada is found wanting. Earlier in the novel, just before the hero's encounter with the irritatingly naive and self-confident foreign journalist he quotes at some length from Revelation (English text, p. 41; Czech text, p. 60). The passage is from Chapter XX, and is primarily concerned with the defeat of Satan who "shall go out to deceive the nations which are in the four quarters of the earth". Obviously the "fire and brimstone" tone of this passage can serve as a mockery of the journalist, who has little chance of even understanding the truth, let alone passing it on to the world at large, but it is no less a piece of self-mockery on the narrator's part. His own attempts to ensure the victory of truth are, like Kafka's, grounded in reflective self-analysis and self-effacement, not in fire and brimstone. This passage, together with several other references to the Apocalypse, takes on even more significance, when one recalls the circumstances under which the last Book of the New Testament was written.

Though Revelation purports to have been written by John, the "beloved disciple" of Christ, Biblical scholars generally agree that the work is a compilation by several unknown authors, and was produced during the last quarter of the first century AD. This was a time of extreme persecution of the early Christians by the Romans, and the Book of Revelation was designed to reinforce the true faith. The relevance of such "morale-boosting" for a beleaguered intelligentsia, or indeed for anyone trying to cling to a set of personal principles, in a society 'normalized" by Brezhnev's tanks, needs no explanation.

Another aspect of the religious question in the novel occurs in the discourses on Paradise. When the hero first becomes emotionally involved with Daria, he recalls his family tree. His maternal grandfather believed in the Messiah, but purely in terms of the coming socialist revolution, and urged the hero to work for a paradise on earth and for social justice. However, one night the hero hears his grandfather praying to God in a language the boy does not understand (presumable Hebrew), and then he realizes that "the depth of the human soul is unfathomable" (p. 14) (dno lidské duše se nedá dohlédnout – p. 29). Later, after a quarrel with Daria, we are treated to a disquisition on Paradise in a passage that is based on the *Talmud* (English text, pp.172–3; Czech text, pp. 203–4).[13] Given the context that this account of the Garden of Eden finds itself in – a row between a man and his mistress – the emphasis on specifics (wine, honey, balsam, milk, five hundred thousand kinds of fruit, the three ages of man, the seven categories into which the just and faithful are divided), is nothing short of comic.

In general then, the religious passages in *Love and Garbage* and *Judge on Trial* are offered to the reader in a spirit of affectionate scepticism. The author is only too aware of the spiritual dimension in man, but sees the dangers inherent in any attempt to deify man's spiritual yearnings. Rada's Catholicism, grandfather's admixture of Judaism and socialism – we may even include here father's communist ideals, which bring so much persecution from the communist rulers – Christ's ultimate victory, as recounted in Revelation, or the innumerable delights of Paradise, as detailed in the *Talmud*, all these undoubtedly appeal to the hero, but he knows too much of the street, or more particularly of the gutter, to be taken in by them. Towards the end of *Love and Garbage* the hero essays a more positive appraisal of the paradise concept:

> Man dreamed of returning, after his death, to God's garden or of fusing with the universe or of returning to the creator in a different shape. He surmised that at least his soul would get close to God.
>
> But over the years as the human race grew older and memories became confused, man exchanged the idea of blissful innocence for that of happiness through pleasure. Ageing man confused the soul with the body and believed he could enter paradise in his lifetime. As soon as he succumbed to the old man's error of believing he could return to the state of childlike innocence he actually entered the age of foolishness and totally succumbed to it in his senile childishness. Man thinks he's building paradise by inventing motor-cars, aircraft, plastics, nuclear power stations or underwater tunnels, whereas in reality he invents and brings about the Apocalypse. (p. 207)

> Člověk [...] snil tedy o tom, že se po smrti vrátí do zahrady Boží, tam se setká se všemi, které miloval anebo splyne se všehomírem, anebo se k Tvůrci vrátí jinak, tušil, že aspon jeho duše by se mohla dostat do boží blízkosti.
>
> Ale během věků se vzpomínky stále více mátly, lidstvo už se podobá starci, ten si zaměnil duši s tělem a pošetile uvěřil, že může vstoupit do ráje ještě

zaživa, že jej zbuduje na Zemi. Staví tedy velkolepá díla, pokořuje přírodu, rozbíjí hmotu, vyrábí a užívá drogy, dovolí a a omluví si každý čin, odpustí si každou proradnost, vecpe se do každého lůžka, kde se naděje rozkoše, řítí se od zážitku k zážitku, od zábavy k zábavě, už se ani nemá čas se zastavit, aby se zeptal, k čemu to vše činí, k jakému ráji to vlastně směřuje.

Ve skutečnosti nepřibližuje ráj, přibližuje apokalypsu. (p. 245)

There are considerable differences between the two passages. In the Czech edition the second and third paragraphs of the extract run roughly as follows in my translation:

But over the centuries memories became dimmer – mankind now resembles an old man who has confused his soul with his body, and has foolishly come to believe that he can enter paradise while still alive, and can build it on Earth. So he builds magnificent things, subdues nature, destroys matter, produces and uses drugs, permits and excuses himself every act, forgives himself every perfidy, jumps into every bed in lustful expectation, rushes from experience to experience, from pleasure to pleasure, he doesn't even have time to stop and ask himself what it's all for, what kind of paradise he is actually heading for.

In fact he is not bringing paradise nearer, but the apocalypse. (p. 245)

While the gist of each version remains the same, one might detect in the former a slightly more pointed attack on the economic policies of the great powers, and in the latter a note of censure at once more general and more self-castigating – the hero's guilt feelings at his marital infidelity will never desert him. It would be simplistic to attribute such discrepancies between the two texts to the different target audiences. It is more likely that Klíma, like his beloved Kafka, strives to be honest and not to go beyond his self. At the same time he admits all manner of influences in his quest. (In *Love and Garbage* we find allusions to Buddha and Kierkegaard, along with the other points of reference discussed here in more detail.)

Klíma is only too aware that he is an intellectual and a realist, not a saint. It is therefore fitting that we should address another first love of his: the incongruous, all those things that are not, despite the best efforts, amenable to rational explanation. Klíma, like Kafka, insists on the mysterious not for its own sake, but in the belief that in the baffling world of today it is the only honest thing one can do.

Hence we have a street-cleaning gang comprising an intellectual who takes on the job for no real reason; a coarse, wrinkled woman with a good figure, always telling the most lurid stories, but also possessing some genuine sensitivity, whom the hero nicknames "Venus"; a "sea captain" who goes in for the most outlandish scientific experiments and ends up in a psychiatric unit; a foreman full of the most engaging war reminiscences;

Rada, a religious man, who has been to prison for his beliefs but whose brother has become a Party member; and a young man who can no longer play jazz because of a liver disorder and who disappears before the hero can pass on to him a drug that may help him.

Moreover, if incongruity is the very stuff of everyday life, it will certainly find a place in Klíma's world of art. As the street-cleaning gang makes its way through Prague, it regularly passes an artist's studio, where a constantly changing exhibition is to be seen in the window. The first time the hero sees it, he is shocked at the depiction of a hanged man. Towards the end of the novel, the artist makes a personal appearance wearing a fool's cap and bells, a sackcloth, a laurel wreath and carrying a bunch of what the hero takes to be deadly nightshade. The hero "in his fool's orange vest" (v oranžové, šaškovské vestě) identifies with him (English text, p. 192; Czech text, p. 225). The final exhibition is of the street-cleaning gang itself, and this time the hero is convinced that the resident artist has ceded his place to a sculptress (Daria, no doubt):

> I realized that all these faces were, in their likeness, both real and unreal. They seemed younger and more attractive, as though nothing of the working of time or life had marked them [. . .] I was still looking for myself among the sculptures, but I didn't see my own face; there was only a tall pillar, as if hewn from stone, but I couldn't see its top through the window. (pp. 208–9)

> Tu jsem si uvědomil, že všechny tváře jsou ve své podobě skutečné i neskutečné, vyhlížejí mladší a líbeznější, jako by na nich neulpělo nic z práce času a života. [. . .] Hledal jsem ještě mezi sochami sám sebe, ale vlastní tvář jsem nezahlédl, jen vysoký sloup jakoby z kamene vytesaný čněl vzhůru, ale oknem jsem jeho vrchol nemohl zahlédnout. (pp. 242–3)

Thus the self remains a mystery, but a closer knowledge of it can be acquired through the interaction of the artist's sensibilities and the apparent banality and sordidness of life – love and garbage are mutually dependent.

In February 1990 Philip Roth visited Klíma in Prague, and wrote a lengthy report of his encounter with his old friend for *The New York Review of Books*.[14] In Roth's view, *Love and Garbage* is "a wonderful book . . . a nice antidote to all that magic in magic realism . . . The book is permeated by an intelligence whose tenderness colors everything and is unchecked and unguarded by irony. Klíma is, in this regard, Milan Kundera's antithesis." It may well be the case that the irony in Klíma is not as cutting as in Kundera, but the foregoing discussion has attempted to show that it is most certainly there. It bears witness to the writer's special relationship to reality and it transforms Klíma's lyricism – which some have found so uncomfortable – into the very tenderness that Roth so accurately identifies.

Short Prose

It might be argued that Klíma is really at his most powerful when he restricts himself to shorter forms. His first major prose success, *A Ship Named Hope* is of novella length, but raises all manner of questions concerning man's destiny and freedom. There are strong religious overtones in the text too. The Kafkaesque mystery was generated by a perfectly realistic event: when on one occasion in the1960s Klíma was crossing the English Channel to Dover, the emergency siren was sounded and all the passengers were ushered to one area on the ferry and cordoned off. Through a combination of poor acoustics and possibly the author's (then) limited English, he did not know what was happening and speculated that those in charge of their safety could have so easily mown them down with machine guns.[15] No doubt, Klíma's wartime experiences also played a part. The story, dated 1967, would perhaps have been especially poignant in 1969 when it first appeared in a Czechoslovakia once again forcibly directed by a foreign power towards a goal that to ordinary people as well as to the cynical politicians of the day was ill-defined and unattainable. The story was originally published with *The Jury* (*Porota*), but this work was dropped by the author in the post-communist period in favour of *The Island of the Dead Kings* (*Ostrov mrtvých králů*). The third story that makes up the new collection, *The Washing Machine* (*Pračka*), makes for a somewhat grotesque murder mystery, not unlike one of Roald Dahl's *Tales of the Unexpected*.

The pinnacle of Klíma's achievement in the short story genre must reside in the three collections that he produced while still a proscribed writer, *My Merry Mornings* (*Má veselá jitra*), *My First Loves*, (*Moje první lásky*) and *My Golden Trades* (*Moje zlatá řemesla*).[16] The first and last of these use the bric-à-brac of his twilight existence during the "normalization" period as a springboard for serious inner and external contemplation. However, the four stories that make up *My First Loves* provide a sentimental education which takes us from the narrator's childhood in Terezín to his courtships as a grown man in the communist era. The collection possesses universality, yet at the same time offers a subtle personalized history of the author's homeland.

We can deduce that the first story, "Miriam" (Myriam), is set in May or June 1944, since there is mention of the British offensive in Italy and the defeat of the Germans at Sevastopol (English text, p. 8; Czech text, p. 8) – Sevastopol had fallen to the Germans in July 1942 and was recaptured by the Russians in May 1944; this would make the narrator about thirteen or fourteen if his age is the same as his creator's. Miriam/Myriam, who for a time gives him extra rations of milk and a warm smile, is put at somewhere between sixteen and eighteen (English text, p. 13; Czech text, p. 13). The narrator becomes infatuated with her, and at the end of the story when the extra portions cease, he faints with grief, explaining to the adults around him that his indisposition is due to his aunt being deported (no doubt to Auschwitz) (English text, p. 20; Czech text, p. 21). All the drama is in the boy's imagination, and indeed in his misunderstanding the situation. Klíma tells us in an essay that he tried to imply that the aunt had instructed Miriam to give him extra rations, but as none of the reviewers of the story spotted this, he must have buried the detail too deeply.[17] None the less, the ironies abound: the hero suffers more from unrequited love than from confinement to the ghetto, while the adults fail to register the real cause of his anguish.

The theme of emotional turmoil is continued in the next story "My Country" (Má vlast), one of the richest of Klíma's texts. First, the title recalls Smetana's patriotic suite, which is mentioned in the text along with various nationalist songs (English text, p. 35; Czech text, p. 38). The temporal setting, to judge by some of the things that the narrator's father and the schoolmaster say about the abolition of capitalism and inequality, and the mention of rationing (English text, p.43; Czech text, p. 46), can be gauged as the late 1940s, possibly just before the 1948 coup. This was a time when Czechoslovak nationalism, later to be duly constrained in Soviet-socialist-internationalist garb, flourished. It was also a time of peace and fleeting independence:

> [Mother] . . . urged us to watch how the sky was turning pink and red, how the sun dipped into the tops of the indistinguishable trees, and asked if we knew or could picture anything more noble or perfect than this spectacle, and whether we could envisage a land more beautiful than our own. (p. 29)

> [Matka] . . . přiměla nás, že jsme sledovali, jak nebe růžoví a rudne, jak se slunce zasunuje do kornoutu nerozeznatelných stromů, a zeptala se nás, jestli známe anebo si dovedeme představit něco vznešenějšího, něco dokonalejšího než je taková podívaná, a jestli si dovedeme představit krásnější zemi, nežli je naše. (p. 31)

These notions are buttressed by the geographical setting: a tiny, rural holiday resort, where work and play can intertwine (the boy's reading serious literature, his father's preoccupation with his engineering project) and people of contrasting outlooks and manners are drawn into close proximity. Apart from the serene setting of the resort, the snatches of Hussite hymns and Mr Anton's affectionate reminiscences about the Czech Lands prior even to the First World War, when he worked as a major-domo for the Emperor in Vienna, all contribute to the sense of national pride and tradition.

The hero-narrator will now be sixteen or seventeen ("I too was seventeen once" (p. 67) (taky mi bylo sedmnáct – p. 71) the doctor says to him and we are told explicitly that the lady for whom he falls, the wife of the vulgar doctor Slavík and mother of twins, is nearly twenty-five (English text, p. 74; Czech text, p. 78). The physical side of their affair amounts to one brief hand-holding session, one kiss and a slight touching of hands at the funeral of her former lover. Their conversations are of necessity short and controlled by circumstance. As in "Miriam", the passion is in the hero's mind:

> I felt her fingers brushing over mine, interlinking with mine, and our fingers rapidly turned into a joint bird's wing, on which we were able to soar up, to rise, to hover above the nocturnal tops of chestnuts and limes, under the summer stars, sink down on the moss and cover ourselves with it to conceal our total nudity, our sin, our passion. (p. 77)

> Jsem ucítil, [. . .] jak její prsty přejíždějí po mých, proplétají se s mými, naše prsty se rychle měnily v jedno společné křídlo, na němž jsme zavěšeni mohli stoupat, vznést se, setrvávat nad nočními korunami kaštanů a lip, pod letními hvězdami, klesnout do mechu a přikrýt se jím, abychom zahalili svou úplnou nahotu, svůj hřích, svoji vášeň. (p. 82)

The hero's school teacher has shown some of his literary efforts to a literary editor, who has been mildly impressed and has urged him, in a style somewhat reminiscent of Soviet practice, to learn from the great writers – in this instance, Balzac, Stendhal, Maupassant, Gorkii and Sholokhov. Herein lies the real strength of Klíma's story. The three great French realist writers and two Russian realists – both canonised in the 1930s in the Soviet Union and among left-wing intellectuals everywhere as *socialist* realists – are quoted at some length and in such a way as to make them seem sensationalist and shallow in comparison with what is going on in the mind of the smitten adolescent. This literary exercise contrasts effectively with the scurrilous ditties that the doctor (singularly misnamed Slavík – "nightingale" – the English translation has to spell this out in a way that the original needs not (English text, p. 42; Czech text, p. 45)) regularly mouths and which outrage the hero's prudish mother. The five classics represented are, for the record: Balzac's *Illusions Perdues*, Stendhal's *Le Rouge et Le Noir*, Maupassant's *Bel Ami*, Gorkii's story "The Watchman", sometimes published in foreign language editions as part of a sequel to *My Universities*, and Sholokhov's *The Quiet Don*, and each extract involves unimpaired sexual activity that might be characterized as: orgy (Gorkii), one-sided passion (Stendhal and Balzac), gang-rape (Sholokhov) and illicit love by mutual consent (Maupassant). Two ironic and unstated questions arise: whatever is the youthful aspiring writer to learn from passages such as these? and what would the hero's mother say to these universally accepted classics, given that she bridles at anything mildly *risqué*? "My

Country" amounts to a vigorous assertion of what literature is, where its wellsprings are to be found and how it can be so frequently misconstrued, especially as a crude instrument of moral edification. There is an additional irony in the figure of the literary editor, who exhorts the hero to put his awful wartime experiences behind him, yet is blithely directing him to scenes of rape and licentiousness.

There is a further arresting image in the work (which is in part taken up in the final story "The TightropeWalkers"): the hero sees a beautiful girl acrobat climb out of a hot air balloon and perform, to his horror, some seemingly perilous manoeuvres from a rope ladder. He thinks he sees her on a second occasion, this time riding a horse, but he isn't sure. She makes a final, definite, appearance at the funeral, this time performing her act in black as if in deference to the deceased. While the young hero fixes his gaze above, the heroine's weeping eyes are trained on the ground. When the balloon disappears, his emotional state seems similar to that which obtained when he first saw the performer: "All at once I felt like crying with the loneliness that had suddenly overwhelmed me on that wide, parched, dusty field" (pp. 66-7) (a mně se chtělo najednou naříkat, jaký do mě vstoupil stesk v tom šírém, rozpáleném, prašném poli – p. 70). The second, mistaken, appearance is interlaced with his father's idealistic assertions about the future joys of socialism. One could characterize this motif as a straightforward political allegory, but it is no less tempting to see it as the author's endeavours to unite the ethereal and the earthly, to record the wonder, danger and fragility inherent in human aspirations. Of course, it also chimes perfectly with the hero's sentimental education. It might be added that such dense imagery is more successful than some of the author's extended ruminations, which are to be found in some of his other works.

We can deduce that "The Truth Game" (Hra na pravdu) takes place from about 1953 through to the early 1960s, for there is mention of Stalin's death (March 1953) and later, of the removal of his body from the Mausoleum (October 1961). Yet in other respects Klíma is as coy about the temporal setting as he is in the other stories. The title of the story might derive from the party game that was popular in student circles in the 1960s, whereby an empty wine bottle was spun and whoever it ended up pointing at had to reply truthfully to a number of questions. At one point the hero and heroine play the game, but without the bottle.

The hero has been given a manuscript of a dissident biography of Stalin, which catalogues the Soviet dictator's crimes and compares him to Hitler. Now the hero's old perceptions of history have been shattered. At the same time he encounters a girl with whom he enjoys a full physical relationship, the only one in the collection. Yet paradoxically, he learns nothing for certain about her. She regales him with lurid stories of relationships with other men, of murdering her own child, of an ex-SS man forcing her to supply him with plans of the factory where she says she works. But ultimately the hero can pin down neither her proper name nor real address, and she simply disappears. Years later he runs into her by chance, she says she is anxious to see him again, but gives him a false address.

The story can be read as much as a paradigm of the enhanced scepticism and even cynicism which swept through the Eastern bloc during the de-Stalinisation period and, with that, the increased concentration by individuals on themselves and their inner world. There is undoubtedly a didactic element in Klíma's writing and the lesson in this work would seem to be that genuine knowledge comes from self-knowledge, which derives in turn from interaction with other individuals more than from political or social life. The hero of "The Truth Game" is of course older than his counterparts in the previous stories; he is also less vulnerable and more self-assured. To any thinking Czech of Klíma's generation the historical backdrop, always implicit and never trumpeted, in *My First Loves* is unmistakable: fascist occupation, followed by a liberal, fragile democracy, followed by Stalinism, de-Stalinisation and then neo-Stalinism.

"The Tightrope Walkers" (Provazochodci), without the forgoing stories might be simply dismissed as a latent love-triangle story, with the hero attracting, and being attracted to, Dana, the girlfriend of his best friend, Ota. She writes him poetry, while he writes her a story. She is sickly and is taken ill on one occasion while with him – the strain of trying to choose between the two men has apparently exacerbated her condition. Ota accuses the hero of seeking nothing but his own gratification, whereas to judge by the narrator's own account it is clearly Dana who has been making the running. The story closes with the situation unresolved. The physical contact between the couple has amounted to a couple of kisses. These events are framed by the hero's vision of a troupe of tightrope walkers, once seen just a year after the war. On the second occasion – when the audience is invited to join the performers on the high wire and the hero almost takes up the challenge – the spectacle drives him to philosophical contemplation:

> It seemed to me that I was beginning to understand something of the secret of life, that I would be able to see clearly what until then I had been helplessly groping for. I felt that life was a perpetual temptation of death, one continual performance above the abyss. (p. 162)

> Zdálo se mi, že začínám chápat něco z tajemství života, že svedu rozsoudit to, před čím jsem až do teď bezradně tápal. Cítil jsem, že život je věčné pokoušení smrti, jediné nepřetržité představení nad propastí. (p. 172)

There is, in this last story in the collection, a realisation on the hero's part that he is learning to cope with life's uncertainties.

Taken together, the two collections *My Merry Mornings* and *My Golden*

Trades, constitute one of the most eloquent and evocative accounts of ordinary life in Czechoslovakia through the 1970s and 1980s. After the collapse of communism Klíma was finally able to bring out in Czechoslovakia, after a fifteen-year hiatus, a collection of "fairy stories" by a group of the leading Czech writers of the day, which depicted a land where all the people were doing jobs totally at variance with their training and aptitudes.[18] The book was of course a transparent political satire on the normalization process post-1968, which had led to something like a third of the teaching profession and other white collar workers losing their jobs. These professionals were forced to pursue their trade at a lower level or in a less congenial part of the country. Worse still, many intellectuals found themselves doing manual jobs, while the jobs for which they were trained and suitable, were filled by people possessing little conscience or intelligence who were only capable of mouthing the correct political slogans. In *Professional Foul*, Tom Stoppard's television play of 1977 set in Prague, a Czech national who has a first class degree in philosophy from Oxford is a cleaner at the bus station, solely because of his political views. As Klíma writes in "Tuesday Morning: A Sentimental Story":

> My former Chief Editor, a literary critic by training, has for seven years now been employed washing shop windows. Another friend, a well-known philosopher, is digging tunnels for the metro. The theatre director who dared put on my last play [. . .] is serving a prison sentence. (p. 32)

> Můj bývalý šéfredaktor, vzděláním literární ktitik, už sedm let umývá výklady. Jiný můj známý filosof hloubí metro. Ředitel divadla, který uvedl moji poslední hru [. . .] sedí v kriminále. (p. 39)

Klíma's own circumstances were not quite this harsh. He was proscribed at home, but was able to obtain some income from foreign royalties, and his wife was fully employed as a psychiatrist. There was, though, always the technical problem of self-imposed unemployment, which – in a socialist country that boasted a planned economy and a job for everyone – was a crime. Indeed the Friday story contains a specific reference to the hero taking the hospital orderly's job to avoid being accused of parasitism (English text, pp. 89–90; Czech text, p. 99). In practice, many of the leading intellectuals enjoyed some immunity through their international reputations; for the government to force them into menial jobs might create more of a political backlash than simply to let sleeping intellectual dogs lie. Václav Havel's manual labouring in the Trutnov brewery in the early 1970s had created waves on the international scene, and his imprisonment (more than four months in 1977, a brief spell in 1978 and then from 1979 to 1983) and failing health eventually caused such international concern that he became more of a nuisance to the authorities in prison than at large.[19] In an

Afterword which appears in the English version of *My Golden Trades* Klíma tells us that he did actually engage in most of the activities the book describes (smuggling books, digging at an archaeological site, land surveying, driving a locomotive). In the case of *My Merry Mornings*, the celebrated story about his selling the carp (traditional Czech Christmas fare) led the author to protest that his friends found it hard to believe that this was one job which he had not actually done (see p. 140 above). No doubt, Klíma's motivation in taking on these diverse tasks was partly to obviate any charges of parasitism, but he was bound, along the way, to find some rich pickings for his literary pursuits. The stories also illustrate some of the notions that Havel expressed in his open letter of 1975 to President Husák that on the surface Czechoslovakia in those years represented a normal country ("people build houses, buy cars, have children, amuse themselves, live their lives"), but that underneath there lurked fear and disturbing anomalies ("Every day someone takes orders in silence from an incompetent superior [. . .] solemnly performs ritual acts which he privately finds ridiculous."[20] Klíma presents us with a world in which corruption and absurdity exist at every level.

Bearing in mind Klíma's near obsession with Kafka, the title of the collection is highly charged: morning time in Kafka's works spells danger and disorientation, despite the matter-of-fact way that his threatened characters may behave. In Klíma's collection, each of the seven mornings that take us through the week – not a single week, to be sure – shows us the narrator exerting a degree of free will in a fairly mundane situation, only to uncover various layers of reality, which usually leave him, if not in a commanding position, then at least in a more edified position.

On a Monday he takes a tough and defiant five year old boy who has jumped out the window to hospital, only to find himself viewed as a child abuser by the medical staff, and then to watch the lad finally dissolve in tears when he is united with his mother. The lad's father beats him regularly and trades in stolen goods, but the narrator – a good citizen by any normal standards – is, *à la* Kafka, the one who stands accused. Routinely refusing the father's offers of quality goods on the cheap, at this stage the hero remains relatively untainted. Tuesday's "sentimental story" shows the brief rekindling of a relationship with a girl of twenty years earlier, though this time there is no opportunity for physical intimacy. Having defected to the West, Lída is now rich and free to globetrot, while he has had his passport confiscated and is under surveillance. There is even an oblique reference to Jan Palach's suicide and the copycat self-immolations that followed, when the hero tells her that in the absurdity of the then Czechoslovakia all you can do is set fire to yourself or make a joke of it (English text, p. 33; Czech text, p. 40). The torment in this story comes from Lída's inability – or worse still, unwillingness – to comprehend the continuing distortions that originally drove her from her homeland and the hero's decision to stay there. "Life often presents you with only two kinds of suffering, two forms of nothingness, two varieties of despair" (p. 40) ("Člověk často nemá v životě jinou volbu než mezi dvěma druhy utrpení, dvěma podobami marnosti, dvěma obměnami zoufalství" – p. 46) he reflects, and tells her he does not know why he has made the decision he has, resigned to the fact that she will not understand.

Any feeling of moral superiority that our hero might be experiencing at this stage is neatly counteracted in the next story, Wednesday's "Christmas Conspiracy" (Vánoční spiklenecká povídka). The scam to sell carp which the narrator is cajoled into by his pal Petr he justifies to himself by intending to give the proceeds to the wife of a jailed dissident friend. Despite all the intricacies of overcharging and under-weighing the fish, the slick sales patter they are instructed in and the various bribes they have to hand out, they end up losing their investment and are down on even their takings. Clearly, other, more seasoned, con men providing the fish have won out. There is an erotic element too, in which the attractive salesgirl, Daniela, offers her favours to the hero (who, we note, is only too ready to accept, the clear reference to his wife and children at the start of the story notwithstanding). Daniela's ulterior motive is to get the intellectual hero, who she assumes to be well off, to set her up in a garage business. Klíma identifies the ubiquitous corruption and the moral turpitude as follows:

> Not that I thought of it as some kind of Mafia; none, or at least certainly not the majority, of its members had any criminal intent, nor were they intentionally dishonest. They were, rather, ordinary, average people who had not been offered a single idea, a single worthwhile goal that would have given meaning to their life, and they themselves had not found the strength of character to discover them on their own. This is how a whole community of the defeated had come into being, bringing together a motley crew of butchers, greengrocers, Party secretaries and factory managers, bribed supervisors and coalmen and corrupt newspapermen and, no doubt, also those who had been appointed to uncover and smash this conspiracy. (pp. 58–9)

> Není to ovšem žádná mafie. Nikdo, anebo aspoň většina z jeho členů netouží ani po zločinu a dokonce ani po nepoctivosti. Jsou to jen průměrní lidé, kterým vzali anebo spíš, kterým nenabídli ani jedinou myšlenku, ani jedinou hodnotu, jež by daly smysl jejich životu a oni nenašli v sobě dost sil, aby si je sami objevili. Tak vzniklo společenství přemožených a kupodivu se v něm směstnali řezníci a zelináři a tajemníci a ředitelé podniků a podplacení kontroloři a uhlíři a zkorumpovaní novináři a nejspíš i ti, kteří byli pověřeni bojem proti tomuhle spiklenectví. (p. 65)

A popular piece of graffiti around this time in Prague was "He who doesn't steal is robbing his family" (Kdo nekrade, okrádá rodinu). The references to Hašek and Kafka at the start of the story (English text, p. 47; Czech text, p. 54) prove all the more apt; and if one needed to look for more irony in the work, one could reflect that the action takes place at Christmas, with all that the season of good will ought to imply, and that the Czech for "Christmas Day" literally translates as "generous day" (Štědrý den).

Thursday's "erotic tale" (erotická povídka) has a blatantly ironic title, for the only "first hand" sexual encounters occur perfunctorily, if fairly publicly, in view of the narrator when he arrives at a workshop in search of a water pump for his car and again at the close of the story. There is something of a joke in the name of the manager, who only appears at the end, Mr Holý (bare). Elsewhere there is talk of all the copulating that goes on in the local gymnasium. The real substance and comedy in the work is encapsulated in the various eccentrics who appear, in particular Augustin Hovorka, the "Private Doctor of Philosophy". He launches into a delightful diatribe against the phallic symbols of factory chimneys and the like, and rails against materialism and all mechanised transport, against the noise and pollution of industry, which produces nothing of value. His words would not be out of place in any industrialized country today; yet perhaps the essence of this story is in the celebration of the individual. In a society where genuine public debate is denied, individuals will create their own private alternative lifestyles, be they sexual or metaphysical. The human comedy played out in this story, involving all the foregoing and altercations over a car crash, takes place to all intents and purposes, with no regard either for society at large or for the state apparatus. The sign TRESPASSERS WILL BE PROSECUTED (NEPOVOLANÝM VSTUP ZAKÁZÁN!), which opens and closes the narrative, stands as a defiant endorsement of individual freedom.

Friday's story, "An Orderly's Tale" (Sanitářká povídka) has the hero yet again beset by ubiquitous corruption, theft and callousness. At the outset the staff nurse catalogues the numbers of items stolen from the hospital, ranging from pillowcases to doors, while later, the orderlies display utter insensitivity over a bereavement. Finally, the hero learns from the affectionate nurse Tanya (Táňa) about the routine killing of terminally ill patients and he reflects that Věra, the nurse with the "angelic" face, is mixing a lethal dose. All this evil, of varying degrees, is relieved only by the author's story, which he has written expressly for Tanya, and which lightly fictionalises the relationship between the aged Mr Lhota and his dying wife, a patient at the hospital. The story-within-a-story technique, as applied here, makes out a case for literary creativity *per se* and illustrates the therapeutic power that fiction, in certain circumstances, might exert. Perhaps slightly more than in some of the other stories, this one, which allows us a brief peek into Klíma's workshop, also contains fleeting references to specifics of totalitarianism and the author's own life: we have already noted the ever-present risk of being dubbed a parasite that a banned writer might run; there is a passing allusion to religion as the opium of the people (in Marx's notorious phrase) (English text, p. 105; Czech text, p. 114); and the author talks of his time lecturing in Michigan, the American première of his play (presumably *The Castle* – *Zámek*, his dramatization after Kafka), and of his return to Czechoslovakia in spring 1970 (English text, pp. 91 and 97; Czech text, pp. 101 and 106).

In Saturday's and Sunday's stories ("a thief's tale" and "a foolish tale"; "zlodějská povídka" and "bláznovská povídka") one might detect some symbolism in the titles. Saturday sees the hero, together with three acquaintances, building garages for themselves, and encountering all the – then – familiar hassles over obtaining materials, with all the palm-greasing and old-boy network that was associated with the shadow economy. On Saturday one traditionally works for oneself, but in the case of the narrator/banned writer, every day feels perhaps like a Saturday. Certainly, in this story the other participants in the building project feel that he has enough free time (English text, p. 119; Czech text, p. 129) and he is designated chief procurer of the materials they need. The Sunday story sees the hero in church and associating with a protestant clergyman.

Yet both stories contain an ironic streak: one of the amateur builders, Dr Merunka, is a Catholic and talks of a vision of the Virgin Mary and a miracle cure he once undertook for an ailment he contracted while forced to work in the mines (clearly a reference to the 1950s). He and the hero filch some discarded timber from a nearby site, and during the operation, the latter spies his former fellow student Libor (his chief supplier of goods and a most successful wheeler-dealer) together with a few other men enjoying a private striptease. Girls routinely have to offer him, as a chief housing official, their favours to gain an apartment. Merunka's moral misgivings about taking the planks of wood are more than outweighed by the thoroughgoing corruption that Libor personifies. At the same time, it seems that such corruption is indispensable even to the most high-minded.

The final story has the hero at a country retreat, a loaned cottage, where he hopes to be able to gain peace and quiet to write. There are allusions to Charter 77,[21] and some comic scenes involving the philosophy professor and courier of dissident texts who struggles to remember the number for the combination lock on his briefcase. He turns up in the locality to see the hero just as the area is experiencing some serious floods. The closing scene of the story, and of the entire collection, is of the two men and the delinquent girl in a boat, as the flood waters rise and the professor is hoping to open his case. Expensive *objets d'art* float out of the house of a well-heeled football coach's house, but, in an uncharacteristic fit of non-materialism, the girl rejects the suggestion that she should take some. The hero concludes: "And now I understood that by some miracle we three were well met in that rowboat" (p. 154) (A já pochopil, že jako divem jsme se na té loďce všichni tři dobře sešli – p. 165). The image is in the same class as those noted occasionally in *My First Loves*, involving acrobats and circus performers. Despite the danger and apparent incongruity, there is also a moment of understanding, a perception of a link between the material and the spiritual, a momentary bonding between heaven and earth, between life and death.

Conclusions

In *My Golden Trades* Klíma continued the themes established in the two previous collections. Activities as an archaeologist, a train driver, a courier and a land surveyor gave him scope through the workaday world to reflect on truth, freedom and religion. He delights in the occasional eccentric, while always allowing that, to those he encounters, he is no less odd – usually he is a teetotal, non-smoking bookworm. "The Land Surveyor" (Zeměměřičská povídka) obliquely reminds us of Kafka's *The Castle* and of Klíma's own dramatisation of this work premiered at the Vinohrady Theatre in Prague in 1964. One might reflect that Klíma is not dissimilar to Kafka in temperament in the way that he contemplates spiritual matters while performing menial tasks conscientiously. There is even a notion that he is able to be a more conscientious worker than many of those he meets precisely because he has a contemplative side. At the same time, the casual recording of developments in Czech life (the Vietnamese immigrants, growing materialism and the quest for foreign goods, foreign popular culture, be it films like *E.T.* or pop music) cannot dispel the underlying sense of stagnation, a feeling that nothing worthwhile is happening and that the individual can play no real role in the socialized world.

One detects in Klíma's fiction a growing despondency. The wry humour and congenial eccentricity of *My First Loves* and *My Merry Mornings* are crowded out by moral considerations. The long novel *The Ultimate Intimacy* (*Poslední stupeň důvěrnosti*) of 1996 seizes on a theme that has attracted such authors as Graham Greene in works like *The Heart of the Matter* and *The End of the Affair*: the religious man caught in a love triangle. In this work too we have, moreover, a clergyman's daughter getting pregnant by a drug dealer, whom the hero is trying to rehabilitate. The young delinquent's scheme to go back to drug dealing in order to finance a religious magazine seems highly contrived. There is real concern in the novel about the proliferation of unconventional religious sects in the Czech Republic.

More successful is *Waiting for the Dark, Waiting for the Light* (*Čekání na tmu, čekání na světlo*) of 1993. This novel captures splendidly the essence of the Velvet Revolution and catalogues its costs and achievements. The hero, having had some difficulties with the authorities in the past, has for years now made a reasonably comfortable living by producing hack documentary films – all his really interesting footage gets routinely spiked. He is overly fond of strong drink. After the collapse of communism, he finds himself making advertisements and pornography. Yet it could be argued that the spiritual side in him does survive, through the agency of his imagination and his personal ties to others. At the end of the book he "feels as if he can almost rise above the earth, rise above his own life as though it belonged to someone else" (může se téměř vznést nad zem. Vznést se nad vlastní život, jako by to byl zcela cizí život).[22] Conceivably, there is a moral sleight of hand here, as the author strives to salvage something of his hero's integrity. Yet in a remarkable passage earlier on, Klíma sets out the moral anguish which totalitarianism visited on every thinking individual and he produces an image at once curiously at variance with the moral conundrums that much modern Czech fiction, Klíma's own included, frequently throws up:

> Peter began to talk about himself [. . .] he had neither the inclination nor the desire to play the judge. We all lived in this country. Given the conditions that existed here, every one of us came out of it scarred in some way. And who can establish a borderline between guilt and innocence, when that borderline runs somewhere right down the middle of each and every person? People overthrew the old in the hope that they would finally see justice done. There would have to be an attempt at some kind of judgement. "Someone can probably be found who can establish that borderline," Peter said, "but it won't be me. The job will probably be done by someone who will use it to cover up his own guilt.
>   What was justice? (pp. 173–4)

> Petr teď začal mluvit o sobě [. . .] on nechce a nemůže dělat soudce. Všichni jsme žili v téhle zemi. Při poměrech, které tu vládly, každý vyšel nějak poznamenaný. A kdo vůbec může stanovit nějakou hranici viny, když hranice většinou běží někde uprostřed každého člověka a je sotva postřehnutelná. Pokud se bude hledat příliš rozhodně, kdo obstojí? Pokud se nebude hledat vůbec, neobstojí spravedlnost. A lidi přece svrhávají starý režim v naději, že se konečně dočkají spravedlnosti. "Někdo se asi najde, kdo tu hranici stanoví," řekl ještě Petr. "Ale já to nebudu. Nejspíš se do toho pustí někdo, kdo se tím pokusí zakrýt vlastní viny."
>   Co je spravedlnost? (p. 157)[23]

Solzhenitsyn writes in *The Gulag Archipelago*:

> Gradually it was disclosed to me that the line separating good and evil passes not through states, nor between classes, nor between political parties either

– but right through every human heart – and through all human hearts. And even within hearts overwhelmed by evil, one small bridgehead of good is retained. And even in the best of all hearts, there remains . . . an unuprooted small corner of evil.[24]

The crucial difference between the two writers is that Klíma's character goes on to avoid making judgements and is left lamely asking what justice is, whereas the Russian writer wastes no time in claiming the moral high ground. Klíma has a very traditional view of what the writer's function is. As he spells out in an essay of 1988 "The Literature of Secular faith":

> The writer who accepts an alien view of the world (especially one associated with power), who allows his language to be taken away from him, denies the precondition of all creation: the truthfulness he alone, in his conscience, can guarantee. It also calls into doubt the basic assumption of creation, which lies, after all, in the writer's attempt to enrich the sum total of human awareness and knowledge, of human experience, by adding to it his own search and his own discoveries.

> Spisovatel, který přijme cizí – dokonce mocenský – pohled na svět, který si dá vzít svoji vlastní řeč, se zříká předpokladu každé tvorby – pravdivosti, jejímž jediným garantem je on – jeho svědomí. Zpochybní i základní smysl tvorby, ten přece tkví v tom, že tvůrce se pokouší obohatit úhrn společného poznání a vědění, společné zkušenosti o vlastní hledání a o vlastní nálezy.[25]

In this Klíma is close to Solzhenitsyn and to his beloved Čapek. Such a stance can lead to some inconsequential, open-ended moralising. At the same time, as we have noted, Klíma can frequently mobilize ironies and absurdities to banish didacticism.

Waiting for the Dark, Waiting for the Light is a large canvas of public life and topical issues in Czechoslovakia before and after the demise of communism: the problems of pollution and industrial diseases are aired; the hero visits a factory where Semtex, the notorious explosive, most favoured by terrorist groups, is manufactured. The passage cited above is just one instance of the problems and dilemmas raised by the post-communist policy of "lustrace", that is, the "outing" of individuals who appeared to have co-operated with the old regime and especially with its security organs. There is a close-up portrait of Gustav Husák, the last communist president, which in some ways bears comparison with Solzhenitsyn's depiction of Stalin in *The First Circle*: there is the same remoteness, paranoia, arrogance and cynicism. The President reflects at some length on the death of his wife. (Husák's wife was killed in a helicopter crash in October 1977. This led to some unkind popular jokes and, many believed, his partial withdrawal from public view).

The recurrent themes in Klíma oeuvre are religiosity, love triangles, distress over encroaching materialism and environmental destruction, horror at the debasement of the language, particularly at the behest of ideologues. All of these are played out against a recurring motif, the image of rising water. The outlook is as bleak as is suggested by the same spectacle at the close of Čapek's *War with the Newts*.

Daniela Hodrová (1946–)
Michal Viewegh (1962–)
Jáchym Topol (1962–)
New voices?

The collapse of communism in Czechoslovakia was, as far as literature was concerned, accompanied by continuity and change. On a visit to Britain in the early 1990s Ivan Klíma stated that in the new freedom he simply continued to write as he had written before. The only difference was that now he was published legally at home. Yet it was to be expected that the new political era would also see a new wave in the arts and literature. Where was the "new" generation? The three writers discussed in this chapter have been chosen because they came on stream in the early 1990s, were regarded by many readers of serious fiction as worthy of note and because they are reasonable representative of wider literary trends. It should be noted too that they were operating in a cultural environment that was quickly being dictated by commercial considerations. This meant that low brow fiction, down market foreign imports and pornography were much in evidence. Publishing was privatised, with all the pluses and minuses that that involved. Moreover, many writers of the older generation who had been proscribed were now once again in the bookshops. All this meant that any serious new wave would have a lot of competition.

Daniela Hodrová's major early fictional writings were not published until after the Velvet Revolution, her *magnum opus* to date being the trilogy *Trýznivé město* (*City of Pain*) comprising *Podobojí* (*In Two Kinds*) – written 1977–84, published 1991), *Kukly* (*Masks* – written 1981–3, published 1991), and *Théta* (written 1987–90, published 1992).[1] The partial overlap in the composition of these works gives us an insight into her artistic method and outlook. In addition, it should be noted that her creative writing has gone hand in hand with the production of extensive

---

162

works on the theory and history of the novel. Hodrová's plots, if that is what they are, are labyrinthine and richly cross-referenced, and the overall aesthetic effect might best be grasped in terms of "poetry in prose". This is the strength and the weakness of her work, for she develops images and motifs which insist on a life of their own (as does Hrabal), but which might appear all too free-standing. Her interest in the theory of the novel has overly conditioned her practice of the genre. That said, the self-containment in her fiction is more than understandable, coming as it does from a heavily politicized cultural context.

Podobojí – which translates as "In Two Kinds" (as in the phrase "communion in two kinds", partaking of the flesh and blood of Christ) – signals the dualism that runs throughout the trilogy. Individual characters, events and objects repeatedly change their aspect and throw up ambiguities, but lend the work, both within each constituent volume and across all three, a coherence and cohesion. We are undoubtedly dealing with a Prague of the twentieth century, but the chronology of its history and of characters' lives is consciously disrupted. Past, present and possible futures mingle to produce a kaleidoscope. As Vladimír Macura says in his Afterword to the first novel: "In the logic of the novel the difference between past, present and future, between the old and the new, the living and the dead is annulled" (V logice románu se tak zcela ruší rozdíl mezi minulostí, přítomností a budoucností, mezi starým a novým, ale i mezi živým a mrtvým – p. 178). Macura also makes the point, readily in evidence to any Czech native, that the action takes place, with minor exceptions, in Prague, and more particularly, on the borders of the Vinohrady and Žižkov districts. This gives the novel an intimacy and very localized atmosphere. Certain street and other place names make up the fine stitching in the book: Kouřimská and Zásmucká Streets, Komenský Square, and especially the Olšanský Cemetery. We are repeatedly reminded that Hagibor was used as a torture chamber by the Germans. There are numerous and intriguing references to Bartolomějská Street (where the security police headquarters are located), but more often than not the allusion is to the persecution of the Huguenots and the massacre on St Bartholomew's Night (24 August 1572).

The "two kinds" of the title is spelled out on several occasions. It first occurs where the young seminarist Jan Paskal is in love with one Anna Houbová, from an institute for the deaf and dumb. The passage is worth quoting at length for the insights it affords into Hodrová's method:

> Anna Houbová smells of coffee and bread and Jan Paskal breathes in the smell and longs for Anna Houbová's body. And that's the real reason why Paskal will come to think that he will convert to the faith in two kinds, now it is still possible, yes, it's not too late yet. And he will get married to the deaf and dumb Anna Houbová in whose lap Vojtěch Paskal is already growing.

So what if they had dismissed him from the seminary of Saint Anna, when any day he could hold Anna Houbová in his arms, silent Anna, smelling of bread and coffee.

And then they travel to Hradec together, Anna is by now about to give birth, every movement causes her difficulties. And Jan Paskal, holding her up, has the mark from a cleric's collar round his neck, really quite faint, no one in the Lutheran institute will take any notice, no. How could Jan Paskal be a Catholic priest when his lineage was full of evangelical ancestors? And when it even maintains that there was even a certain Jean de Pascal in it, a Huguenot, who on St Bartholomew's Night fled from Paris. Huguenot blood runs in the Paskal veins. So what if now Anna Houbová had got it circulating in her?

And many years later, when there are long since only dust and ashes left of Anna Houbová, and Nora Paskalová is bringing up the adolescent Vojtěch, every time that Pastor Paskal performs the Sacrament of the Altar, he gives the believers the body and blood of the Lord (as he does, he never omits to wipe the chalice with the cloth), he recalls another Communion, he recalls the bread and coffee of Anna Houbová.

Anna Houbová voní kávou a chlebem a Jan Paskal tu vůni vdechuje a touží po těle Anny Houbové. A to je pravý důvod, proč si Paskal vymyslí, že přestoupí na víru podobojí, teď ještě je to možné, teď ještě ano. A ožení se s hluchoněmou Annou Houbovou, v jejímž klíně už roste Vojtěch Paskal. Co na tom, že ho vypověděli od Svaté Anny, když může den co den držet v náručí Annu Houbovou, mlčenlivou Annu, vonící chlebem a kávou?

A pak spolu cestují do Hradce, Anna je už před slehnutím, každý pohyb jí činí potíže. A Jan Paskal, který ji podpírá, má na krku rýžku po kolárku, docela nepatrnou, ale v Lutherově ústavu ne. Jakýpak by mohl být Jan Paskal katolický kněz, když je jeho rod plný evangelických předků? A dokonce tvrdí, že tu byl i jistý Jean de Pascal, hugenot, který o Bartolomějské noci prchl z Paříže. V Paskalových žilách koluje hugenotská krev. Co na tom, že ji rozproudila teprve Anna Houbová?

A ještě po letech, kdy z hluchoněmé Anny je dávno prach a popel a Nora Paskalová vychovává dorůstajícího Vojtěcha, pokaždé, když pastor Paskal udílí svátost oltářní, podává věřícím tělo a krev Páně (nikdy přitom neopomene utřít kalich ubrouskem), vzpomene na jiné přijímání, na chléb a kávu Anny Houbové. (pp. 18–19)

The phrase crops up a few chapters and years later when Jan Paskal's German neighbour from the fifth floor, Herr Hergesell, receives Holy Communion from him and engages him in explanations about the faith in two kinds (p. 33). Through a series of oblique, but unmistakable, references, it is clear that it is during the German occupation. Herr Hergesell is to be feared, Anna has been murdered in Auschwitz (has "flown out the chimney in Poland" (vyletěla v Polsku komínem – p. 33) – a phrase ubiquitously used, often with grim humour, in Holocaust literature, not least in the works of Arnošt Lustig). Theirs is a "very special friendship" (prazvláštní přátelství – p. 33). They eat mutton, and Hergesell puns on his guest's surname and the Lamb of God. Here, and throughout the work, he is likened to, or becomes, a wolf (p. 34).

Locations also come in two kinds: there are good and evil places, chosen places and places of loss (p. 55). Hagibor, we are told, is a wasteland named after a Jewish house standing on its edge, but the local children call it Hadibor or Haďák, which derives from the word for snakes (hadi), and snakes guard the entrances into the underworld. Life is in two kinds (p. 158), as when we are told that Nora Paskalová is pregnant and her baby may turn out to be a lamb of a wolf, or that Herr Hergesell (whom Jan Paskal has killed), now in the form of an eagle, may be killed again – by her. If characters, places and events come in two kinds, it is no surprise that reality and moral considerations are likewise subject to similar ambiguities. We are informed that Jan adopted the faith in two kinds merely because of the sins of the flesh and that he invented the story of his Huguenot ancestor, but "somewhat differently" (trochu jinak – p. 161). Probably the most salient occurrence of the phrase is the chapter "The People" (Národ). (Frequently, the omniscient narrator adopts first person narration and the persona of an object, place, concept or character in the book):

> I am the people. I have fallen into a new Egyptian captivity. I profess the faith in two kinds, I accept the body and blood of the Lord. I have my stable lads and my onion soup. I have my revolutions and my heroes. One of them went up in flames on a pyre that he'd made himself – between the National Museum and Main Grocery Store [. . .]
> I am the people, disillusioned with my revolutions and invasions, as well as with my burnt offerings. I am the people which converted. I am Jan Paskal, priest of the Czech Brethren, currently a trader in feathers and pelts of all kinds, a frequent guest in Bartholomew Street. I am Bartholomew Paskal – a cat's skin.

> Jsem národ. Upadl jsem v nové egyptské zajetí. Vyznávám víru podobojí, přijímám tělo i krev Páně. Mám své pacholky a svou cibulovou polévku. Mám své revoluce a své hrdiny. Jeden z nich vzplál na hranici, kterou si sám navršil – mezi Národním muzeem a Domem potravin [. . .]
> Jsem národ vystřízlivělý ze svých revolucí a ze svých okupací, i ze svých zápalných obětí. Jsem národ, který konvertoval. Jsem Jan Paskal, českobratrský kněz, nyní výkupce peří a kožek všeho druhu, častý host v Bartolomějské. Jsem Bartoloměj Paskal – jedna kůže kočičí. (p. 120)

The resonances here come thick and fast. There is of course the assonance of Jan Paskal and Jan Palach, and the clear indication of the latter's suicide (see p. 87). Paskal is now a typical social and professional outcast in post-1968 Prague, and as a political suspect will be frequently hauled in for questioning by the police. There is the closing opposition between a cat's skin and the name of one of the apostles, a meeting of the sublime and the banal. The passage continues with the narrator assuming the identity of nearly twenty of the characters in the book: Diviš Paskal, Alice Davidovičová, Pavel Santner etc.

From the foregoing brief examination of the title of the first volume in the trilogy is should be clear that any question of conventional plot hardly arises. Rather, we are dealing with a multitude of incidents and characters, objects and abstract notions which keep re-inventing themselves and/or popping up in different contexts. The perfectly realistic geographical settings, historical events and the many and oft-invoked everyday objects (Alice's muff, Jura's pin and his mouse-coloured coat, the smell of onions) are transformed into a supra-metaphor connoting a collective memory and identity.

Moreover, events, characters and objects enjoy equal status. Alice commits suicide by jumping from her window rather than face the transport (presumably to Terezín and then Auschwitz), yet her muff lives on, a whole chapter, narrated for the most part in the first person, devoted to it. The caretaker Šípek steals it, passes it on to the newsagent Tomáš Hamza, who sells it on to Mr Köck from Kouřimská Street, who gives it to his daughter. It is made of genuine Astrakhan and provides warmth and protection in a wolves' world' (pp. 74–9). Note the contrast with the cat's skin referred to above as well as the unremitting opposition of the wolf and the lamb. Alice's fatal descent stands in clear juxtaposition to the numerous images of ascension. We have noted Herr Hergesell as an eagle, but there are other birds and a butterfly, and characters often take off to soar over the city of Prague. Another recurrent image connected with notions of flying is that of the "melancholy angel" (melancholický anděl), the statue with only one wing in the cemetery, where Mr Turek hides from the Germans and Mr Klečka brings him food, while tame squirrels run about (e.g. pp. 26–7).

Hodrová's choice of proper nouns also bears traces of mystification. We have already alluded to Bartholomew and Paskal (there are references to Blaise Pascal too). The caretaker Šípek's son Jura, who is almost invariably in the pose of an eternal child (e.g. p. 27) is often called Šípková Jura, which makes for a neat pun, if one recalls that he pricks Alice with a pin. Šípek is a dog rose, šipka is a dart and Šípková Růženka is Sleeping Beauty, which of course continues the notions in the text of resurrection and immortality. The pair of minor characters Roháček (roháč – stag beetle) and Boháček (boháč – rich man) suggest a comic pantomine or fairy tale duo, although their names are common enough, and on occasion they acquire the French names Mortier and Sanglier (e.g. pp. 60, 63, 81). A pair of Russians Platon Lvovič Glinka and Kosťa Suchoručkov (p. 40) celebrate victory with Šípek.

As liberators, not only do they counteract the ominous Herr Hersegell, they also echo the slightly comic contrast in the Czech names Roháček and Boháček. Glinka claims descent from the composer and his full, high-sounding, name and patronymic are given, whereas his companion has to make do with a diminutive of his Christian name and a surname that sounds painfully mundane (literally, "dry hand"). At one point Jura mistakes Roháček for Kosťa (p. 84). Kosťa makes other appearances, notably when, the "plague peasants" (moroví pacholci) on their tanks ride down "Stalin Street" – "actually Vinohradská these days" (a deliberately contrived *faux pas* on the part of the narrator to illustrate that not much has changed since Stalin's day) (pp.107–8). This is an obvious reference to the 1968 invasion, and on this occasion Jura and Kosťa recognize each other, but Kosťa pretends not to. (One recalls that samizdat leaflets distributed illegally on the anniversary of the invasion were headed "The Day of Shame" – Den hanby.)

The concepts of a collective identity and a collective memory, which we signalled above, are also reflected in the various passages that deal with the transmigration of souls, the "bitter transience of worldly things" (hořká pomíjivost věcí – e.g. p. 79), the what-might-have-beens that, for example, Granny Davidovičová goes in for (p. 90). She muses that if there had been no war Alice and Pavel would have been married and had children, but then Alice would have felt just as tired and she would have grown old and ugly, so perhaps it would all have turned out the same.

Literary theorists will delight in decoding Hodrová's text in terms of Post-modernism and magical realism. Yet the question must remain as to whether the work's ludic qualities, to use the current jargon, which are so much to the fore, are only that. On the other hand, in a chapter entitled "Remains and Symbols" (Ostatky a symboly) the author makes out a compelling case for something more:

Souls cling to life through things or rather through the remains of things. These remains are as it were a sort of promise of rebirth, a guarantee of a new life. It is in fact that aura, that very special fluid, which surrounds things and animates them, and which the dead perceive much more sensitively than the living. Touching things is almost the same as touching life itself.

Look at Tomáš Hamza's hankerchief, which got torn. Look at the button which Pavel Santner found and threw and which Nora Paskalová keeps to this day, turning it over and remembering. Look at Granny Davidovičová's Sabbath cloth and her Astrakhan muff, which experienced several changes into a Persian lamb. For a thing in the world of the dead can for a time cease to be a thing and become an image, a symbol, a pure word. All these changes of things into images and images into things are, however, only temporary and things soon fall back into their earthly, mundane context. Of an image, of a form there will then remain only nostalgia, a sort of strange nostalgia.

Daniela Hodrová, Michal Viewegh, Jáchym Topol *New voices?*

Dušičky se upínají k životu skrze věci či spíš skrze ostatky věcí.Tyto ostatky jako by byly jakýmsi příslibem znovuzrození, zástavou nového života. Je tu přece ona aura, ono prazvláštní fluidum, které věci obklopuje a oživuje a které mrtví vnímají mnohem citlivěji než živí. Dotýkat se věcí je téměř jako dotýkat se samého života.

Hle, kapesník Tomáše Hamzy, jenž byl přetržen. Hle knoflík, který nalezl Pavel Santner a pohodil a který dosud drží Nora Paskalová, otáčí jím a vzpomíná.

Hle, šíbesový ubrus babičky Davidovičové a její perzianový štucl, jenž zažil několikerou proměnu v jehňátko perské. Nebot věc ve světě mrtvých může na čas přestat být věcí a stát se obrazem, symbolem, pouhým slovem. Všechny tyto proměny věcí v obrazy a obrazů ve věci jsou však jen dočasné a věci brzy upadají nazpět do svých přízemních, pouze věcných souvislostí. Z obrazu a tvaru zůstane pak jen stesk, takový divný stesk. (pp. 162–3)

The idea of turning objects into symbols and "pure words" must be the primary function of literature. Hodrová allows that the process might be difficult and that the immediate results may be temporary, but no doubt she would also admit that the cumulative result is an enduring culture. Naturally, culture will challenge everyday political, social and economic concerns. In a society where the purpose of literature and the arts was viewed by the establishment as being militantly utilitarian, the urge to the metaphorical in Hodrová's trilogy is perfectly understandable. After the 1968 invasion Czechoslovakia was subjected to processes of "normalization" and "consolidation". In the chapter headed "Consolidation in Olšany" the author comes close to stating her own agenda:

A consolidation process is going on. It's going on in the Spanish Hall [i.e. in Prague Castle – the seat of government] and also at Olšany.Vinohradská Street is being consolidated and so is Zásmucká Street. Such little streets that lead from nowhere and to nowhere are always under suspicion and there can be all sorts of danger hidden in them.

Probíhá konsolidační proces. Probíhá ve Španělském sále a probíhá také u Olšan. Konsoliduje se ulice Vinohradská a Zásmucká. Takové uličky, které vedou odnikud nikam, jsou vždycky podezřelé a může se v nich skrývat všelijaké nebezpečí. (p. 149)

The strength of Hodrová's prose, which seemingly "leads nowhere and to nowhere" (the Afterword notes the circular structure of the book and points to Joyce's *Ulysses* and *Finnegan's Wake* p. 179), resides in its vehement independence and self-containment. Its "danger" is well attested by the fact that it was not published until after communism collapsed.

The subsequent volumes in the trilogy do not differ in substance from the first. We have many of the same characters, objects and locations, but new ones appear. There are changes of emphasis and focus. In *Kukly* one

Sofie Syslová is now as prominent as was Alice in the first book. Characters become interchanged and there is a strong element of role-playing. Characters assume guises (the "masks" of the title) and there is a significant symbolism involving puppets. Sofie Syslová habitually turns into a swan in her bath. She is persistently referred to as the dressmaker in the Land of the Puppets (švadlenka v Říši loutek.- e.g p. 49). *Podobojí* has chapter headings, whereas *Kukly* is made up of a hundred and twenty-six "images" or "pictures" (*obrazy*).

Both books strive to link the Czech present with her past. *Podobojí* has a lengthy reference to the leading lights of the National Revival, Palacký, Kollár, Jungmann, Šafařík (pp. 96–8). *Kukly* persistently returns to the composer František Brixi (1732–71), who some two hundred years before was in the hospital where Sofie visits her mother regularly. The mother is scraping a hole in the wall to try and make contact with him. One of the main characters is Hynek Machovec, who is from Most and is "primarily a poet" (hlavně je básník – p. 26); he studied at the Philosophical Faculty in the "stormy sixties" (v bouřlivých šedesátých letech – p. 49) and was involved in the theatre then. Sofie thinks she sees him at one point, but then realizes it is none other than Karel Hynek Mácha, "the poet of *Máj*" (básník Máje – p. 95). We have some punning at this stage, since Machovec bought his coat, which somewhat resembles Mácha's, we are told, in the shop "Máj"(pp. 94–5). When she catches sight of him on another occasion, she wonders if he mistakes her for Mácha's bride-to-be, Lori Šomková (pp.166–7)!

Puppets, costumes, stage make-up, masks, games, roundabouts, swings, hot air balloons – given all these motifs in the text, it is not difficult to guess that Hodrová's father Zdeněk Hodr was a distinguished actor at the Vinohrady Theatre. Yet the overall effect is not to remind us of the author's family background, but rather to generate questions of human identity. Čapek uses his "substitute" human beings (robots, newts) to temper mankind's arrogance. Hodrová, less didactically, re-asserts Heisenberg's uncertainty principle, and asserts her freedom as an author to create and manipulate, puppet-like, her characters.

In the final volume *Théta*, Hodrová invites us into her workshop. The text is seamless, apart from frequent page-breaks. Chapter headings and "images" give way to first person *apologia*: on the first page we have the celebrated words from Dante's *Divine Comedy* which among other things provide the title for the whole trilogy (*città dolente*), and soon the author is offering workaday explanations:

> After *In Two Kinds* and *Masks* I intend to write a novel that might reflect itself. By intimation. If the whole thing were conceived as anti-illusion, who would enjoy reading it? We always need at least a shadow of an illusion of

reality. In certain places I will attempt to create a text that is, so to speak, autobiographical. Characters and objects from the preceding novels and from others' novels will appear. It seems that now that I have entered the city of pain, I must once again walk through those places which I have already written about, and meet the characters who have passed through them before me. In the end the Olšansky Comedy or the City of Pain (both these titles for the trilogy have occurred to me) will have perhaps a hundred characters.

Po Podobojí a Kuklách mám v úmyslu napsat román, který by reflektoval sám sebe. V náznaku. Kdyby byl celý pojat antiiluzívně, kdo by jej se zalíbením četl? Vždycky potřebujeme alespoň stín iluze skutečnosti. Na některých místech se pokusím o text takřka autobiografický. Objeví se tu postavy i předměty z předchozích románů, také z cizích románů. Vypadá to tak, že když jsem vstoupila do trýznivého města, musím znovu procházet místy, o nichž jsem už psala, a potkávat se tam s postavami, které jimi prošly přede mnou. Na konci bude mít Olšanská komedie nebo Trýznivé město (ty dva názvy pro trilogii mě napadají) možná stovku postav. (p. 9)

The book might best be read as a companion volume to the other two. The hero, for want of a better word in Hodrová, Eliška Beránková, is the author's alter ego. There is also pan Chaun, a puppet maker. There are numerous references to her father and his circle, to his death in 1984 (p. 16). Milada Součková, best known to English-speaking scholars of Czech literature for her work on the Czech Romantic poets and volumes on Czech literature from 1938 through into the Communist era, is discussed frequently, and Milada Horáková, the politician hanged for high treason in 1950 also looms large. Allusions to world literature abound, not just to Dante, but to Homer (p. 180), Proust (p. 40), T. S. Eliot, notably *The Wasteland* (pp. 152–3), Umberto Eco (p. 154) and many more.

The puzzling title of the work receives its exegesis only some three quarters of the way through the text. Theta is the Greek letter θ which, we are informed, was used by medieval scribes as a shorthand for "dead" (thanatos) and written against the names of monks who had passed away (p.154). "Eliška Beránková, she into whom I have disguised myself, and in whom I await with anxiety my last transformation, has long since known how to write the letter θ" (Eliška Beránková, ta do níž jsem se zakuklila a v níž očekávám s úzkostí svou poslední proměnu, umí už dávno psát písmeno θ – p. 155). Elsewhere she writes: "I am writing a novel so that I do not change – into a bird, into a puppet, into someone's phantasmagoria. The City of Pain has become the city of changes (Píšu román, abych se neproměnila – v ptáka, v loutku, v něčí fantasmagorii. Trýznivé město se stalo městem proměn – p. 137). At moments like this Hodrová seems to be rejecting what some critics might see as the purely ludic qualities of her fiction. Discoursing on the uncertainty of her position in her own text she writes:

Daniela Hodrová, Michal Viewegh, Jáchym Topol *New voices?*

I just want to say that I do not choose this position as a soft option. Or even because it is in fashion, (anyway anti-illusive poetics has already gone out of fashion, according to the post-modernist theorist John Barth, and the novel is returning to its illusivity, even though it is not to the illusivity of the realistic novel of the nineteenth century).

Chci tím prostě říci, že si tuto pozici nevolím pro snadnost, či dokonce pro její módnost (ostatně antiiluzívní poetika už vyšla z módy, román se podle Johna Bartha, teoretika postmodernismu, vrací ke své iluzívnosti, i když už to není iluzívnost realistického románu 19. století). (p. 28)

In the light of these remarks, are we not, in Hodrová, dealing with the time-honoured function of any serious writer simply to cheat death?

One of the first "new" voices to be heard on the literary scene after the collapse of communism was that of **Michal Viewegh.** His bitter-sweet novel *Splendid Dog Days* (*Báječná léta pod psa*) tells the story of a not untypical middle class family of intellectuals surviving the Czech version of what Gorbachev had dubbed the period of stagnation, that is, in the case of the Czechs, from late 1968 through to 1989. The bulk of the narrative is presented as the creative work of Kvido, the elder son, but is punctuated with brief exchanges between him and his editor, who is operating under the constraints of the communist regime. The work closes with the Velvet Revolution and the author at last able to submit his manuscript for publication. Eschewing the traditional disclaimer that his characters are invented and bear no resemblance to real people, Viewegh, in his Foreword, informs us that it is difficult to distinguish the fiction from the reality in his work, noting that many readers often insist that fictional characters are in fact real, while many authors maintain the opposite. This playful tone is sustained throughout.

There is something of Sue Townsend's Adrian Mole cycle of novels in the way that this ordinary and somewhat extended family way battles with work, domestic upheaval, marital infidelity, growing children and exasperating grandparents and in the way that all these universal tribulations are compounded by specific wider political and social developments. Adrian Mole insists he is an intellectual – even if on occasion he admits that he is not a very bright one. Kvido's precocity knows no such boundaries. He comes to tell his younger brother Paco that nine months ("two hundred and seventy days, all identical" – dvě stě sedmdesát naprosto stejných dní) of pregnancy for an intellectual embryo amounts to "Terrible boredom [. . .] without a decent book to read" [. . .]. The last three months I was just praying that mother would finally break one of those senseless taboos and take me for a ride on a motorbike along some country unmade-up road or would send a couple of drags of tobacco smoke my way, if she wasn't going to put down a glass of white vermouth" (strašlivá nuda [. . .] bez jediné slušné knihy [. . .]. Poslední tři měsíce jsem se už jenom modlil, aby matka konečně porušila některé z těch nesmyslných tabu a svezla mne na motorce po neudržované polní cestě nebo mi poslala dva tři pořádné šluky, když už ne rovnou dvě decky bílého vermutu).[2]

Through Kvido's precocity we are treated to a witty and wonderfully perceived social comedy, occasionally tinged with darkness, which touches on cultural considerations, psychological pressures and recent history.

One of mother's former roles was that of Hettie in Wesker's *The Kitchen* (p. 10). The mention of this play plus some of the other references to more popular culture (films like *Jaws* and *Planet of the Apes* p. 162 and p. 187) offer a fair indication of what the cultural diet was like. Escapism and/or Leftish-leaning classics were available, especially if the two genres combined in a kind of anti-American-militarism, as is the case with the second film quoted above. *Waiting for Godot* – in the novel being staged in 1962 – would present more ideological difficulties to a communist regime, but it could always be passed off as being the result of Western, capitalism-induced angst. Foreign culture was though not always free of control: when one of Kvido's grandfathers dies, the Shakespeare sonnet (no. 66) he has wished to be recited at his funeral is "not on the list of permitted quotations" (na seznamu povolených citátů – p. 149) and Mother concludes angrily that " a person cannot even die freely" (ani umřít nemůže člověk svobodně – p. 150). The real restraints on culture in Czechoslovakia were to be found in the domestic product. Kvido is told by his editor that he cannot be born in his novel during *Waiting for Godot* because that is an existentialist play. "That idiot would probably want me to be born during *The Bartered Bride*" (Ten idiot by snad chtěl, abych se narodil na Prodaný nevěstě – p. 199), Kvido complains to his wife.

The main cultural constraint in the novel, however, is the family's – particularly Mother's – lingering association with the writer Pavel Kohout. The editor wishes to excise all references in Kvido's book to this firebrand communist of the post-war years, who then became an outspoken supporter of the Prague Spring and then a leading signatory of Charter 77, which eventually led to his having to emigrate to Austria. (Incidentally, there are some delightfully ironic allusions to Kohout in Havel's plays *Audience* and *Private View*; in the latter, for example, the bourgeois-in-all-but-name couple, doing very nicely under the Moscow-backed post-1968 communist regime tell the tongue-tied banned writer that he shouldn't associate with such "communists" as Kohout.) Kohout's reappearance in the life of the family after a two-year break precipitates Father's paranoia. He whispers to himself, smashes glasses, hides books and photographs. He increasingly devotes himself to DIY in his workshop, where he manufactures himself a coffin and periodically lies in it. He becomes convinced they are under surveillance from the KGB (p. 155) – this was the old Soviet secret service (currently the FSB), and presumably more to be feared than the homespun Czech equivalent, the Stb (Státní bezpečnost).

These darker considerations are neatly enmeshed with routine family concerns, which results in some hilarious family altercations. Father argues that Mother could have easily avoided bumping into Kohout in the supermarket by the frozen foods. This leads to him saying that he prefers old meat to fresh vegetables; and this leads to his wife countering that the exception would be the young Yugoslav female colleague he got involved with (S výjimkou jugoslávského leča; "lečo" is literally a spicy vegetable dish – p. 127).

Apart from the briefest of references to Kohout's Stalinist past, we have no firsthand evidence of what he has written or what he stands for. His deep involvement in Charter 77 is all that counts in the eyes of the authorities and Kvido's family is deemed guilty by association. The moral dilemmas and the risks attached are ubiquitous. "Participate in further and successful normalization (everybody)" (Podílet se i nadále na úspěšné normalizaci (všichni) – p. 107) writes Mother on the family memory Board, which father has pinned on the wall, and this leads to one of the grimmest rows:

"I have a clean sheet. I've never done a single nasty thing in my life!"

Kvido's mother frowned unhappily. Now she regretted that she had given in to a momentary impulse and written those words; it was an expression of her momentary depression at life in this country, which did not want to take any discussion any further – she well knew the feelings that awaited a person at the end of such debates. It was just that the supposed certainty of Kvido's Father had irritated her too much.

"And you've never in your life stopped anything. Never even tried." She said.

"I don't know about anything like that."

"So such things don't even go on," said Kvido's Mother slowly. "As if you don't know about them. Everything's all right. Nothing's happening to anybody. They didn't chuck Dad out of work. Lawyers aren't working as gardeners. Hospital consultants aren't working as cinema usherettes. History is progressing normally. Farmers are bringing in the harvest as normal, the wheels in the factories are turning and our promising engineers are blithely flying across the so-called iron curtain in order to assure for us a bright future by securing excellent contracts."

"Give me a break! I meant simply that I don't know of anything that I could or could not have prevented. And as to whether the history of this country has stopped or not, I'll leave that to your Prague intellectuals."

"Mám čistej stůl. Nikdy v životě jsem neudělal jednu jedinou levárnu!"

Kvidova matka se nešťastně zamračila. Litovala už, že podlehla chvilkovému popudu ona slova napsat; byl to výraz její momentální deprese

z života v této zemi, kterou nechtěla nějakou delší rozpravou prohlubovat –
znala už dobře pocity, které na člověka čekají na konci takových debat.
Jenomže domnělá jistota Kvidova otce ji příliš dráždila.
   "A nikdy v životě žádný nezabránil. Ani se o to nepokusil," řekla.
   "O žádný takový nevím!"
   "Takže se vlastně ani nedějou," řekla zvolna Kvidova matka. "Když o nich
nevíš. Všechno je v pořádku. Nikomu se nic neděje. Tátu nevyhodili.
Právníci nedělaj zahradníky. Primářky nedělaj uvaděčky v kinech. Dějiny
normálně pokračujou. Zemědělci normálně sklízejí úrodu, kola v továrnách
se točí a přes takzvanou železnou oponu klidně létají naši perspektivní
inženýři, aby nám prostřednictvím skvělých kontraktů zajistili skvělou
budoucnost."
   "Neštvi mě! Myslel jsem přirozeně, že nevím o ničem, čemu bych mohl
zabránit a nezabránil. A pokud jde o úvahy na téma, zda se naše dějiny
zastavily, nebo ne, přenechávám je tvým pražským intelektuálům." (p. 108)

In these exchanges there are a number of allusions to specific characters
in the novel. One of them, the psychiatrist whom Mother engages to treat
father, is working as a stoker in a cinema (p. 163). When he states that
Father needs a successful counter-Revolution to get cured, he is probably
right. Which is not to say that personal and social problems will disappear.
Splendid Dog Days as a title, if nothing else, has a universality about it.
When the Velvet Revolution arrives, Kvido's younger brother Paco, by
now a university student, quickly gets disillusioned, goes to the USA,
becomes an anarchist and then ends up with a well-paid job in commerce.
Father lands a job in the foreign trade ministry. But then he falls victim to
the processes of "lustrace" (see p. 160). His erstwhile boss Šperk attempts
suicide and then opens a restaurant. Mirjana, Father's Yugoslav old flame,
flees Serbian nationalists and Mother offers her political asylum.
   These absurdities and anomalies are hardly any different from many
with which the novel opens. Kvido's grandfather Josef is deeply sceptical
towards all things communist (p. 10), and really wanted to be a hotelier,
yet is in fact a miner. When official high-ranking delegations visit, he is kept
out of the way and is nicknamed Cinderella by his work mates (p. 14).
Granny Líba, on the mother's side, is a vegetarian and loves travelling, not
least in Russia. At the close of the novel she is caught stealing spoons from
a hotel in Leningrad (now Petersburg). Kvido's career at school entails
some DIY sex education with Jaruška, who later becomes his wife – it starts
with him trading in the dessert from his school lunch for a look at her geni-
tals. He lands the family in political hot water by breaking the photograph
of President Svoboda at school. Later his brother Paco manages the same
feat with the picture of President Husák.
   Father's being is as much taken up with his attempts to learn to drive and
to become a professional footballer. His professional life is perhaps at its

zenith when he has a business trip to England, and is perhaps at its nadir when he becomes the doorman at the block where his wife works. Kvido abandons his studies and assumes this job too, in order to have more time to write.

It is in this capacity that we see him in a particularly telling scene. Climbing on to the roof of the block during his evening shift, he can see his house, the house of Šperk, the functionary, and Pavel Kohout's villa (pp. 178–9). Given the practical joke that he subsequently plays, one is tempted to see not a little symbolism. As night watchman, one of his tasks is to illuminate the slogan on the roof: SLÁVA KOMUNISMU (GLORY TO COMMUNISM). He takes to standing in front of the letter I and thus "winking" to his mother and wife, who know he is up there. One night he finds some tarpaulin and blanks out the last five letters, sending out the message SLÁVA KOMU (GLORY TO WHOM). The reader might wonder whether the glory should go to the party boss, the persecuted dissident or the family.

Ultimately, perhaps no one in this novel earns any glory. The hero's novel gets censured as much by his mother as it did by the communist editor, concerned as she is, among other things, that he has told all their friends about the state of their toilet – he should have cleaned, it rather than just writing about (pp. 201–2). The precocious hero, whether as boy or man, is prey to his parents, grandparents and editor, just as his country was prey to an insidious and corrupting tyranny.

Viewegh's other novels possess the same social comedy as *Splendid Dog Days*, but they lack the same degree of incision and irony. Perhaps only the sudden demise of communism and the two decades that led up to it could provide the necessary spark for real pithy social and psychological comment. *Bringing Up Girls in Bohemia* (*Výchova dívek v Čechách*) has a familiar plot line: utterly disaffected teenage girl, Beáta, refusing even to talk to, let alone co-operate with, parents and teachers; gifted young male teacher and struggling young novelist is engaged for a scandalously high remuneration by wealthy, mafia-connected, father to sort her out; sexual chemistry between mentor and charge leading to domestic friction in hero's life; at least there is no happy ending this time – the girl eventually commits suicide. To a degree the story might be seen as a darker and more detailed variation on Paco's post-1989 experience. Certainly it was the case that particularly among the younger generation the euphoria of the Velvet Revolution quickly gave way to disillusion as economic problems began to bite and routine re-established itself over heroism.

Opinions About A Murder (*Názory na vraždu*) was Viewegh's first book to be published before the success of *Splendid Dog Days*. Something of a comedy thriller/Whodunnit, it has understandably been overshadowed by subsequent work. *Participants in an Excursion* (*Účastníci zájezdu*) is a lengthy, light read concerning a crowd of tourists and is reminiscent of David Lodge's *Paradise News*. The work contains a fair number of "gags", such as at the start of the book when the tourist coach deliberately fails to pick up a waiting contingent of holiday makers, because the author has decided he already has enough characters for his novel. There are frequent attacks by one of the protagonists, the writer Max, on literary critics. *Note-takers of Paternal Love* (*Zapisovatelé otcovský lásky*) gives a light airing to the generational problem, makes some free use of current slang and displays a degree of sexual uninhibitedness which seems to be *de rigueur* in much contemporary culture everywhere.

Of more interest is the collection of pastiches *Ideas of a Kind-hearted Reader* (*Nápady laskavého čtenáře*). Viewegh is fond of peppering some of his other works with literary allusions and quotations, usually in a playful attempt to highlight the gap between the ethereal and the everyday. In *Bringing Up Girls in Bohemia* the author offers us writers from Komenský to Kundera, Gertrude Stein to Věra Linhartová, in depicting his hero's endeavours to battle with the unmanageable Beáta. *Ideas of a Kind-hearted Reader* more readily leads us to ponder the various functions of parody. Obviously, there is the satirical purpose, but the most enduring parodies spring from affection rather than from opposition. Viewegh's first three chapters, guying Hrabal, Kundera and Škvorecký respectively, denote the simple fact that all three writers have more than risen above the varying degrees of cloud-cover under which they have had to operate in their country of birth and the parody testifies to their strength and stature. "Kruciprdel" (Damnarse?) (p. 15) is a nice skit on Hrabal's "Kurva fix" (see p. 57). The Kundera piece has a sentence almost identical to the opening of *The Joke* and has a leather armchair coming from Brezhnev via Aragon to Kundera – a clear reference to Clementis's hat, which ends up on Gottwald's head in all the official photographs while its real owner is executed and air-brushed from history in *The Book of Laughter and Forgetting*; or it could equally refer to the bowler hat motif in *The Unbearable Lightness of Being*. Viewegh's Kundera spends most of his time correcting his translator's mistakes . . .

The English-speaking student of Czech will delight in the Škvorecký send-up, though one dreads to think what such dialogues as the following will do to his/her grasp of the language:

> "Ty lajkuješ swimování?" zeptala se s úsměvem.
> "Nemám plavky," řekl jsem opatrně. "I've no trunks."
> [. . .]
> "Ty nenýduješ tranky," rekla. "Džojnuj se k nám na klouzačku.
> [. . .]
> " Máš krásnou pinkovou skin," rekla obdivně a rozepnula mi příklopec.

"Jááúúúú!" zařval jsem.
"Oh, shit! zvolala. "Lúkněte na toho ilavýho bérdíka!" (p. 27)

Fuks, Páral and other Czech writers come in for some teasing for their artistic methods, as do Tigrid and Havel for their political and moral analyses. Viewegh also targets a good number of foreigners (e.g. Hemingway, Moravia, Kazantzakis, Henry Miller).

All these parodies require a lot of knowledge of their originals to be fully appreciated and that is their weakness. The most successful parodies will take on an independent life. In this connection we should note in particular the pastiche of Vítězslav Rzounek's critical writings. Here, Viewegh is at his most politically scathing, but needs most exegesis for those not in the know. Rzounek made his career in the post-1968 era as Professor of Czech literature at Charles University, and was fairly notorious for his utterly communist orthodox views, to which all students and colleagues were expected to comply. Confidential "readers' reports", which publishers the world over frequently rely on, were, in the case of the communist bloc, designed to check out ideological worthiness at least as much as anything else. Viewegh's Rzounek produces a positive recommendation for the manuscript of a cookery book and a negative report for one on hair care, all based on ideological considerations.

One novel which attracted enormous interest in the early 1990s was **Jáchym Topol**'s *Sister* (*Sestra*), published in English under the title *City Sister Silver*, the headings of its three parts (*Město Sestra Stříbro*). Such are the complexities of this work that it makes more sense to discuss the author's second novel *Angel* (*Anděl*), a shorter and simpler work, first.

> In the old days, petitions used to circulate here under the tables, now drugs had taken their place. Now no one here thought about society as a monster, it was more a question of coping with the monster in yourself. Sometimes coping with its roaring. At home there were only walls waiting for you, and maybe also the person you're living with. Or at any rate the horror on the television. In the morning you can wake up here or somewhere else, on your own or with someone else. It will be only you again. And you can put off that moment here. This was one of the places where that was possible.
>
> Once upon a time the underground small fry used to practise here, today youth took its own measurements for its coffin. The people from the former underground, who had now carved out a niche for themselves in politics or somewhere writing their culture columns in magazines, came here just on an occasional excursion, to remember the good old days. Across the formica tabletops, to those who had stayed here, it was more obvious how much they had come up in the world.
>
> Former allies from psychiatric units, from cops shops and demonstrations all tried out their new way of talking, from the drug pusher to the senior civil

servant. For everyone of them the world had fallen apart, everyone of them had to recreate it and in a different place. The underground with its classical stage sets had returned to one of its oldest sources; it had become the under-world.

Dřív tu pod stoly kolovaly petice, nahradily je drogy. Nikdo tu neuvažoval o společnosti jako o bestii, šlo o to, vydržet s bestií v sobě. Někdy s řevem. Doma tě čekají jen stěny a možná na tebe ještě čeká ten, s kým žiješ. Každopádně horor v televizi. Ráno se můžeš vzbudit tady nebo jinde, sám nebo s někým. Budeš to zas jen ty. A tu chvíli je možný oddálit. Tohle je jedno z míst, kde to jde.

Kdysi tu cvičil undergroundový potěr, dnes si mládež brala míru na máry sama. Ti z bývalého undergroundu, co se chytili v politice nebo někde po kulturních rubrikách, sem chodili jen na výlety, zavzpomínat. Nad umarkatem a s těmi, kteří tu zůstali, jim bylo zřejmější, jak vysoko postoupili.

Bývali spojenci z psychiatrií, fízláren a demonstrací tu na sebe zkoušeli mluvit každý svou novořečí, prodavač drog s ministerským úředníkem. Každému z nich se rozpadl svět, každý z nich si ho musel vytvořit znova a jinde. A underground se ve svých klasických kulisách vrátil k jednomu ze svých nejstarších ohnisek; stal se podsvětím.[3]

This extract from *Angel*, which appeared in 1995, gives a fair indication of the disorientating and disturbing world Topol establishes in his fiction. Here we are in Prague in the not too distant future from the time when the novel was written and published. One scene takes place in Paris in 1997 (p. 46), and there is mention of a supposedly Gulf War veteran, aged sixteen, (p. 79), which puts the action post-1992, as well as of a branch of MacDonalds (p. 58) where a piece of graffiti on the synagogue opposite informs us that someone was there in 1942 and 1997; and there is mention of a Lenin poster which has been defaced with swastika eyes and horns on its head (p. 23).

Random characters in the first few chapters have unlikely (nick?)names (Elefanta, Black Delilah [Černá Dalije], Dead Monkey [Mrtvá Opice], Guinea Pig [Morče]) and the plot is deliberately fragmented. But we are by no means in the kind of dream world that Hodrová creates. The main protagonists – Jatek, his girl Ljuba, their friends Pernica, Věra and Vladimír, the businessman Machata, the dumb girl Naďa, whom Machata and his wife abuse – are grimly offered in good faith. The main events are perfectly deducible. The action frequently centres around the bars and gambling dens in Smíchov at a location by the metro station called Angel Exit (formerly Moskevská). Jatek and his circle are drug users and are engaged in perfecting a special concoction. At one time Jatek worked in a foundry, where his work mates teased him for his reading ("only gays read books" – "knížky čtou jen teplouši" – p. 22) and at his squeamishness when they toss a cat in the furnace. He is even robbed on one occasion. He spends time in a psychiatric hospital; Ljuba, pregnant, probably by him – but it could be Pernica's – loses the child, whose blood is to be used as an essential ingredient in the drug preparation.

In a finale worthy of *Hamlet*, Jatek finds Naďa apparently strangled in the bath by Machata's wife, Pernica swallows all of the drug preparation and Machata sets fire to the building, presumably destroying himself in the process. Jatek flees, but not before lobbing more petrol canisters into the conflagration and pulling down the steel shutters, so that those still alive cannot escape. He returns to the crossroads at Angel Exit, and the novel closes with images that recall some of its opening and earlier scenes: the reddening morning sky and the blood that forever seems to fill Jatek's vision. "It was a new time, and it was like the beginning of everything and it was the first day" (Byla to nová doba a bylo to jako na počátku všeho a byl to nový den – p. 135).

One of those trapped by Jatek in the fire is Lurija, a member of an extreme religious sect, who together with a female companion Jerija clandestinely sets up distorted religious statues all over town.

> In the society of Those True to The Living Advent all the women were called Jerija. All the men were called Lurija. The Lord made no other distinctions within His flock. For the time being they lived in darkness, because the world was in the hands of Satan. Only now and then were they able with a slight gesture to remind other people, eaters of animals, miserable and perverted creatures, chasing after money and orgasms, that for them time was running out.

> Ve společnosti Věrných Živému Příchodu se Jerija jmenovaly všechny ženy. Lurija se jmenovali zas muži. Jinak Pán své stádo přece nerozdělil. Zatím žili v temnotách, protože svět byl v moci Satana. Jen občas mohli skrovným gestem připomenout ostatním lidem, pojídačům zvířat, mrzkým a zvráceným stvořením, ženoucím se za penězi a orgasmem, že čas se naplňuje. (p. 87)

It would be easy to read Topol's text as merely a sensationalized record of what was happening in Czech society in the 1990s – free enterprise, drugs, crime, extreme alternative religions. Yet the graphic shock-horror tactics he employs suggest an affinity with "punk" culture as well as *fin de siècle* preoccupations in general. A number of recent English-language novels bear comparison, perhaps some of Ian McEwan's works at their darkest, e.g. *The Child in Time* (1989) and *Black Dogs* (1992). Irvine Welsh's *Trainspotting* was published in 1993, just two years before *Angel*. Beyond its immediate subject matter of drug abuse, it stands as a celebration of a defiant counter-culture. Welsh's heroes, like Topol's, have grimly outlandish nicknames: Rent Boy, Sick Boy, Spud, Beggar, while his racy, unremittingly foul-mouthed narrator, operating in a Scottish vernacular, generates a mixture of horror and comedy.[4]

The linguistic register of *Trainspotting* finds something of a counter-point in Topol's major novel *Sister*, first published in 1994. Moreover, the shifts between dream and reality, the plethora of characters, some assuming various guises, many still remaining mysteries, the settings of criminality, drugs and subcultures, all these elements led the critic Sergej Machonin for one to draw comparisons with Jean Genet and Jack Kerouac. The novel won the Egon Hostovský Prize. The author trimmed the text by some thirty pages for a second edition, which appeared in 1996, and, in close collaboration with Topol, further cuts were made for the English transla-tion.[5]

City Sister Silver can be read as an extended, bewildering and at times stomach-turning metaphor for all the confusion, moral and otherwise, that the closing decade of the twentieth century has come to mean. It is poetry in prose, in the manner of, but not as lyrical as, Hrabal and Hodrová; indeed on a few occasions it breaks into free verse. But beneath all this there is a conventional, even deliberately banal, plot. The hero-narrator Potok is an actor and artist by profession, who has spent time in prison and psychi-atric hospitals under the communists. He and his circle of acquaintances witness the flood of East Germans in Prague escaping into the West German Embassy, abandoning their possessions and even there Trabant cars, that cheap and not too cheerful symbol of Communist mediocrity. These scenes were watched on television throughout the world in 1989, and they presaged the tearing down of the Berlin Wall and the creation of a new Europe. Dramatic they may have been, but perfectly real. However, in Topol nothing is "real" for long.

Potok and his friends are "People of the Secret"(p. 13) (lidi Tajemství – p. 7) as the first words of the novel inform us. They are also described as the Organization, and in the new era of economic and political freedom, they engage in shady deals to get rich, bribing civils servants to acquire properties which they rent out to Asians, retailing cheap goods from the Far East, dealing in pornography. Yet there are limits to their criminality: "no weapons or drugs, no porno with fleas" [i.e. prostitution] (p. 64) (žádný zbraně, drogy, žádný porno s blechama – p. 52). A constant refrain is "the metal flowed" (kov tek), i.e. the money rolled in. However, Potok is eventually induced by Hadraba and Jícha, who have a "private persecu-tion agency" (p. 181) (soukromá stihací agentura – p. 164) called "Dostoevsky", to help them defeat rival mobs ("Zones"). Later still, he is recruited by a government agency to track down one General Vang. "Vang and his men are kidnapping communists, Vietnamese secret police, embassy staff. They dope em up, interrogate em, and then they kill em" (p. 267) (Vang a ti jeho unášej komunisty, členy vietnamský tajný policie a

ambasádníky. Vyslýchaj je pod drogama a pak je zabijou – pp. 247–8). It is
not clear from the text why a Czech government that has just thrown off
the yoke of communism should want to prevent Vang, and the whole
episode is simply part of the confusion factor operating throughout the
book. The hero eventually flees this assignment, finds himself in various
remote retreats – including staying with a rustic family from a previous era,
among tramps on a rubbish dump, being cared for in a convent.

All these events are in fact secondary to Potok's hunt for his great love.
At the start of the novel she is called the Little White She-Dog (p. 16) (Malá
Bílá Psice – p. 8); her real name appears to be Barbara Zavorová (English
text, p. 153; Czech text, p. 139); most commonly she is referred to as Černá
(the translator leaves this name in the original, but footnotes the literal
meaning, black). At the outset she promises Potok a sister, and she and the
sister become one and the same or interchangeable. She is a singer in a night
club and on occasion a prostitute. When with the hero, she is an eager lover
and a stout travelling companion. In the final pages of the novel they are
united, but this cliché, like so many others in the book (racketeers, information on the girl's whereabouts in exchange for co-operation on nefarious
activities) is subverted: Potok copulates simultaneously with Černá and
another girl and the doorbell interfers with their love-making. The ideal
represented by the notion of his sister-lover fixation (platonic intimacy and
carnality) remains unattainable.

The narrative slides between dream and waking in such a way as to imply
that there are no certainties in the world. In a sequence somewhat reminiscent of an episode in Dostoevsky's *The Idiot*, three of the main
characters, Bohler, David and Potok each tell of a dream in which they
appear most evil. Potok's lengthy account of his dreamed trip to Auschwitz
and his being taken on a conducted tour by Josef Novák, a talking skeleton,
is another instance of a cliché subverted. Striding over acres of human
bones and skulls, the gruesome tour guide informs the hero of how
Mengele escaped to Argentina, cured a "negro" (sic) (English text, p. 118;
Czech text, p. 105) of cancer and eventually went to Heaven. Even in the
waking scenes, there is more emphasis on what seems than what is. The
hero has various guises – at one point there is even talk of him having
regular monthly men's cycles (pravidelný chlapský měsíční kruhy – p. 69)
and being pregnant. Towards the close of the novel he appears in a series
of film advertisements, at one stage as Popeye the Sailor. Elsewhere, the
various legends, Biblical and otherwise, that are recounted become a
curious amalgam of continents and epochs, as Zulus and Bedouins,
Spartacus and Merlin are juxtaposed, with the computer playing its part.

The problems of rendering the text in English are formidable, since the
real strength of the work resides in the special linguistic register that Topol
has created. The vernacular and obscenities in the manner of *Trainspotting*

were mentioned above, but to these Topol brings neologisms and more or less recognizable distortions. There is a mention of a "Yanis Yoplin" record (p. 77) (Jenis Jo, p. 67, in the original). Prague is most frequently referred to as The Pearl (Perla), while Berlun is obviously post-1989 Berlin. "The Monster" of the English translation is Zrůda in the original, with connotations of "rudý" (red), so might it allude specifically to The Reds (Red Army, Red Menace)? The Sewer(Period) ("Kanál" in the original) is a felicitous and accurate rendition, but loses the alliteration with "Communism" to which it clearly refers. Only those with a knowledge of Slavonic languages will get the correct resonance of "Bog" (the Russian for God), as the Almighty is referred to in both the original and the translation. Using the Russian rather than the Czech word adds a faintly alien, sinister touch. Čehůni for Czechs (Bohos, i.e. Bohemians, in the translation) has a pejorative ring, as does the Russian "droog" ("friend"). Here, incidentally is a parallel with Anthony Burgess's novel *A Clockwork Orange*, which similarly utilizes a futuristic slang based on Russian. One notes that there is a tangential reference to this novel in the phrase "Mechanický pomidor" (p. 125, rather freely rendered as "Clockwork pomegranate" in the translation – p. 139). The linguistic inventiveness bears out the contention that "Czech had exploded along with time" (p. 41) (s časem tehdy vybouchla i čeština – p. 31).

It would scarcely be an exaggeration to say that the multitude of arresting and sometimes harrowing images, the linguistic virtuosity and the wide range of literary and cultural references add up to a work that effectively eclipses the rebelliousness of the 1960s in the West, the Punk era and the disorientation of the newly emerging Europe. There are occasional cultural landmarks (one, for instance, involves the *Bambino di Praga*, mentioned when Potok is being cared for in the convent (English text, p. 460; Czech text, p. 417) and which figures in several of the works discussed earlier in this book. Yet in *City Sister Silver* other motifs are more prominent, while being more temporary and mystifying: the peculiar well that seems to spirit away cats, dogs and even humans; the rubbish dump, where Potok dwells with the tramps for a time and is the scene of gruesome murders; the Rock out of town where he and his associates occasionally gather; the silver Black Madonna that the hero wears.

It could well be that Topol, more than any of his contemporaries, is turning Czech literature in a new direction and that he is fulfilling the promise he makes:

> On the body of a changed world, in the ruins of the former time, I'll open the first glorious chapter of Kanak literature! I'll write the book in raw post-Babylonian, the way I heard it on my wanderings through the past, present and future. (p. 243)

> Na těle měněného světa, na troskách bejvalýho času bych započal slavnou

kapitolu kanackýho písemnictví! [. . .]. Napíšu tu knihu surovou post-babylónštinou, tak jak jsem ji pochytil na svejch toulkách v minulosti, přítomnosti i budoucnosti. (p. 226)

Notes

Preface

1   S. Baranczak, *Breathing Under Water and Other East European Essays*, Cambridge, Massachusetts and London: Harvard University Press, 1990, p. 236.

Introduction

1   R. Wellek, *Essays on Czech Literature*, The Hague: Mouton, 1963, p. 30.
2   J. Cuddon, *A Dictionary of Literary Terms*, revised by Claire Preston, Oxford: Blackwell, 1998, p. 87.
3   H. Bergson, "Laughter" in *Comedy* (with "An Essay on Comedy" by George Meredith), New York: Doubleday Anchor Books, 1956, pp. 62–3. Translator unnamed.

Jaroslav Hašek: *Surviving the century*

1   R. Pynsent, *Czech Prose and Verse*, London: The Athlone Press, 1979, p. lviii.
2   R. Pynsent, "Jaroslav Hašek" in G. Stade (ed.), *European Writers: The Twentieth Century*, vol. 9, New York: Scribner, 1989, pp. 1091–1118, p.1116.
3   M. Kundera, *The Art of the Novel*, trans. L. Asher, London: Faber and Faber, 1988, p. 9.
4   Quoted in P. Steiner, *The Deserts of Bohemia: Czech Fiction and its Social Context*, Ithaca and London: Cornell University Press, 2000, p. 29. This is just one of several delightful examples in Steiner's engrossing analysis of the text.
5   G. Skilling, *Czechoslovakia's Interrupted Revolution*, Princeton: Princeton University Press, 1976, p. 16.
6   E. Marsland, *The Nation's Cause: French, English and German Poetry of The First World War*, London: Routledge, 1991, p. 240.
7   R. Graves, *Goodbye to All That*, Harmondsworth: Penguin, 1960, p. 157. Subsequent page references are in the text.
8   T. E. Lawrence, *Seven Pillars of Wisdom: A Triumph*, Harmondsworth: Penguin, 1962, p. 17. Subsequent page references are in the text.

9 Incidentally, after the death in a car accident of Princess Diana in 1998 there were press items attempting to draw parallels, a hundred years apart, between her fate and Elizabeth's.

10 J. Hašek, *Osudy dobrého vojáka Švejka za světové války*, vol. 1, Československý spisovatel, 1971, p. 13; *The Good Soldier Švejk and his Fortunes in the World War*, trans. C. Parrott, Harmondsworth: Penguin Books, 1974, p. 5. Subsequent page references will be in the text.

11 M. Sholokhov, *Quiet Flows the Don*, trans. R. Daglish, Moscow: Raduga, 1984, vol. 1, p. 27. Subsequent page references are in the text.

12 V. Bělohradský, "The Retreat into the Uniform and the Disintegration of Order. Švejk as an Integral Part of Central-European Literature", *Scottish Slavonic Review*, no. 2, 1983, pp. 21–40, p. 27.

13 R. Pytlík, *Toulavé house: život Jaroslava Haška*, Vimperk: Emporius, p. 200. Subsequent page references are in the text.

14 See R. Hayman, *K.: A Biography of Kafka*, London: Weidenfeld and Nicholson, 1981, p. 69. Entry to this prestigious firm was not easy and Kafka had to submit applications in Czech and German.

15 R. Gray, *Franz Kafka*, London: Cambridge University Press, 1973, p. 34. Subsequent page references are in the text.

16 F. Kafka, *Diaries*, ed. M. Brod, trans. Martin Greenberg, London: Secker and Warburg, 1949, p. 75.

17 I. Klíma, *Love and Garbage*, trans. Ewald Osers, London: Chatto and Windus, 1990, p. 111.

18 K. Kosík, "Hašek and Kafka", trans. A. Hopkins, *Cross Currents: A Yearbook of Central European Culture*, *Michigan Slavic Materials*, no. 23, University of Michigan, 1983, pp. 127–36, p. 136. Subsequent references are in the text.

19 M. Kundera, *The Art of the Novel*, trans. L. Asher, London: Faber and Faber, 1988, p. 49.

20 C. Parrott, *Jaroslav Hašek: A Study of "Švejk" and the Short Stories*, Cambridge and London: Cambridge University Press, 1982, pp. 133–4.

21 J. Hašek, *Dějiny strany mírného pokroku v mezích zákona*, Československý spisovatel, 1977, pp. 296–8.

22 Bernard Levin, "Mockery that Helped Topple an Empire", *The Times*, 18 January 1990, p. 12.

Karel Čapek: *Whose point of view?*

1 B. Bradbrook, *Karel Čapek: In Pursuit of Truth, Tolerance and Trust*, Brighton and Portland: Sussex Academic Press, 1998, p. 6.

2 See J. Sturrock, "Why the Tortoise Lost", *London Review of Books*, 18 September 1997, pp. 10–12, p. 12.

3 B. Russell, *History of Western Philosophy*, London: Unwin Paperbacks, second edition, 1961, p. 757.

4 See A. Thomas, *The Labyrinth of the Word: Truth and Representation in Czech Literature*, Munich: Oldenbourg, 1995 for a penetrating discussion of Čapek's responses to Masaryk's humanism (*Humanita*) and how this humanism relates to religion. Thomas argues (pp. 119–31) that the term is diffi-

cult to define and that it is fundamentally flawed. However, it "privileges man rather than God as the source of moral truth" (pp.120-1). In Thomas's view Čapek's fiction is more durable than Masaryk's philosophy.

5 For a full account of the relationship with Chesterton see B. Bradbrook "Letters to England from Karel Čapek", *Slavonic and East European Review*, December 1960, pp. 61–72 and "The Literary Relationship between G. K. Chesterton and Karel Čapek", *Slavonic and East European Review*, June 1961, pp. 327–38.

6 Karel Čapek, *Three Novels: Hordubal, Meteor, An Ordinary Life*, translated by M. and R. Weatherall, Introduction by William Harkins, New York: Catbird Press, 1990, p. 469. Čapek, K., *Spisy*, vol. VIII, Československý spiso-vatel, 1984, p. 400. Subsequent page references will be noted in the text.

7 See W. Harkins, *Karel Čapek*, New York: Columbia University Press, 1962, p. 130.

8 See Umberto Eco, *The Search for the Perfect Language*, trans. J. Fentress, Oxford: Blackwell, 1995, p. 276 and p. 281.

9 Karel Čapek, "Jak se dělá světová literatura", *Lidové noviny*, 19 January 1936, reprinted in *Spisy*, XVII, vol. 3, p. 677.

10 Boris Pasternak, *Doctor Zhivago*, trans. M. Hayward and M. Harari, London: Fontana, 1961, p. 292.

11 Karel Čapek, *Válka s Mloky*, Československý spisovatel, 1972, p. 213; *War with the Newts*, trans. E. Osers, London: Picador, 1991, p. 214. Subsequent page references will be in the text.

12 J. Tolkien, *The Lord of the Rings*, "Preface", London: Allen and Unwin, 1969, pp. 8-9.

13 It is interesting to note that Ivan Klíma, in an Afterword to a 1966 edition of *R.U.R*, tells us that Čapek's play, judged as a technical utopia, is "inconsistent, if not naïve" (nedůsledné, ne-li naivní), given that the robots are manufactured from a single chemical formula. Given what we know now about DNA, the play in fact seems remarkably prescient. See *R.U.R.*, Československý spiso-vatel, 1966, pp. 185–200, p. 193.

14 Karel Čapek, *Spisy*, vol. VI, "Šlépěje", Československý spisovatel, 1993, p. 109; *Tales from Two Pockets*, "Footprints", trans. N. Comrada, New York: Catbird Press, 1994, p. 132. "Poslední soud", pp. 131–2; "The Last Judgment", p. 159. Subsequent page references will be in the text.

15 See R. Pynsent, *Czech Prose and Verse*, London: The Athlone Press, 1979, pp. lxii–lxiii.

Bohumil Hrabal: *Small people and tall tales*

1 I. Hájek, "Czech Republic and Slovakia", in *The Oxford Guide to Contemporary Writing*, J. Sturrock (ed.), Oxford: Oxford University Press, 1996, p. 104.

2 R. Pytlík, *Bohumil Hrabal*, Československý spisovatel, 1990, p. 116. Subsequent page references are in the text.

3 M. Jankovič, *Kapitoly z poetiky Bohumila Hrabala*, Praha: Torst, 1996, pp. 26–7.

4 B. Hrabal, *Pábitelé*, Praha: Mladá fronta, 1964, dust jacket. Also *Sebrané spisy*, vol. 12. pp. 293–5. Several of the stories appeared in English in the collection *The Death of Mr. Baltisberger*, trans. Michael Heim, London: Abacus, 1990.

5 B. Hrabal, *The Little Town Where Time Stood Still* (with *Cutting It Short*), trans. J. Naughton, London: Abacus, 1993.

6 B. Hrabal, *Něžný barbar* (with *Městečko, kde se zastavil čas* and *Příliš hlučná samota*), Praha: Odeon, 1992, p. 119.

7 B. Hrabal, *Sebrané spisy*, Praha: Pražská Imaginace, 1991–, vol. 4, p. 150. Unless stated otherwise, further references, by volume and page number, will be in the text to this Collected Works.

8 "Diadur" is a technical term, a carbide used in the production of high-performance machine parts such as drills and cutters.

9 M. Polizzotti, *Revolution of the Mind: The Life of André Breton*, London: Bloomsbury, 1995, pp. 264–73 and pp. 281–5.

10 Umberto Eco, *The Search for the Perfect Language*, trans. J. Fentress, Oxford: Blackwell, 1995, pp. 122–3.

11 B. Hrabal, *Closely Observed Trains*, trans. E. Pargeter, London: Abacus, 1990, p. 7. Subsequent page references will be in the text.

12 M. Kundera, *The Book of Laughter and Forgetting*, trans. M. Heim, London: Faber and Faber, 1982, p. 66.

13 B. Hrabal, *Sebrané spisy*, vol. 6, p. 195. Quoted in Jankovič, p. 97.

14 B. Hrabal, *Městečko u vody: Postřižiny, Krasosmutnění, Harlekýnovy milióny*, Československý spisovatel, 1982, p. 34. *The Little Town Where Time Stood Still* (with *Cutting It Short*), trans. J. Naughton, London: Abacus, 1993, p. 28.

15 B. Hrabal, *Městečko, kde se zastavil čas, Něžný barbar, Příliš hlučná samota*, Praha: Odeon, 1992, p. 52.

16 R. Pytlík, p. 90.

17 B. Hrabal, *I Served the King of England*, trans. P. Wilson, London: Chatto and Windus, 1989, p. 9.

18 *The Little Town Where Time Stood Still*, trans. J. Naughton, Introduction, p. xvii.

19 Quoted on the cover of the English translation, *Too Loud a Solitude*, trans. M. Heim, New York: Harcourt Brace and Co., 1990.

20 *Městečko, kde se zastavil čas, Něžný barbar, Příliš hlučná samota*, Praha: Odeon, 1992, pp. 248 and 251. Also *Collected Works*, vol. 8, pp. 299 and 302. Readers in the 21st century perhaps need reminding that Brezhnev was the Soviet leader from 1964 till his death in 1982, an era of political stagnation that saw among other things the suppression of the Prague Spring.

21 *Too Loud a Solitude*, p. 44. One notes also that the Collected Works has the professor working for *Divadelní listy* whereas the Odeon text noted above has *Divadelní noviny* (p. 208).

Josef Škvorecký: *Fascism, Communism and all that jazz*

1 J. Škvorecký, *Zbabělci*, Československý spisovatel, 1966, p. 61. *The Cowards*, trans. Jeanne Němcová, Harmondsworth: Penguin Books, 1972, p. 68. Subsequent page references will be in the text.

2 S. Solecki, *Prague Blues: The Fiction of Josef Škvorecký*, Ontario: ECW Press, 1990, pp. 132–3 and p. 247, note 5.

3 P. Trensky, *The Fiction of Josef Škvorecký*, London: Macmillan, 1991, pp. 52–3.

4 M. Kundera, "Préface" to *Miracle en Bohème*, trans. Claudia Ancelot, Gallimard, Paris, 1978. Reproduced in English translation in S. Solecki (ed.), *The Achievement of Josef Škvorecký*, Toronto: University of Toronto Press, 1994, pp. 25–31, p. 30.

5 J. Škvorecký, *Mirákl: Politická detektivka*, Praha: Ivo Železný, 1997, pp. 342–3; *The Miracle Game*, trans. P. Wilson, London: Faber and Faber, 1991, pp. 277–8. Incidentally, the English translation makes a marginally better job of transliterating the Cyrillic than does the author's original text. Subsequent page references will be in the text.

6 P. Trensky, p. 110.

7 J. Škvorecký, *Dvě legendy: Red Music, Legenda Emöke, Bassaxofon*, Toronto: Sixty-Eight Publishers, 1982, pp. 133–4; *The Bass Saxophone: Red Music, Emöke, The Bass Saxophone*, trans. K. Polackova-Henly, London: Picador, 1980, pp. 95–6. Subsequent page references will be in the text.

8 B. Thomson, *Lot's Wife and The Venus of Milo: Conflicting Attitudes to the Cultural Heritage in Modern Russia*, Cambridge: Cambridge University Press, 1978, pp. 12–13.

9 It was in fact on 26 October 1932 that Stalin apparently called writers "engineers who build human souls", see V. Terras (ed.), *Handbook of Russian Literature*, New Haven and London: Yale University Press, 1985, p. 429.

10 S. Baranczak,"Tongue-Tied Eloquence" in S. Solecki (ed.), *The Achievement of Josef Škvorecký*, Toronto: University of Toronto Press, 1994, p. 15–24, pp. 20–1.

11 *Příběh inženýra lidských duší, Entrtejment na stará témata o životě, ženách, osudu, snění, dělnické třídě, fízlech, lásce a smrti*, Toronto: Sixty-Eight Publishers, 1977, vol. I, p. 94; *The Engineer of Human Souls: An Entertainment on the Old Themes of Life, Women, Fate, Dreams, The Working Class, Secret Agents, Love and Death*, trans. P. Wilson, London: Chatto and Windus, 1985, p. 64. Subsequent page references will be in the text.

12 Presumably the translator and author, working quite closely and probably with published translations in Czech of some of the works that make up the fabric of *The Engineer of Human Souls*, agreed an English version rather than a literal translation in places. Sections of the English text appear in different places from the Czech version. Note also for instance that the correspondence in the English version is all dated, whereas in the Czech version the reader, having the right cultural backgound, is left to guess for himself when the various letters are written. There is also some deft footwork when it comes to names: Dotty, for example, is Blběnka in the original.

13 Stalin was hardly being original here. Thomas Paine wrote of the "just war" during America's struggle for independence from the English. A parallel phrase "A just cause" was also used during the Second World War and is often attributed to Molotov.

14 The story is also reproduced in Milan Kundera. See *Immortality*, trans. P. Kussi, London: Faber and Faber, 1991, p. 56.

15 There is a joke here which those Czechs of Škvorecký's generation and many Canadian Czechs, will instantly respond to. "Sandnerka" as it was colloquially referred to, was *Kuchařka: Kniha rozpočtů a kuchařských předpisů* by Marie Janků-Santnerová and František Janků. First published in Prague in 1924 and much reprinted, once in Montreal by International Book Service in 1952, this was the Czech equivalent of Mrs Isabella Beeton's celebrated publications, notably *The Book of Household Management*.

16 See R. Porter, "Zinovy Zinik's Gothic Suburbia" in A. McMillin (ed.), *Reconstructing the Canon: Russian Writing in the 1980s*, Amsterdam: Harwood Academic Publishers, 2000, pp. 125–46.

17 J. Škvorecký, *Scherzo Capriccio: veselý sen o Dvořákovi*, Praha: Odeon, 1991, p. 22. *Dvořák in Love: A Light-Hearted Dream*, trans. P. Wilson, London: Hogarth Press, 1989, p. 10. Subsequent page references will be in the text.

18 A more literal translation here would be "The Enigma of the Ending", *kadence* being the Czech for "cadenza". However, the translation is perfectly understandable, given the context. On a more general level and as with *The Engineer of Human Souls*, it might be more appropriate to speak of an English *version* rather than a word-for word translation: the original makes liberal use of italics for some passages and is handsomely adorned with period illustrations. The English version dispenses with these latter, but tries to make the text more accessible by rearranging the order of the chapters occasionally.

19 Jeannette Thurber was born 29 January 1850 and died 2 January 1946, just weeks away from her 96th birthday. This might explain the discrepancy between the Czech and English texts here (z dálky svých šestadevadesáti let (p. 206); from the distance of her ninety-five years – p. 271). The English version also here omits the reference in the Czech to Dvořák smoking a large cigar. Incidentally, this chapter has been transposed from 9th place in the Czech to 22nd in the English version.

20 J. Škvorecký, *Nevěsta z Texasu*, Toronto: Sixty-Eight Publishers, 1992, p. 106. *The Bride of Texas*, trans. K. Polackova-Henly, Faber and Faber, 1996, p. 104. Subsequent page references will be in the text.

Ota Pavel: *Laughter in the dark*

1 O. Pavel, *Smrt krásných srnců*, Praha: Mladá fronta, 1971. *Jak jsem potkal ryby*, Praha: Mladá fronta, 1974. *Fialový poustevník*, Praha: Edice Máj, 1977. Page references will be to this edition. Translations are my own. A selection of Pavel's prose has appeared in English: *How I Came to Know Fish*, trans. J. Badal and R. McDowell, New York: New Directions Books, 1990.

2 B. Svozil, "Svět próz Oty Pavla", in *Fialový poustevník* as above, p. 171.

3 O. Pavel, *Cena vítězství*, Praha: Máj, 1968. Page references are in the text.

4 O. Pavel, *Pohádka o Raškovi*, Praha: Olympia, 1974. Page references are in the text.

Ivan Klíma: *Conscience and moral conundrums*

1 I. Klíma, *Láska a smetí*, London: Rozmluvy, 1988. *Love and Garbage*, trans. E. Osers, London: Chatto and Windus, 1990. Page references are in the text. There are some substantial differences between the English and Czech versions. An interview "Tea and Biscuits in the City of Sadness" *The Guardian*, 17 April 1990, p. 31, alludes to a forthcoming revised edition. In fact there was a misunderstanding as to which draft the translator should work from. None the less our references to the different versions should be instructive.

2 J. Naughton, "Desiring to Meet," *Times Literary Supplement*, 30 March/5 April 1990, p. 338.

3 K. Chvatík, "Poznámky o české literatuře v zahraničí (podruhé)," *Tvorba*, 28 March 1990, pp. 14–15.

4 M. Williamson, "Time in a Net," *The Observer*, 25 March 1990, p. 66.

5 M. Williamson, p. 66.

6 *Soudce z milosti*, London: Rozmluvy, 1986. *Judge on Trial*, trans. A. Brain, London: Chatto and Windus, 1991. Page references are in the text.

7 I. Klíma, *Má veselá jitra*, Toronto: Sixty-Eight Publishers, 1979.

8 I. Klíma, *Moje první lásky*, Toronto: Sixty-Eight Publishers, 1985.

9 Note that the Czech text differs markedly from the English, omitting the comments on war and revolution.

10 Note that the second paragraph quoted here is omitted from the Czech text.

11 "Dlhý čas čakania", *Literárny týždenník*, 26 January 1990, p. 6.

12 The novel is set in 1983 or 1984 (English text, p. 15; Czech text, p. 23, where the hero talks of being in America fifteen years ago), and this was a particularly harsh time for religious believers in Czechoslovakia. By 1985 as many as 30,000 people were reported to have signed a petition inviting Pope John Paul II to visit the country, and this despite wide-scale repression: "There was a large scale police operation against priests and believers in October 1981. During another severe crackdown in March 1983 . . . some 250 people were taken into custody and interrogated. During house searches conducted in more than a dozen cities, religious literature, money, and typewriters were confiscated. This action sparked off a letter of complaint to Cardinal Tomášek signed by nearly 4,000 Protestants and Catholics . . . An estimated 150,000 people took part in the Methodius celebrations in Velehrad, southern Moravia, on 7 July 1985 . . . about two thirds of the attendants were young people", see J. Bugajski, *Czechoslovakia: Charter 77's Decade of Dissent*, New York: Praeger, 1987, pp. 63–4.

13 According to a letter to me from the author the source is the edition of the *Talmud* by A. Cohen, London: A. Dent and Sons, 1971, p. 387.

14 P. Roth, "A Conversation in Prague," *The New York Review of Books*, no. 37, 6 April 1990, pp. 14–22.

15 I. Klíma, *Loď jménem Naděje* (with *Pračka* and *Ostrov mrtvých králů*), Praha: Hynek, 1998, p. 215.

16 I. Klíma, *Moje první lásky*, Toronto: Sixty-Eight Publishers, 1985; *My First Loves*, trans. E. Osers, London: Chatto and Windus, 1986. *Má veselá jitra*,

Toronto: Sixty-Eight Publishers, 1979; *My Merry Mornings*, trans. G. Theiner, London: Readers International, 1985. *Moje zlatá řemesla*, Brno: Atlantis, 1989; *My Golden Trades*, trans. P. Wilson, Harmondsworth: Penguin Books, 1992. Page references will be in the text.

17 I. Klíma, "A Rather Unconventional Childhood" in *The Spirit of Prague*, trans. P. Wilson, London: Granta Books, p. 18.

18 I. Klíma, *Uzel pohádek* (Havel, Kliment, Klíma, Kohout, Pochop, Sidon, Skácel, Trefulka, Vaculík, Vladislav, Werich), Praha: Lidové noviny, 1991.

19 See J. Keane, *Václav Havel, A Political Tragedy in Six Acts*, London: Bloomsbury, 1999, pp. 296–7.

20 V. Havel, *Open Letters*, selected and edited by P. Wilson, London: Faber and Faber, 1991, pp. 50, 78.

21 *Charter 77* was a statement, compiled by a group of disaffected intellectuals and issued in January 1977, which called for the observation of basic human and political rights in Czechoslovakia. Its three initial spokesmen were Václav Havel, Jiří Hájek and Jan Patočka. It was very quickly endorsed by hundreds of prominent people in Czechoslovakia and abroad. The ringleaders were subject to severe police harassment.

22 I. Klíma, *Čekání na tmu, čekání na světlo*, Český spisovatel, 1993, p. 211; *Waiting for the Dark, Waiting for the Light*, trans. P. Wilson, London: Granta Books, 1994, p. 234. Subsequent page references are in the text.

23 The addition and omission of certain phrases here suggest that, as with *Love and Garbage*, the translator was working from a text other than the published one.

24 A. Solzhenitsyn, *The Gulag Archipelago*, Vol. 2, trans. T. Whitney, London: Collins/Harvill, 1975, p. 597.

25 "O literatuře světské víry" in *Už se blíží meče*, Novinář, Praha, 1990, pp. 56–64, pp. 63–4. "On the Literature of Secular Faith" in *The Spirit of Prague*, trans. P. Wilson, London: Granta Books, 1994, pp. 131–45, pp. 144–5.

Daniela Hodrová, Michael Viewegh, Jáchym Topol: *New voices?*

1 D. Hodrová, *Podobojí*, Ústí nad Labem: Severočeské nakladatelství, 1991. *Kukly*, Praha: Práce, 1991. *Théta*, Československý spisovatel, 1992. Page references will be in the text.

2 M. Viewegh, *Báječná léta pod psa*, Český spisovatel, 1992, pp. 11–12. Subsequent page references will be in the text.

3 J. Topol, *Anděl*, Praha: Hynek, 1995, p. 77.

4 When Topol visited the University of Glasgow on 30 April 2001, he confirmed that he had no knowledge of Welsh's novel in the early 1990s, but suggested that a recent Czech translation of the work drew heavily on his own, Topol's, prose for an appropriate linguistic register.

5 J. Topol, *Sestra*, Brno: Atlantis, 1994. Revised edition, Brno: Atlantis, 1996. *City Sister Silver*, trans. A. Zucker, North Haven: Catbird Press, 2000. Page references will refer to the second Czech edition and the translation.

Select Bibliography

Primary texts and translations are to be found in the Notes, as are some incidental items of secondary literature. Wherever practically possible, I have tried to use Collected Works or prominent editions.

Suggested Background Reading

General

In English

Hájek, I., "Czech Republic and Slovakia" in *The Oxford Guide to Contemporary World Literature*, J. Sturrock (ed.), Oxford and New York: Oxford University Press, 1997, pp. 101–12.

Harkins, W. and Trensky, P. (eds), *Czech Literature since 1956: A Symposium*, New York: Bohemica, 1980.

Novák, A., *Czech Literature*, trans. P. Kussi, edited and with a Supplement by W. Harkins, Ann Arbor: Michigan Slavic Publications, 1976.

Pynsent, R., *Czech Prose and Verse: A Selection with an Introductory Essay*, London: The Athlone Press, 1979.

Součková, M, *A Literary Satellite: Czechoslovak-Russian Literary Relations*, Chicago and London: University of Chicago Press, 1970.

Steiner, P., *The Deserts of Bohemia: Czech Fiction and Its Social Context*, Ithaca and London: Cornell University Press, 2000.

Thomas, A., *The Labyrinth of the Word : Truth and Representation in Czech Literature*, Munich: R. Oldenbourg, 1995.

Wellek, R., *Essays on Czech Literature*, introduced by P. Demetz, The Hague: Mouton, 1963.

In Czech

Blahynka, M. (ed.), *Čeští spisovatelé 20 století: slovníková příručka*, Československý spisovatel, 1985.

Brabec, J. and others, *Slovník českých spisovatelů: pokus o rekonstrukci dějin české literatury 1948–1979*, Toronto: Sixty-eight Publishers, 1982.

Čulík, J. *Knihy za ohradou: česká literatura v exilových nakladatelstvích 1971–1989*, Praha: Trizonia, 1991.

Holý, J. *Česká literatura: od roku 1945 do současnosti*, Český spisovatel, 1996.

Měšťan, A, *Česká literatura 1785–1985* , Toronto: Sixty-Eight Publishers, 1987.

Select Bibliography

Hašek

In English

Parrott, C., *The Bad Bohemian : The Life of Jaroslav Hašek*, London: The Bodley Head, 1978.

Parrott, C., *Jaroslav Hašek: A Study of 'Švejk' and the Short Stories*, Cambridge: Cambridge University Press, 1982.

Pynsent, R., "Jaroslav Hašek" in *European Writers*, G. Stade (ed.), Vol. 9, New York: Scribner, 1989, pp. 1091–1118.

In Czech

Pytlík, R., *Kniha o Švejkovi*, Československý spisovatel, 1983.

Pytlík, R., *Toulavé house: život Jaroslava Haška, autora Osudů dobrého vojáka Švejka*, Vimperk: Emporius, 1998.

Čapek

In English

Bradbrook, B. *Karel Čapek: In Pursuit of Truth, Tolerance and Trust*, Brighton: Sussex Academic Press, 1998.

Harkins, W., *Karel Čapek*, New York and London: Columbia University Press, 1960.

Matuška, A., *Man against Destruction*, (English version of item listed below) London: Allen and Unwin, 1964.

In Czech

Klíma, I., *Karel Čapek*, Československý spisovatel, 1962.

In Slovak

Matuška, A., *Člověk proti skaze*, Bratislava: Slovenský spisovatel, 1963.

Hrabal

In English

Kadlec, V., "Bohumil Hrabal" in *Dictionary of Literary Biography, Vol. 232: Twentieth-Century East European Writers*, S. Serafin (ed.), Detroit: The Gale Group, 2001, pp. 146–57.

In Czech

Jankovič, M., *Kapitoly z poetiky Bohumila Hrabala*, Praha: Torst, 1996.

Kladiva, J., *Literatura Bohumila Hrabala: struktura a metoda Hrabalových děl*, Praha: Pražská imaginace, 1994.

Select Bibliography

Pytlík, R., *Bohumil Hrabal*, Československý spisovatel, 1990.
Roth, S., *Hlučná samota a hořké štěstí Bohumila Hrabala*, Praha: Pražská imaginace, 1993.

Škvorecký

In English

Pilař, M. and Čulík, J., "Josef Škvorecký" in *Dictionary of Literary Biography, Vol. 232: Twentieth-Century East European Writers*, S. Serafin (ed.), Detroit: The Gale Group, 2001, pp.336–51.
Solecki, Sam, *Prague Blues: The Fiction of Josef Škvorecký : A Critical Study*, Toronto: ECW Press, 1990.
Solecki, S. (ed.), *The Achievement of Josef Škvorecký*, Toronto: University of Toronto Press, 1994.
Trensky, P., *The Fiction of Josef Škvorecký*, London: Macmillan, in association with the School of Slavonic and East European Studies, University of London, 1991.

In Czech

Chvatík, K. "Velký vypravěč Josef Škvorecký", *Česká literatura*, 1991, no. 1, pp. 41–54.
Kosková, H., "Bořitel falešných mýtů Josef Škvorecký" in her *Hledání ztacené generace*, Toronto: Sixty-eight Publishers, 1987, pp. 109–52.
Trenský, P., *Josef Škvorecký*, translated by A. Haman, Praha: H & H, 1995. (Czech language version of *The Fiction of Josef Škvorecký* as listed above).

Pavel

In English

Lustig, A., "The Short Life of a Czech Writer", *World Literature Today*, 1981, pp. 412–16.
Svobodová, H., "The Death of a Beautiful Fish", translated by P. Wilson, *Cross Currents: A Yearbook of Central European Culture*, Ann Arbor, 1983, pp. 285–90.

In Czech

Svozil, B., "Svět próz Oty Pavla", Afterword to O. Pavel's *Filalový poustevník*, Praha: Mladá fronta, 1977, pp. 168–85.
Vlašín, S., "Povídky o tatínkovi", *Tvorba*, no. 3, 1971.

Klíma

In English

Holý, J. and Čulík, J., "Ivan Klíma" in *Dictionary of Literary Biography*, Vol. 232:

Select Bibliography

Twentieth-Century East European Writers, S. Serafin (ed.), Detroit: The Gale Group, 2001, pp.173–9.

Porter, R., "Ivan Klíma's Other First Loves" in *Czechoslovak Central and East European Journal*, vol. 10, 1991, no. 2, pp. 118–30.

Ward, I., "Ivan Klíma's *Judge on Trial*: A Study of Law and Literature", *Scottish Slavonic Review*, no. 20, 1993, pp. 23–44.

In Czech

Kosková, H., "Perspektiva mravní odpovědnosti" in her *Hledání ztracené generace*, second edition, Praha: H+H, 1996, pp. 165–73.

Pechar, J., "Krize racionalistického idealismu v díle Ivana Klímy", in his *Nad knihami a rukopisy*, Praha: Torst, 1996, pp. 47–64.

Suchomel, M., "Hodina ticha" and "Hledání tvaru" in *Literatura z časů krize* edited by J. Bednářová, Brno: Veta Via, 1995, pp. 62–6 and pp. 112–13.

Hodrová

In Czech

Bartůňková, J., Zachová, A., "Problém dvojnictví v trilogii Daniely Hodrové", *Česká literatura*, no. 5, 1994, pp. 522–32.

Knapp, A., "Sukces trýznivé imaginace: Daniela Hodrová a Jáchym Topol v překladech do němčiny", *Nové knihy*, no. 28, 1998, p. 8.

Viewegh

In Czech

Hoffmann, B., "Michal Viewegh – autor postmoderních bestsellerů", in *Přednášky z literární vědy, kultury a historie*, vol. 2, LŠSS, 1999, pp. 99–117.

In Slovak

Minár, P., "Poznámky k čítaniu textov Michala Viewegha Názory na vraždu a Báječná léta pod psa", *Česká literatura*, no. 3, 1996, pp. 294–301.

Topol

In English

Reviews of the English translation of *Sestra* (*City Sister Silver*) include:
Anders, J., in *The New Republic* 19 June 2000, pp. 45–9.
Bose, S. in *Washington Post Book World*, 9 July 2000.
Crossley, J., in *Review of Contemporary Fiction*, Autumn, 2000.
Hampl, P., in *Los Angeles Times Book Review*, 6 August 2000.
Smale, A., *New York Times, Arts Section*, 30 March 2000.

Select Bibliography

In Czech

Knapp, A., "Sukces trýznivé imaginace: Daniela Hodrová a Jáchym Topol v překladech do němčiny", *Nové knihy*, no. 28, 1998, p. 8.

Rulf, J., (Interview) "Bůh tam patu nevsune", *Reflex*, vol. 9, no. 3, 1998, p. 16–19.

Sarvaš, R. (Interview) "Vojáci a andělé na rozkývaném topolu", *Koktejl*, vol. 8, no. 9, 1999, pp. 15–22.

Ševel, V., (Interview) "Narazit na spodní proud", *Mladá fronta*, vol. 9, no. 12, supplement Magazín MF Dnes, vol. 6, no. 2, 1998, pp. 20–2.

Index

Abe (character), 43
abstract expressionism, 74
Adam, Paul, 43
Adolf Hitler: My Part in His Downfall
    (Milligan), 5
affection, 2
Aldington, Richard, 8
All Quiet on the Western Front (Remarque),
    8
All the Sad Young Men (Fitzgerald), 111
allegory, 42
Altman, Robert, 5
ambiguity, Čapek, 42, 49
American Civil War, Škvorecký, 119–21
Analytical Cubism, 29
Anděl (Topol), 177–80
Angel (Topol), 177–80
Anouilh, Jean, 1–2
Anthologie de l'humeur noire (Breton), 2
anti-fascism, Čapek, 42, 44, 47
anti-intellectualism, Hašek, 25
anti-semitism, Pavel, 129
Anton, Mr (character), 149
Apocalypse Now, 113
Aragon, Louis, 73
Arashidov (character), 93
Aristophanes, 116
Arlott, John, 124
The Art of the Novel (Kundera), 4
artistic tradition, 1
At the Mountains of Madness (Lovecraft),
    111–12
"An Attempt at Murder" (Čapek), 48
Auda, 9–10, 13–14
Audience (Havel), 172
Auschwitz, 102, 127, 149, 164, 166, 181
Automat "Svět" (Hrabal), 59–60
avant-garde, Čapek, 27, 46–7

Babel, Isaac, 130
bábení, 54
Báječná léta pod psa (Viewegh), 171–5
Balada o Juraji Čupovi (Čapek), 50
"The Ballad of Juraj Čup" (Čapek), 50

Balmont, Konstantin, 105, 106
Baloun (*The Bride of Texas* character), 120
Baloun (*The Good Soldier Švejk* character),
    13, 22, 24, 25
Balzac, Honoré de, 150
"Bambini di Praga 1947" (Hrabal), 60–5
Baranczak, Stanislaw, vii, 104, 105
Barth, John, 171
The Bass Saxophone (Škvorecký), 88,
    97–102, 104
Battle of the White Mountain, 47
Beáta (character), 175
Beatles, 95
Bel Ami (Maupassant), 150
Bellamy, David, 44
Bellamy, Edward, 44
Bellissimo W. W. (character), 107, 115
Bělohradský, Václav, 17
Beneš, Dr Eduard, 130
Benno (character), 96–7, 112
Beránková, Eliška (character), 170
Berlin, Isaiah, 87
Bertram, Sir John (character), 43
Berty (Bertík) (character), 89
Bible
    Čapek, 28, 37
    Klíma, 142, 144
Biegler, Cadet (character), 24–5
Bílá Hora, 142
Bílá nemoc (Čapek), 41
Bílé hřiby, 126
birth control, 45
Bizet, Georges, *Carmen*, 60
Black Dogs (McEwan), 179
black humour, 1–3
Blake, William, 116
bláznovská povídka (Klíma), 157
Blok, Alexander, 90
Boccaccio, Giovanni, 25
Boháček (character), 166, 167
Bohler (character), 181
Bondy, Egon, 57, 75
Bondy, G. H. (character), 43, 46

Index

The Book of Laughter and Forgetting (Kundera), 73–4, 176
Booker (character), 112
Born, Adolf, 135
Bosch, Hieronymus, 102
Brahe, Tycho, 110
Brecht, Bertolt, *Švejk in the Second World War*, 5
Breton, André
  Anthologie de l'humeur noire, 2
  Dadaism, 73
  Nadja, 58–9
  Surrealism, 73
The Bride of Texas (Škvorecký), 118, 119–22
Bringing Up Girls in Bohemia (Viewegh), 175, 176
Brixi, František, 169
Brod, Max 18
Brooke, Rupert, "The Soldier", 7
Brueghel, Pieter, 102
Bucifal, Mr (character), 61, 64
Buddha, 146
Bukavec (character), 93
Burgess, Anthony, 182
Burnside, Ambrose, 120
byt, 98

"Cafe 'World'" (Hrabal), 59–60
Camus, Albert, 78, 85, 116, 134
Čapek, Josef, 27
Čapek, Karel, 1, 2, 27–51, 160, 169
  ambiguity, 42, 49
  anti-fascism, 42, 44, 47
  "An Attempt at Murder", 48
  avant-garde, 27, 46–7
  "The Ballad of Juraj Čup", 50
  Bible, 28, 37
  "The Crime on the Farm", 49
  Cubism, 27, 28–9, 74
  "The Disappearance of an Actor", 49, 51
  "Footprints", 49
  "The Fortuneteller", 48–9
  From the Life of Insects, 30, 42, 45
  God, 28, 31, 49–50
  Hordubal, 29–33, 37, 50
  influences on, 27–9
  Krakatit, 42
  "The Last Judgement", 49–50
  The Makropulos Secret, 42
  Meteor, 29–30, 33–7, 38
  Mother, 41
  "Mr Janik's Cases", 49
  "Oplatka's End", 49
  An Ordinary Life, 29–30, 37–41
  preoccupation with technology, 27–8, 45
  relativism, 35–6, 49, 50, 51

Rossum's Universal Robots, 30, 42, 45, 46, 185*n*
The Tales from Two Pockets, 29, 48–51, 92
War with the Newts, 41–8, 51, 161
The White Plague, 41
capitalism, 42, 74
Carnegie, Dale, 131
"Carp for the Wehrmacht" (Pavel), 130
The Castle (Kafka), 158
The Castle (Klíma), 157, 158
Catch-22 (Heller), 5, 88
Catholic Church, 28, 29, 71, 91–2
Čekání na tmu, čekání na světlo (Klíma), 158–60
Čenkovič, Vratislav (character), 117
Čepička, Alexej, 93
Černá (character), 181
Cervantes Saavedra, Miguel de, 20
chance, 20
Charter 77, 157, 172, 173, 191*n*
Chataway, Chris, 135
Chaucer, Geoffrey, 25
"Chcete vidět zlatou Prahu?" (Hrabal), 63
Chesterton, G. K., 29, 48, 51
Chief Salamander (character), 41, 43
The Child in Time (McEwan), 179
"Christmas Eve" (Hrabal), 57
cinema, 73
City of Pain, (Hodrová), 162, 163–71
City Sister Silver (Topol), 177, 180–3
Cleaver, Eldridge, 118
"Climbing the Eiger" (Pavel), 133
A Clockwork Orange (Burgess), 182
cloning, 45
Closely Observed Trains (Hrabal), 65–72, 75, 85
collage
  Dadaism, 73
  Hrabal, 56, 57, 81
comedy, 1–3
communism
  Hrabal, 81
  Škvorecký, 116
complacency, dangers of, 44
Confrontation (Hájek), 123
Conrad, Joseph, 104, 105, 113–15, 116, 117
  Heart of Darkness, 113
  Under Western Eyes, 113
The Cowards (Škvorecký), 88, 89–91, 93, 94, 96–7, 102, 104, 106, 121
Crane, Stephen, 104, 109–11, 116, 120
  The Red Badge of Courage, 109, 110
creativity, 27, 45
"The Crime on the Farm" (Čapek), 49
Cubism, Čapek, 27, 28–9, 74
curiosity, 44

Index

Cutting it Short (Hrabal), 56, 75
cynicism, 2, 29
Czech Musicians' Union, 76

Dadaism, 73
Dahl, Roald, 148
"Dáma s kaméliemi" (Hrabal), 64
Dana (*The Engineer of Human Souls* character), 111
Dana (*My First Loves* character), 152
Dancing Lessons for the Elderly and Advanced (Hrabal), 57
Daniela (character), 155
Dante Alighieri, 169
Daria (character), 137, 144, 145
David (character), 181
Davidovičová, Alice (character), 166, 167
Davidovičová, Granny (character), 167
Davis, Angela, 118
De Gaulle, Charles, 80
death, Hrabal, 78
Death of the Beautiful Roebucks (Pavel), 124, 125–6
decency, 3, 51
decisiveness, 20
Démanty noci (Lustig), 128
Desnos, Robert, 81
despair, 2
detective stories
  Čapek, 48, 49
  Škvorecký, 92
Dewey, John, 28
dialogue, Čapek, 49
Diamantové očko (Hrabal), 60
"Diamond Eye" (Hrabal), 60
Diamonds of the Night (Lustig), 128
Dickens, Charles, 72
A Dictionary of Literary Terms and Theory, 2
didacticism, Čapek, 28, 51
Diderot, Denis, 20
Dimmesdale (character), 107
"The Disappearance of an Actor" (Čapek), 49, 51
disillusionment, 2
Dítě (character), 76–82, 86
Divine Comedy (Dante), 169
Dlouhá míle (Pavel), 130
Dlouhý Honza (Pavel), 131–2
"Do You Want to See Golden Prague?" (Hrabal), 63
Doctor Zhivago (Pasternak), 39
Dodge, Sir Oliver (character), 43
Dolores, Maria (character), 37
Don Quixote, 17, 20
Dorsey, Tommy, 119
Dostoevsky, Fyodor, 46, 71, 72, 181

Dotty (character), 112
Drake, Sir Francis (character), 44
dreams, 73
Dub, Lieutenant (character), 21, 24
Dubček, Alexander, 93, 118
Dvořák in Love (Škvorecký), 118–19, 120
Dyk, Viktor, 116

Eco, Umberto, 170
education
  Čapek, 28
  Hrabal, 55
Edward VIII, 64, 80
Einstein, Albert, 30
Eisenstein, Sergey Mikhailovich, 73, 134
Eliot, T. S., 170
Eluard, Paul, 73
Emöke (Škvorecký), 97, 102–4
emotion, 2
The End of the Affair (Greene), 158
The Engineer of Human Souls (Škvorecký), 88, 91, 94–5, 103, 104–18, 119, 120, 121
The Enthusiasts (Hrabal), 54
epic tradition, 3, 6
Erasmus of Rotterdam, 55, 85
erotická povídka (Klíma), 156
Esenin-Volpin, Alexander, 105, 106
eternity, Hrabal, 78, 84–5
evolution, 27
existentialism, 18, 78, 127–8
experience, Pragmatist philosophy, 28
expressionist movement, 74

"The Fairy Tale about Raška" (Pavel), 134, 135
faith, 31–2
The Fall of the House of Usher (Poe), 105
Falstaff, 6
fantastic, 2, 42
fantasy
  Čapek, 36–7
  Klíma, 137
  Surrealism, 73
fascism
  Čapek, 42, 44, 47
  Hrabal, 81
  Škvorecký, 116
"Father Brown" stories, 29, 48
Faulkner, William, 114, 117
feeling, absence of, 2
Ferdinand, Archduke, 9
Ferdinand Maximilian, 10
Fialový poustevník (Pavel), 124–32
Fielding, Henry, 20
Fikejz, Milan (character), 107
Finnegan's Wake (Joyce), 168
The First Circle (Solzhenitsyn), 160

Index

First World War Literature, 6–12
"Fishing with a Submarine" (Pavel), 131
"Fishing-Rod Thief" (Pavel), 132
Fitzgerald, Ella, 102
Fitzgerald, F. Scott, 104, 111, 116
Fleming, Alexander, 133–4
footnotes, 46–7
"Footprints" (Čapek), 49
Ford, Ford Maddox, *Parade's End*, 7–8
Forever Flowing (Grossman), 113
"The Fortuneteller" (Čapek), 48–9
Foxley, Julian (character), 43
France, Anatole, 116
Frank, Mrs (character), 132
French Symbolists, 35, 75
Freud, Sigmund, 73
"Friday's Orderly's Tale" (Klíma), 156–7
From the Life of Insects (Čapek), 30, 42, 45
Frynta, Emanuel, 56
FSB, 173
Fuks, Ladislav, 177

"The General" (Sassoon), 7
Genet, Jean, 180
genetic engineering, 45
Germans, 47
Gershwin, George, 119
Gigli, Benjamino, 63
Glinka, Platon Lvovič, 166–7
God, (Čapek), 28, 31, 49–50
Goethe, Johann Wolfgang von, 84, 85
Gogol, Nikolay Vasilyevich, 72
Going for Broke (Pludek), 123
The Good Soldier Švejk (Hašek), 2, 4–6, 9,
    10, 12–13, 15–26, 56, 120
"Goodbye to All That" (Graves), 7
Gorbachev, Mikhail, 171
Gorkii, Maxim, 150
Goths, 13
Grass, Günter, 82
Graves, Robert, "Goodbye to All That", 7
Gray, Ronald, 19
The Great Gatsby (Fitzgerald), 111
Greek epics, 6
Greene, Graham, 87, 158
Griffin, 101
Grossman, Vasilii
    Forever Flowing, 113
    Life and Fate, 6
grotesque, 2
The Gulag Archipelago (Solzhenitsyn),
    159–60
"Gypsies" (Pushkin), 60

Habakuk, Uncle (character), 121
Hades, 102
Hadraba (character), 180

Hafie (character), 30, 33
Hagibor, 163, 165
Haile Selassie, 80
Hájek, Igor, 52
Hájek, Jiří, 123, 191*n*
Hakim, Larry (character), 105, 112–13, 115
Hamlet, 41
Hamza, Tomáš (character), 166, 167
Hanňťa (character), 83, 85
Hanuš (character), 143
Hanzlitschek, Captain (character), 121
Hardubej, Juraj, 31
Hardy, Oliver, 20
Harkins, William, 32, 51
Harlequin (Soffici), 116–17
Hašek, Jaroslav, 1, 4–26, 39, 56, 66, 156
    The Good Soldier Švejk, 2, 4–6, 9, 10,
        12–13, 15–26, 56, 120
Havel, Václav, 26, 87, 93
    Audience, 172
    Charter 77, 191*n*
    first official trip abroad, 47
    manual labouring, 153
    open letter to Husák, 154
    Private View, 172
    and Viewegh, 177
Havelka, Police Captain (character), 50
Hawthorne, Nathaniel, 104, 116
    The Scarlet Letter, 105, 106–8
Heart of Darkness (Conrad), 113
The Heart of the Matter (Greene), 158
Hebrew language, 63
hedonism, 24
Hegel, G. W. F., 94
Heim, M., 83, 84–5
Heisenberg, Werner, 169
Hejl (character), 93
Hellenic world, 85
Heller, Joseph, 66
    Catch-22, 5, 88
Hemingway, Ernest, 106, 134, 177
Hergesell, Herr (character), 164–5, 166, 167
Hermes Trismegistos, 62
Hester (character), 107
Heydrich, Reinhard, 5, 107
Higgins (character), 109
L'Histoire du Surrealisme, 81
history
    Hašek, 6
    Hrabal, 69–70
History of the Czech Nation (Palacký), 90
Hitler, Adolf, 41–2, 83, 89, 128, 151
Hodge, Sir William, 43
Hodr, Zdeněk, 169
Hodrová, Daniela, 1, 162–71, 180
    City of Pain, 162, 163–71
    Kukly, 162, 168–9

Index

Podobojí, 162–8, 169
Théta, 162, 169–71
Holan (character), 128–9
Holan, Vladimír, 116, 118
Holý, Mr (character), 156
Homer, 6, 170
Honza (character), 131–2
Honzlová, Jana (character), 107
Horáková, Milada, 170
Hordubal, (Čapek), 29–33, 37, 50
Hordubal, Juraj (character), 29–33
Houbová, Anna (character), 163–4
Hovorka, Augustin (character), 156
"How Dad and I Served Eels" (Pavel), 127
How I Met the Fish (Pavel), 124, 125, 127–8
How to Win Friends and Influence People
   (Carnegie), 131
"How Zátopek Ran on that Occasion"
   (Pavel), 134–5
Hra na pravdu (Klíma), 151–2
Hrabal, Bohumil, 1, 39, 52–86, 163, 180
   "Bambini di Praga 1947", 60–5
   biography and lifestyle, 52–3
   "Cafe 'World'", 59–60
   "Christmas Eve", 57
   Closely Observed Trains, 65–72, 75, 85
   collage, 56, 57, 81
   Cutting it Short, 56, 75
   *Dancing Lessons for the Elderly and
      Advanced*, 57
   "Diamond Eye", 60
   "Do You Want to See Golden Prague?",
      63
   I Served the King of England, 60, 64, 72,
      75–82, 85
   "Jarmilka", 57–9
   "The Lady of the Camellias", 64
   The Little Town Where Time Stood Still,
      56, 74, 75, 83
   "The Lost Little Street", 65
   "The Notary", 59
   pábení, 52, 53–6, 61–2, 65, 72, 76
   Pábitelé, 54–5, 57–65, 70, 72
   "A Pearl on the Bottom", 65
   "Romance", 57, 60
   Surrealism, 59, 73–4, 81–2
   The Tender Barbarian, 57, 83
   Too Loud a Solitude, 72, 74, 75, 82–6
   and Viewegh, 176
Hrabal, František, 52
Hrabalovština, 57
Hrma, Miloš (character), 65–72
Hrzán, Dr (character), 92
Hubička (character), 65–6, 68–9, 70, 71
Huckleberry Finn (Twain), 108, 109
Hus, Jan, 1
Husák, Gustav, 123, 154, 160

Hussite tradition, 28
Huxley, Aldous, 43, 45, 116
Huxley, Julian, 43
Hyrman, Mr (character), 61
Hyrman, Mrs (character), 61

I Served the King of England (Hrabal), 60,
   64, 72, 75–82, 85
Ideas of a Kind-hearted Reader (Viewegh),
   176–7
The Idiot (Dostoevsky), 181
Illusions Perdues (Balzac), 150
imperialism, 42
impulse, 18, 21
In Plain Russian (Voinovich), 88
In Two Kinds see Podobojí
indifference, 2
infinity, Hrabal, 78, 84–5
inquisitiveness, 44
instinct, 18
intellectual openness, 29
intellectual tradition, 1
intelligence, 2
intuition, 21, 48
Irena (character), 89, 91, 96
Irene (character), 105, 111–12, 115, 116
Irish Times, 56–7
irony
   Čapek, 28, 42
   Hrabal, 54
   Klíma, 147
The Island of the Dead Kings (Klíma), 148

*Jak jsem potkal ryby see How I Met the
   Fish* (Pavel)
Jak jsme s tatínkem servírovali úhořům
   (Pavel), 127
Jak to tenkrát běžel Zátopek (Pavel), 134–5
James, William, 28
Jan (character), 108, 113–14, 117–18
Jankovič, Milan, 54
"Jarmilka" (Hrabal), 57–9
Jarry, Alfred, 81
Jaruška (character), 174
Jatek (character), 178–9
Jaws, 172
jazz, Škvorecký, 97–100
Jerija (character), 179
Jesus Christ, 85
Jezulátko, 60
Jícha (character), 180
Jirásek, Alois, 3, 81, 90
Jirka (character), 127
Jirotka, Zdeněk, *Saturnin*, 20
Jódl, Tonda (character), 81
John Paul II, Pope, 190n
The Joke (Kundera), 2–3, 95, 123, 176

Index

Joplin, Scott, 119
Josef (character), 174
Joyce, James, 55, 56, 57, 168
Judaism, 62–3, 138
Judge on Trial (Klíma), 137, 141–3, 145
Julius Caesar, 13
Jungmann, Josef, 169
Jura (character), 166, 167
Jurajda (character), 13, 24
The Jury (Klíma), 148
Jůzl (character), 92, 95

Kabbala, 63
Kafka, Franz, vii
  The Castle, 158
  and Hašek, 18–19
  and Klíma, 137–40, 144, 146, 154, 156, 157
  The Trial, 138
Kainar, Josef, 116
Kákonyi, Mrs (character), 21, 22
Kalandra, Záviš, 73
Kant, Immanuel, 85
Kapři pro wehrmacht (Pavel), 130
Kapesní povídky see The Tales from Two Pockets (Čapek)
Katy (character), 21, 25
Katz, Chaplain Otto (character), 15, 20, 23–4
Kazantzakis, Nikos, 177
Když ti to nejede (Pavel), 134
Kerouac, Jack, 180
Kettelring, George (character), 37
KGB, 173
Kierkegaard, Søren 146
Kindl, Adam (character), 141–3
Kindl, Matěj (character), 143
Kindlová, Alena (character), 142
King Kong, 43
Kistemaeckers, Blanche (character), 45
The Kitchen (Wesker), 172
Klečka, Mr (character), 166
Klíma, Ivan, 1, 51, 123, 136–61, 162, 185n
  Bible, 142, 144
  The Castle, 157, 158
  "Friday's Orderly's Tale", 156–7
  The Island of the Dead Kings, 148
  Judge on Trial, 137, 141–3, 145
  The Jury, 148
  "The Land Surveyor", 158
  "The Literature of Secular Faith", 160
  Love and Garbage, 19, 136, 137–41, 143–7
  "Miriam", 148–9, 150
  "My Country", 149–51
  My First Loves, 137, 148–52, 158
  My Golden Trades, 148, 152–4, 158

My Merry Mornings, 137, 140, 148, 152–3, 154–8
religion, 141, 142, 143–5
"Saturday's Thief's Tale", 157
A Ship Named Hope, 137, 148
A Summer Affair, 137
"Sunday's Foolish Tale", 157
"Thursday's Erotic Tale", 156
"The Tightrope Walkers", 151, 152
"The Truth Game", 151–2
"Tuesday Morning: A Sentimental Story", 153, 154–5
The Ultimate Intimacy, 137, 158
Waiting for the Dark, Waiting for the Light, 158–60
The Washing Machine, 148
"Wednesday's Christmas Conspiracy", 155–6
Klobouček (character), 93
Köck, Mr (character), 166
Kohout, Pavel, 87, 93, 117, 123, 134, 172, 173
Kolář, Jiří, 54, 117
Kollár, Jan, 169
Komenský, Jan, 176
Konfrontace (Hájek), 123
Kosík, Karel, 19, 20
Kosťa (character), 166–7
Koťátko, Mr (character), 62
Kozlík, Karel (character), 141–2
Krahulík, Mr (character), 61
Krakatit (Čapek), 42
Královédvorský manuscript, 43
Kramář, Karel, 90
Krause, Mr (character), 62
Krutch, Joseph Wood, 106
Kubr, Honza, 134
Kühl, Horst Hermann (character), 99–100, 101
Kuchař, Radan, 133
Kukly (Hodrová), 162, 168–9
Kundera, Milan, vii, 21, 52, 87, 93, 112, 147
  The Art of the Novel, 4
  The Book of Laughter and Forgetting, 73–4, 176
  indictment of, 123
  The Joke, 2–3, 95, 123, 176
  Monology, 117
  The Unbearable Lightness of Being, 176
  and Viewegh, 176
Kurtz (character), 113
Kvido (character), 171–2, 175

"The Lady of the Camellias" (Hrabal), 64
"The Land Surveyor" (Klíma), 158
"Lanky Honza" (Pavel), 131–2
Lánská, Mrs (character), 67, 72

Index

Lánský, Mr (character), 70–1
Lao-Tzu, 55, 85
Láska a smetí see Love and Garbage
  (Klíma)
"The Last Judgement" (Čapek), 49–50
laughter, 2–3
  Hašek, 26
Laurel, Stan, 20
Lawrence, T. E., *Seven Pillars of Wisdom*,
  8–12, 13–14, 15, 17, 18
Leavis, F. R., 87
Lee, Laura (character), 121–2
Lee, Laurie, 125, 126
Legenda Emöke see Emöke (Škvorecký)
Leibniz, Gottfried, 35
Levene, Mr (character), 110
Lexa (character), 91, 97
Lhota, Mr (character), 156
Líba, Granny (character), 174
Libor (character), 157
Lída (*Love and Garbage* character), 137
Lída (*My Merry Mornings* character), 154–5
*Life and Extraordinary Adventures of
  Private Ivan
  Chonkin* (Voinovich), 88
Life and Fate (Grossman), 6
The Life of Jesus Christ, 81
Linhartová, Věra, 176
Literárny týždenník, 140
"The Literature of Secular Faith, (Klíma),
  160
The Little Town Where Time Stood Still
  (Hrabal), 56, 74, 75, 83
Living with a Star (Weil), 128
Ljuba (character), 178, 179
*Lod' jménem Naděje see A Ship Named
  Hope* (Klíma)
Lodge, David, 176
Lojza (character), 112
"Long Mile" (Pavel), 130
Looking Backward (Bellamy), 44
The Lord of the Rings (Tolkien), 42
"The Lost Little Street" (Hrabal), 65
Love and Garbage (Klíma), 19, 136,
  137–41, 143–7
Lovecraft, Howard Phillips, 104, 111–13,
  116
  At the Mountains of Madness, 111–12
Lukáš, Lieutenant (character), 20–3, 24, 25
Lurija (character), 179
Lustig, Arnošt, 60, 123, 128, 134, 165
lustrace, 160, 174
Lvíče see Miss Silver's Past (Škvorecký)

Má veselá jitra see My Merry Mornings
  (Klíma)
Má vlast see (Klíma), 149–51

McCaffrey, Sharon (character), 115
McEwan, Ian, 179
Mácha, Karel Hynek, viii, 1, 169
Machata (character), 178, 179
Machonin, Sergej, 180
Machovec, Hynek (character), 169
Macura, Vladimír, 163
Maiakovskii, Vladimir, 46, 98, 134
Majdanek, 102
The Makropulos Secret (Čapek), 42
Mallarmé, Stéphane, 53
The Man Who Was Thursday (Chesterton),
  51
Manya, Štěpán (character), 30, 31, 33
Marek (character), 24
Margitka (character), 109
Margulies, Adèle (character), 118
Marie (character), 111
Marsland, Elizabeth, *The Nation's Cause*, 7
Maruška (character), 142
Marx, Karl, 92, 94, 157
Marxism
  and art, 101
  Čapek, 42
  and war, 120
Mary (character), 37
Máša (character), 65
Masaryk, Tomáš, 1, 28, 43, 64, 80, 90, 110
M.A.S.H., 5
Masks see Kukly (Hodrová)
mass production, 27–8, 45
master-servant relationship, Hašek, 19–23
Matka (Čapek), 41
Maupassant, Guy de, 150
Max (character), 176
Means of Mutual Correspondence
  (Voinovich), 88
mechanism, 27
Mejzlík, Police Captain Dr (character), 49
Melekhov, Grigorii (character), 14–15
Melville, Herman, 114
Mengele, Josef, 181
Menzel, Jiří, 65
Merunka, Dr. (character), 157
*Městečko, kde se zastavil čas see The Little
  Town Where Time Stood Still* (Hrabal)
Meteor (Čapek), 29–30, 33–7, 38
Miles na Gopaleen, 56–7
Miller, Henry, 177
Milligan, Spike, *Adolf Hitler: My Part in
  His Downfall*, 5
Milostné léto (Klíma), 137
Milton, John, *Paradise Lost*, 9
The Miracle Game (Škvorecký), 91–4, 95,
  103, 118
miracle play, 95
Mirákl see The Miracle Game (Škvorecký)

Index

"Miriam" (Klíma), 148–9, 150
Mirjana (character), 174
Míša (character), 31
Miss Silver's Past (Škvorecký), 92, 93
Mladá fronta publishing house, 83
modern symbolist poets, 1
Modernism, 1
  Čapek, 29
Moje první lásky see My First Loves (Klíma)
Moje zlatá řemesla see My Golden Trades
  (Klíma)
Mole, Adrian (character), 171
Molokov, Comrade (character), 44
Molotov, Vyacheslav, 44
Monology (Kundera), 117
Monster Raving Loony Party, 26
montage
  Dadaism, 73
  Hrabal, 56, 81
Moravec, Emanuel, 5
Moravia, Alberto, 177
Mortier (character), 166
Mother (Čapek), 41
"Mr Janik's Cases" (Čapek), 49
Mr X (character), 34–7
Müller, Mrs (character), 16
Musil, Robert, 76
Mussolini, Benito, 116
Můžou tě i zabít (Pavel), 127
"My Country" (Klíma), 149–51
My First Loves (Klíma), 137, 148–52, 158
My Golden Trades (Klíma), 148, 152–4, 158
My Merry Mornings (Klíma), 137, 140, 148,
  152–3, 154–8
My Universities (Gorkii), 150
The Mysterious Stranger (Twain), 108
mysticism, 28

Naďa (character), 178, 179
Nadia (character), 107, 109, 111, 112
Nadja (Breton), 58–9
Nadja (character), 63, 64
Nápady laskavého čtenáře (Viewegh), 176
National Revival, 44, 90
National Theatre, 51
nationalism
  Hašek, 13–16
  Klíma, 149
  Pavel, 125
The Nation's Cause (Marsland), 7
natural science, 30
Nazism, 47
Názory na vraždu (Viewegh), 175–6
Nechleba, Vratislav, 130
negation, Dadaism, 73
Neumann, Stanislav, 117

Nevěsta z Texasu see The Bride of Texas
  (Škvorecký)
The New World Symphony, 119
The New York Review of Books, 147
The New York Times, 82
Něžný barbar see The Tender Barbarian
  (Hrabal)
Nezval, Vítězslav, 59, 73
Nicholas of Cusa, 55
Nietzsche, Friedrich Wilhelm, 85
"Noh", 101
Nosferatu, 102
"The Notary" (Hrabal), 59
Notetakers of Paternal Love (Viewegh), 176
Novák, Josef, 181
novelty, lack of, 27
Novy mir, 93

O'Brien, Flann, 56–7
*Obsluhoval jsem anglického krále see I
  Served the King of England* (Hrabal)
Obyčejný život see An Ordinary Life
  (Čapek)
The Odyssey, 8
Old Czech Legends (Jirásek), 81
One Day in the Life of Ivan Denisovich
  (Solzhenitsyn), 88
Opinions About A Murder (Viewegh),
  175–6
"Oplatka's End" (Čapek), 49
oral tradition, 1
An Ordinary Life (Čapek), 29–30, 37–41
*Ostře sledované vlaky see Closely Observed
  Trains* (Hrabal)
Ostrov mrtvých králů (Klíma), 148
*Osudy dobrého vojáka Švejka za světové
  války see The Good Soldier Švejk*
  (Hašek)
Ota (character), 152
Owen, Wilfred, "Strange Meeting", 7

pábení, 52, 53–6, 61–2, 65, 72, 76
pábitel, 54–5
Pábitelé (Hrabal), 54–5, 57–65, 70, 72
Pachman, Luděk, 93
Paco (character), 171, 174
Palach, Jan, 87, 154, 165
Palacký, František, 1, 90, 169
The Palaverers (Hrabal), 54
Pan Notář (Hrabal), 59
Parade's End (Ford), 7–8
paradise, Klíma, 144–6
Paradise Lost (Milton), 9
Paradise News (Lodge), 176
paradox, 29, 76–80
Páral, Vladimír, 52, 177
parody, Viewegh, 176–7

Index

Parrott, Sir Cecil, 4, 24
Participants in an Excursion (Viewegh), 176
Party of Moderate Change within the Boundaries of the Law, 18–19, 26
Pascal, Blaise, 166
Paskal, Jan (character), 163–6
Paskalová, Nora (character), 165, 167
Pasternak, Boris, 39
Patočka, Jan, 191*n*
patriotism, 7
Paustovskii, Konstantin, 124
Pavel, Ota, 1, 123–35
  biography, 124
  "Carp for the Wehrmacht", 130
  "Climbing the Eiger", 133
  Death of the Beautiful Roebucks, 124, 125–6
  "The Fairy Tale about Raška", 134, 135
  "Fishing with a Submarine", 131
  "Fishing-Rod Thief", 132
  "How Dad and I Served Eels", 127
  How I Met the Fish, 124, 125, 127–8
  "How Zátopek Ran on that Occasion", 134–5
  "Lanky Honza", 131–2
  "Long Mile", 130
  The Price of Victory, 133–4
  "Pumprdentlich", 131
  The Purple Recluse, 124–32
  "They Can Even Kill You", 127
  "When You Just Can't Do It", 134
  "White Mushrooms", 126
Pavlová, Věra, 126
"A Pearl on the Bottom" (Hrabal), 65
Pelikán, Mr (character), 110
Pepek (character), 121
Pepin, Uncle, 56, 75
"Perlička na dně" (Hrabal), 65
Pernica (character), 178, 179
Peters, Jim, 135
"Petlice" editions, 76
Philipe, Gérard, 60
Philo of Alexandria, 62
photography, 73
physics, 30
Picasso, Pablo, 28–9, 85
pièces noires, 2
pièces roses, 2
The Pickwick Papers (Dickens), 143
Pinter, Harold, 123
Pirie, Gordon, 135
The Pit and the Pendulum (Poe), 105, 112
pity, 2
Planet of the Apes, 172
playing, Hrabal, 63, 64
Pludek, Alexej, 123

Podobojí (Hodrová), 162–8, 169
Poe, Edgar Allan, 104, 105, 112, 115, 116, 121
poetic tradition, 1
poetism, 80–1
poetry, First World War, 7
Pohádka o Raškovi (Pavel), 134, 135
Pohorský, Mr (character), 110, 112
Polana (character), 29, 30, 31, 33
Pollock, Jackson, 74, 85
Porota (Klíma), 148
Poslední stupeň důvěrnosti see The Ultimate Intimacy (Klíma)
poshlost', 98
Poslední soud (Čapek), 49–50
Postřižiny see Cutting it Short (Hrabal)
Potok (character), 180–1, 182
Pound, Ezra, 116
Povětroň see Meteor (Čapek)
Povídky z jedné kapsy a z druhé kapsy see The Tales from Two Pockets (Čapek)
Povondra, Mr (character), 46
Pračka (Klíma), 148
practical tradition, 1
Pragmatist philosophy, 28
Prague Spring, Škvorecký, 93–4, 95, 118
Příběh inženýra lidských duší see The Engineer of Human Souls (Škvorecký)
The Price of Victory (Pavel), 133–4
Příliš hlučná samota see Too Loud a Solitude (Hrabal)
Prima sezóna see The Swell Season (Škvorecký)
Případy pana Janíka (Čapek), 49
Private Ivan Chonkin (Voinovich), 5
Private View (Havel), 172
Professional Foul (Stoppard), 153
Promethean threat, 46
Prošek, Karel (character), 125, 128, 129
Proust, Marcel, 170
Prouza (character), 112
Provazochodci see "The Tightrope Walkers" (Klíma)
Prst, Veronika (character), 108, 109, 112, 115, 120
"Pumprdentlich", (Pavel), 131
Purkrábek, Mr (character), 21
The Purple Recluse (Pavel), 124–32
Pushkin, Aleksandr, 46, 60
Pynsent, Robert, 4, 51
Pytlík, Radko
  on Hašek, 20, 23, 26
  on Hrabal, 53–4, 55, 56, 58, 76
The Quiet Don (Sholokov), 6, 13, 14–15, 150

Index

R. U. R. see Rossum's Universal Robots
(Čapek)
Rada (character), 143, 144, 145, 146
railways, Čapek, 39–41
Raška, Jiří, 135
rationalism, Surrealists' rejection of, 73
rationalist tradition, 1
"The Raven" (Poe), 105
reason, 3, 31–2
The Red Badge of Courage (Crane), 109,
110
Red Cavalry (Babel), 130
"Red Music" (Škvorecký), 97
The Red Wheel (Solzhenitsyn), 6
rejection, Dadaism, 73
relativism, Čapek, 35–6, 49, 50, 51
religion, 190n
Čapek, 28
Klíma, 141, 142, 143–5
Remarque, Erich Maria, *All Quiet on the
Western Front*, 8
Rembrandt, 85
reproduction, Čapek, 45–6
The Republic of Whores (Škvorecký), 88,
89, 94, 103
Revelation, Book of, 144
Rickwood, Edgell, "The Soldier Addresses
His Body", 7
Rimbaud, Arthur, 53
Roháček (character), 166, 167
Rollini, Adrian, 101, 102
"Romance" (Hrabal), 57, 60
Une Rose Publique (Eluard), 73, 81
Ross, Alan, 123
Rossum's Universal Robots (Čapek), 30, 42,
45 , 46, 185n
Roth, Philip, 147
Le Rouge et Le Noir (Stendhal), 150
Rudolph, Archduke, 10
Russell, Bertrand, 27, 43
Russian Futurists, 46
Russian Symbolists, 35, 75
Ruthenia, 30, 50
Rzounek, Vítězslav, 177

S ponorkou na ryby (Pavel), 131
Sade, Marquis de, 44
Šafařík, Pavel Josef, 169
Ságner, Captain (character), 25
Saidl, František, 80
Salivarová, Zdena, 87, 116
samizdat publishers, 76, 83
Sancho Panza, 20
Sanglier (character), 166
Sanitářská povídka (Klíma), 156–7
Santner (character in Škvorecký), p. 116
Santner, Pavel (character in Hodrová), 167

Sartre, Jean-Paul, 78, 85
Sassoon, Siegfried, 7
satire, Škvorecký, 93
"Saturday's Thief's Tale" (Klíma), 157
Saturnin, (Jirotka), 20
The Scarlet Letter (Hawthorne), 105, 106–8
scepticism, 18, 28, 29, 44
Scherzo Capriccioso see Dvořák in Love
(Škvorecký)
Scheuchzer, Johannes Jakob (character), 44
Schiller, Friedrich von, 85
Schultze, Andreas (character), 41
Schwarzburg, Major-General von (char-
acter), 21
science fiction, 42
Sestra see Sister (Topol)
Seeger, Pete, 14
self, Hašek, 18–20, 23
Seneca, 85
servant-master relationship, Hašek, 19–23
Seven Pillars of Wisdom (Lawrence), 8–12,
13–14, 15, 17, 18
Shake, Jan Amos (character), 120, 121
Shakespeare, William, 6, 25, 106, 116, 172
Shelley, Mary, 46
Sherman, William, 120
A Ship Named Hope (Klíma), 137, 148
Sholokov, Mikhail, *The Quiet Don*, 6, 13,
14–15, 150
Shryock, Colonel (character), 121
Sinatra, Frank, 135
Šípek (character), 166
Sister (Topol), 177, 180–3
Sitting Bull, Chief, 119
Sixty-Eight Publishers, 87
Skilling, Gordon, 5
Skočdopole, Přema (character), 90, 89, 91,
112
Skřivánek (character), 77, 79, 81
Škvorecký, Josef, vii, 1, 82
  The Bass Saxophone, 88, 97–102, 104
  The Bride of Texas, 118, 119–22
  The Cowards, 88, 89–91, 93, 94, 96–7,
  102, 104, 106, 121
  Dvořák in Love, 118–19, 120
  Emöke, 97, 102–4
  The Engineer of Human Souls, 88, 91,
  94–5, 103, 104–18, 119, 120, 121
  foreign influences and emigration, 115–22
  lyricism, 95, 96–115
  The Miracle Game, 91–4, 95, 103, 118
  Miss Silver's Past, 92, 93
  politics and history, 89–95
  "Red Music", 97
  The Republic of Whores, 88, 89, 94, 103
  The Swell Season, 88, 103
  and Viewegh, 176

Index

"A Slap in Face of Public Taste", 46
Slaughterhouse-Five (Vonnegut), 5, 18
Slavík (character), 150
Šlépěje (Čapek), 49
Slušný (character), 71
Slutskii, Boris, 134
Smetana, Bedřich, 149
Smiřický, Danny (character in *The Bass Saxophone*), 97–101
Smiřický, Danny (character in *The Cowards*), 88, 89–91, 96–7
Smiřický, Danny (character in *The Engineer of Human Souls*), 94–5, 104,105–6, 107–10, 111–15, 116, 118, 120
Smiřický, Danny (character in *The Miracle Game*), 92, 93, 103
Smiřický, Danny (character in *The Republic of Whores*), 103
Smrt krásných srnců see Death of the Beautiful Roebucks (Pavel)
Socialist Realism, 1, 6, 53, 74, 88, 103, 150
Socrates, 55, 85, 134, 142–3
Soffici, Ardengo, 116–17
"The Soldier" (Brooke), 7
"The Soldier Addresses His Body" (Rickwood), 7
Solomon, 62
Solzhenitsyn, Alexander
    The First Circle, 160
    The Gulag Archipelago, 159–60
    One Day in the Life of Ivan Denisovich, 88
    The Red Wheel, 6
songs, 13–16
Sorrell, Walter, 116
Součková, Milada, 170
Soudce z milosti see Judge on Trial (Klíma)
Soviet Union
    Socialist Realism, 1, 6, 53, 74, 150
    Village Prose movement, 124–5
Šperk (character), 174
Splendid Dog Days (Viewegh), 171–5
sport, Pavel, 123–4, 132–5
Staël, Madame de, 116
Stalin, Joseph, 103, 105, 108, 110, 151, 160
Stb, 173
Štědrovečerní (Hrabal), 57
Stein, Gertrude, 176
Stendhal, 150
Štěpán (character), 30, 32, 33
Stoppard, Tom, 153
Strana mírného pokroku v mezích zákona see Party of Moderate Change within the Boundaries of the Law
"Strange Meeting" (Owen), 7
sub-atomic physics, 30

Suchoručkov, Kosťa, 166–7
A Summer Affair (Klíma), 137
"Sunday's Foolish Tale" (Klíma), 157
Surrealism, 59, 73–4, 81–2
The Surrealist Manifesto (Breton), 73
survival instincts, 24
Sutch, Screaming Lord, 26
Svatá, Zdena (character), 65, 69, 71
Svědectví, 82
Švejk (character), 2, 4–6, 9, 10, 12–13, 15–26, 56
Švejk in the Second World War (Brecht), 5
Švejkism, 5
Světová literatura see World Literature
Svozil, Bohumil, 133
The Swell Season (Škvorecký), 88, 103
Sylva (character), 94
symbolism, Čapek, 31
Symbolists, 35, 75
synaesthesia, 35, 75
Syslová, Sofie (character), 169

The Tales from Two Pockets (Čapek), 29, 48–51, 92
Tales of the Jazz Age (Fitzgerald), 111
Tales of the Unexpected (Dahl), 148
Talmud, 62, 145
Taneční hodiny pro starší a pokročilé (Hrabal), 57
Tankový prapor see The Republic of Whores (Škvorecký)
Tanya (character), 156
technology, Čapek, 27–8, 45
teleology, 27
telepathy, 35
The Tender Barbarian (Hrabal), 57, 83
Tender is The Night (Fitzgerald), 111
Théta (Hodrová), 162, 169–71
"They Can Even Kill You" (Pavel), 127
Thomas, A., 184n
Thompson, Boris, 101
Thonet, Michael, 85
Thurber, Jeannette, 119, 189n
Thüring, Hans (character), 44
"Thursday's Erotic Tale" (Klíma), 156
Tietjens, Christopher (character), 7–8
Tigrid, Pavel, 177
"The Tightrope Walkers" (Klíma), 151, 152
time motif, Hrabal, 66–8
The Times, 26
The Tin Drum (Grass), 82
Tolkien, J. R. R., 42
Tolstoy, Leo, 46, 109
    War and Peace, 6, 8
Tom Sawyer (Twain), 143
Tomášek, Cardinal, 190n

Index

Too Loud a Solitude (Hrabal), 72, 74, 75, 82–6
Topol, Jáchym, 1, 177–83
  Angel, 177–80
  Sister, 177, 180–3
total realism, 75, 85
Toufar, Josef, 91–2
Toupelík, Cyril (character), 121
Toupelíková, Lída/Linda (character), 120
Townsend, Sue, 171
Tracy, Lorraine (character), 121–2
Trainspotting (Welsh), 179–80, 182
translations, vii
Treblinka, 102
Trensky, Paul, 93, 97
The Trial (Kafka), 138
"The Truth Game" (Klíma), 151–2
Trýznivé město see City of Pain (Hodrová)
"Tuesday Morning: A Sentimental Story" (Klíma), 153, 154–5
Tůma, Viktor (character), 61–2, 63
Turek, Mr (character), 166
Tvardovsky, Alexander, 93
Tvorba, 76, 136
Twain, Mark, 104, 108–9, 116
  Huckleberry Finn, 108, 109
  The Mysterious Stranger, 108
  Tom Sawyer, 143

Účastníci zájezdu (Viewegh), 176
Uhde, Antonín (character), 61, 63
Uher (*The Engineer of Human Souls* character), 112
Uher, Vladimír (*War with the Newts* character), 43
The Ultimate Intimacy (Klíma), 137, 158
Ulysees (Joyce), 168
The Unbearable Lightness of Being (Kundera), 176
Under Fire (Barbusse), 8
Under Western Eyes (Conrad), 113
uniforms, Hašek, 17–18
Union of Soviet Writers, 53
Union of Writers, 123
United States, Vietnam War, 42
universe, nature of, 30
urbanity, 3
Uršula (character), 63

Vabank (Pludek), 123
Václavík, Dr (character), 130
Vaculík, Ludvík, 123
Válka s Mloky see War with the Newts (Čapek)
Valley, Lily (character), 43
Van Gogh, Vincent, 85

van Toch, Captain J. (character), 42, 43, 44, 46, 47
Vandevilt, Rosemary (character), 118
Vang, General (character), 180–1
Vaníček, Bedřich, 73
Vánoční spiklenecká povidka (Klíma), 155–6
Vašek (character), 57, 58
Věc Makropulos (Čapek), 42
Venus de Milo, 100–1
Věra (character in *Angel*), 178
Věra (character in *My Merry Mornings*), 156
Verlaine, Paul, 53
vernacular
  Čapek, 51
  Hašek, 25
Veselý, Jan, 134
Věštkyně (Čapek), 48–9
Vicky (character), 109
Vietnam War, 42
Viewegh, Michal, 171–7
  Bringing Up Girls in Bohemia, 175, 176
  Ideas of a Kind-hearted Reader, 176–7
  Notetakers of Paternal Love, 176
  Opinions About A Murder, 175–6
  Participants in an Excursion, 176
  Splendid Dog Days, 171–5
Viktorka (character), 66, 70, 72
Village Prose movement, 124–5
visual arts *see* Cubism
Vítek (character), 120
Vladimír (character), 178
Voinovich, Vladimir, 5, 88–9
Vonnegut, Kurt, *Slaughterhouse-Five*, 5, 18
Voženil (character), 112
Vražedný útok (Čapek), 48
Vrchcoláb (character), 93, 94
Výchova dívek v Čechách see Bringing Up Girls in Bohemia (Viewegh)
Výstup na Eiger (Pavel), 133

Waiting for Godot, 172
Waiting for the Dark, Waiting for the Light (Klíma), 158–60
War and Peace (Tolstoy), 6, 8
War of the Worlds (Wells), 43–4
War with the Newts (Čapek), 41–8, 51, 161
The Washing Machine (Klíma), 148
The Wasteland (Eliot), 170
"The Watchman" (Gorkii), 150
"Wednesday's Christmas Conspiracy" (Klíma), 155–6
Weil, Jiří, 128
Wellek, René, 1
Wells, H. G., 43–4, 45
Welsh, Irvine, 179–80

Index

Wesker, Arnold, 172
"When You Just Can't Do It" (Pavel), 134
"White Mushrooms" (Pavel), 126
The White Plague (Čapek), 41
Wihan, Hanoušek 118
Wilson, Colin, 116
Wilson, Paul, 115–16
Wodehouse, P. G., 20
women's gossip, 54
work, Hrabal, 64
World Literature, 87

Xenophon, 13

Zámek see The Castle (Klíma)
Zapisovatelé otcovský lásky (Viewegh), 176
Záruba (character), 127
Zavorová, Barbara (character), 181
Zavřel, František, 116
Zbabělci see The Cowards (Škvorecký)
Zdeněk (character in *The Cowards*), 96

Zdeněk (character in *I Served the King of England*), 79
Ze života hmyzu see From the Life of Insects (Čapek)
Zelenohorský manuscript, 43
Zeměměřičská povídka (Klíma), 158
Žert see The Joke (Kundera)
Zibrin, Zdeno, 133
Zillergut, Colonel (character), 24
Zinik, Zinovy, 118
Zinkule (character), 120
Život s hvězdou (Weil), 128
Zločin v chalupě (Čapek), 49
Zloděj prutů (Pavel), 132
Zlodějská povídka (Klíma), 157
Zmizení herce Bendy see "The Disappearance of an Actor" (Čapek)
Zohar, 63
Zoshchenko, Mikhail, 56
"Ztracená ulička" (Hrabal), 65

Hike
Lake :)
Petr
Vienna?
Poland